Mar & Papp

Susan

Bus

Aug, 8 8

THE MASTER BUILDERS

76 - Ref to another
book "The Moneyspinners
by Rod McQueen

The Acquisitions."
Peter Newman.

A Matter of Trust
Patricia Best &
Ann Shortle

Fortune 1982

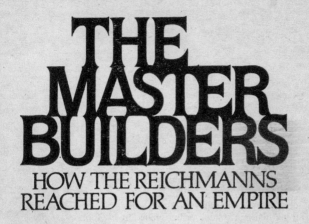

THE MASTER BUILDERS

HOW THE REICHMANNS
REACHED FOR AN EMPIRE

PETER FOSTER

A TOTEM BOOK
TORONTO

To the memory of my mother
First published 1986
by Key Porter Books Limited
This edition published 1987
by TOTEM BOOKS
a division of Collins Publishers
100 Lesmill Road, Don Mills, Ontario

© 1986 by Key Porter Books Limited

Canadian Cataloguing in Publication Data
Foster, Peter, 1947-
   The master builders

1st paperback ed.
Includes index.
ISBN 0-00-217910-5

1. Reichmann family. 2. Olympia & York Developments
· History. 3. Consolidation and merger of
corporations · Canada · History. 4. Real estate
developers · Canada · History. I. Title.

HD316.F68 1987   338.8'6'0971   C87-094921-7

Design: Michael van Elsen Design Inc.

Printed and bound in Canada

CONTENTS

INTRODUCTION

He is tall, around six-foot-three, and walks with a slight, almost deferential stoop. He always dresses in dark suits, white shirts, and black shoes. He is never seen in public without his yarmulke or his homburg, the acknowledgement that he is the servant of his God. But he is seldom seen in public.

He has strong, Levantine features, and his ears stick out at improbable angles, but his black-bearded face is kindly and wise. His eyes show great humanity, and yet they are surrounded by black rings, as if he never sleeps; as if the relentless activity in the brain behind stops them from closing. He speaks softly, sometimes inaudibly, with a slight mid-European accent. When he listens, he inclines his head to one side, as if he were a little hard of hearing, or particularly keen to pay you the courtesy of his full attention.

He is a man who somehow seems outside his time. His education, courtliness, and mode of speech conjure up images of other times and other places. One can imagine him as an advisor to medieval monarchs, or as a Renaissance polymath. In fact, he wanted at one time to become a full-time scholar of the Talmud. But his family wanted him to go into business, and since, in his world, the family is to be obeyed, he did so. And in so doing, he became a monarch himself — a commercial monarch.

Paul Reichmann is perhaps the most important businessman to emerge in Canada since the war. In thirty years, since he arrived as one of several waves that brought his family from their previous home in the exotic Moroccan port city of Tangier, he has been the mastermind behind the creation of one of the world's largest family empires.

From a humble tile business in the Toronto suburbs, and a seminal decision to build a small warehouse for themselves, the Reichmanns — Paul, his elder brother Albert, and his younger brother Ralph — have become a family of billionaires. The world's biggest property developers, they are the largest owners of real estate in New York City, controlling a phenomenal one-fifth of all the primary office space in the financial canyons of lower Manhattan. Through their main company, Olympia & York Developments, they own more than 50 million square feet of space throughout North America. In their best locations, such as Manhattan's elegant World Financial Center — the largest private commercial development in the world — just one of those square feet can command an annual rent of $50. It's an awful lot of money for the space on which to put a waste-paper basket.

But their real estate business, huge as it is, isn't even half the story. Real estate is just where the money comes from. The more fascinating side of the Reichmann story — and by far the more controversial — is where the money has been spent.

Between the summer of 1985 and the summer of 1986, Paul Reichmann masterminded the acquisition of two Canadian companies with total assets of close to $10 billion. The takeovers marked the stunning culmination of diversifications out of real estate that had started in the early 1980s.

The purchase of Gulf Canada, the country's second-largest oil company, made the Reichmanns the first Canadians to buy back a subsidiary of one of the Seven Sisters, the major oil companies that had dominated world oil for much of the twentieth century. Ironically, it was conceived by Paul Reichmann partly as an act of gratitude to his adopted country, a repatriation of part of Canada's resource birthright. But the whole affair became bogged down in controversy. The takeover turned out to be an exercise in Canadian politics at its most Byzantine.

Paul Reichmann's complex acquisition strategy raised many

questions about using public money to achieve private corporate ends. Everybody agreed that the strategy was brilliant from the Reichmanns' point of view, but how did it look for everybody else? The family that for so long had carefully nurtured an arrow-straight business image was suddenly cast as being perhaps a little too clever.

Scarcely was the ink dry on the Gulf acquisition when, in March, 1986, Paul Reichmann launched a bid for Hiram Walker Resources Ltd., which controlled one of the world's largest wine and spirits operations as well as holding extensive petroleum and pipeline interests. That bid sparked a series of corporate manoeuvres and countermanoeuvres the reverberations of which were felt from the City of London to the Melbourne Stock Exchange.

The Walker acquisition turned out to be not merely convoluted but also extremely hostile. Paul Reichmann had always firmly declared that he would never become involved in a hostile takeover, that he would never go after a company he knew would not want him. But somehow lines became badly crossed. Paul Reichmann failed to make his intentions clear, and as a result was paying a heavy price.

By the summer of 1986, Paul Reichmann was responsible for the most significant bout of corporate acquisition in Canadian history, but suddenly it all began to look less like prudent business than a gigantic gamble. There remained many loose ends, and many question marks.

The plummeting of the world oil price had clouded the business outlook of Gulf Canada, while the Reichmann control had left it heavily burdened with debt. Morale within Gulf was at an all-time low. The company had been split up and sold off. Its staff were being severed. As for Hiram Walker, Paul Reichmann had succeeded in gaining control of a company that had already begun the process of self-liquidation, the ultimate act of managerial hari-kari. Their attempts to stop that dissolution had landed the Reichmanns and their empire with a $9 billion lawsuit, the second largest such suit in the world.

These massive acquisitions, meanwhile, had provided further ammunition for growing public concern about corporate concentration in Canada. What were the implications of having so much business in so few hands?

Why had Paul Reichmann become involved in these enormous and controversial takeovers? Had the man and the family held in awe by the whole North American business community really stumbled? Although the house of Reichmann hardly seemed likely to fall, the myth of the family's business invulnerability had been tarnished. Was it just bad luck, or misunderstanding? Or was it something else? Had growth led to a change in—indeed forced a change on — the way the Reichmanns did business? Had Paul Reichmann perhaps become the victim of his own success? Or was it, perhaps, that the Reichmanns had never been the equal to the mythology that had grown around them? Did the events of 1985–86 mean a permanent change in the outlook for the Reichmann empire? Or were they merely valuable lessons from which the Reichmanns would learn and on which they would go on to build an even greater empire?

This book sets out to answer these questions by tracing the fascinating growth, and strange metamorphosis, of the Reichmann family empire.

1
FROM TANGIER TO TILES

Easy money was the basis of Tangier's wealth and excitement. . . . Anybody could open a bank and nobody had to produce balance sheets.

It seems almost as improbable as those innocuous little stores in James Bond movies, the shopfronts that lead to the subterranean command posts of acronymic espionage agencies. It's not sinister, of course. It just seems unlikely that the tip of the Reichmanns' huge financial iceberg should be a large, low-rise suburban tile showroom.

Olympia Floor & Wall Tile Co., at 1000 Lawrence Avenue West in Toronto, is itself more than merely where the house-proud come, with or without their interior designers, to select the marbles, mosaics, and ceramics that will grace their homes. It is the tip of the largest tile and carpet business in North America.

To one side of the reception desk, a chrome and glass staircase leads up to the administrative offices, where Ralph Reichmann has surely the only executive suite in the Toronto suburbs decorated with rococo antique furniture. Beyond the staircase is a pleasant sitting area where you can have a complimentary coffee under a Cinzano umbrella amid the well-tended greenery.

On the other side of the reception desk are museum cases with some items from Ralph Reichmann's personal collection: a little antique oil lamp, an ancient bowl, a priapic Central American figurine, a small classical bust, a group of hand-painted ceramic tiles, a small ceramic sculpture by an artist called Grès.

Like every public facet of the Reichmann empire, quality and taste abound. Arranged around the 19,000-square-foot showroom are a number of set pieces: bathrooms, kitchens, and dining rooms from dream homes. Everywhere there are mounted displays of the company's mainly imported products in all their glazed, unglazed, or vitrified glory.

This is suburban middle-class heaven, but it is tinged with a *frisson* of the exotic — as of course any suburban middle-class heaven should be. Some of the products have an almost poetic ring: tiles called ''Amica Rapsodia Fascia,'' or ''Hellas Prisma Noce.'' And, of course, the marbles — sheets of rich Carrara and Travertine — always carry their own special air of mystery: Arabescato Rosso, detailed as an infra-red satellite picture of the earth; Nero Marquina, with white nebulous wisps against its black background, rich as the night sky. Then there are the more mundane items: the spreaders and trowels, the glues and grouts, the wall-mounted soap dishes and toilet-roll holders.

At the showroom's customer desk, the credit card machines ratchet back and forth. Deeper within the bowels of the building there is another, less plush office, where the cash customers, the contractors, peel off notes with cement-dusted hands. Farther back, there lies a massive labyrinth of warehouse space, with row upon row of steel shelving packed to the ceiling with tiles and accessories. Fork-lift trucks speed up and down the aisles shifting goods. Off to one side of the building, pallets piled with tiles are stacked together beneath signs — ''Vancouver,'' ''Ottawa,'' ''Winnipeg''—waiting for trucks to ship them all over the country. The seemingly endless stacks in the warehouse are in turn filled each day from an even larger 300,000-square-foot warehouse recently built a little farther out on Mississauga's Thompkin Avenue.

In the Lawrence warehouse, on the side of a crate, is stamped the name ''Azuvi.'' It is just one of dozens of suppliers from all over the world whose products the Reichmanns import. But Azuvi is important because the company, situated just outside Valencia, Spain, provides one of the transatlantic links with the Reichmanns' European and North African past.

The Road to Morocco

The Reichmann story begins in Budapest, the Hungarian capital, where, after World War I, Samuel Reichmann founded a successful poultry business which distributed its products across a good part of Europe. Budapest, sitting astride the Danube and commanding the approaches to the Great Hungarian Plain, had already established itself as a bustling commercial metropolis, and Reichmann's business thrived.

However, there was fear in the 1920s, in the wake of the Russian Revolution, of a possible Soviet invasion, so Samuel and his wife Renee decided to move to Vienna. With their three children, Edward, Louis, and Eva, they transported their possessions westward up the Danube to the Austrian capital, another of the great cities of Europe, which had for more than two thousand years been one of the meeting places between East and West. It was in this beautiful city, where the skyline was dominated by the spire of St. Stephen's Cathedral, that the three youngest sons, Albert, Paul, and Ralph, were born at around the time of the Depression in the early 1930s.

Vienna, which the Hapsburgs had ruled for almost seven hundred years until the end of World War I, was a city of enormous cultural, intellectual, and political importance. The home of Mozart and Freud, it contained the world's finest examples of baroque architecture. It was the city where the Congress of Vienna had rewritten the map of Europe after the final fall of Napoleon. But it was also the home of less beneficent influences. During the early years of the Reichmanns' stay, the city's Academy of Fine Arts had a minor employee named Adolf Hitler. The Reichmanns were one of the Jewish families wise enough to flee. When the Nazis annexed Austria in March, 1938, they moved to Paris. Two years later, they fled the French capital just days before the Germans marched into the city. Travelling south, the Reichmanns made it over the Spanish border literally hours before it closed. Samuel decided that safety lay even farther south, and the family headed for the neutral international port of Tangier.

Tangier, overlooking the Atlantic and the Strait of Gibraltar from low sand hills at the extreme northwest tip of Africa, was a very different place from Vienna or Paris. Over the three thousand years of its history, Phoenicians, Carthaginians, Visigoths,

Vandals, the Portuguese, the Spanish, and the English had all raided and held it. But the strongest mark was left by the Arabs.

The city also had a long Jewish history. Local Berbers had converted to Judaism as early as 700 B.C. When the Reichmanns arrived in the city, they could take comfort in the sight, among the turbans, jellabas, burnouses, and caftans of the bazaar, of the dark suits and felt hats of their fellow Jews, worn on even the hottest of summer days.

In the 1930s, the city was renowned as a hotbed of mystery, vice, and skullduggery. But it was also a mecca of commerce, and for the next ten years Samuel Reichmann's commercial interests grew. He began to deal in money and gold, joining the Jewish money-changers who dominated the business in the city, and graduated to the status of banker, becoming the main tenant of the Tangier Stock Exchange. Easy money was the basis of Tangier's wealth and excitement. Currencies of all nations could be seen in the bazaar. The city's free money market, where officially pegged prices meant nothing, proved an irresistible magnet. Anybody could open a bank and nobody had to produce balance sheets.

But there were also ironies in Tangier as a home for those fleeing Nazi persecution. Tangier banks played guardian to huge and ill-gotten German fortunes, which eventually found their way to Switzerland or Montevideo, Uruguay.

After the war, thousands of Europeans and a few Americans were attracted to the city by the low taxes and duties and the free money market. The absence of banking laws and the pittance it cost to form a Tangier corporation were a bonus. Nobody paid any personal or corporate taxes. International holding companies, and people of a thousand different persuasions and lifestyles, flocked to the city. A United Feature Syndicate column of the time declared that "Sodom was a church picnic, and Gomorrah a convention of Girl Scouts" compared to Tangier.

Smugglers used World War II P.T. boats to ferry contraband — cigarettes, nylons, soap, whisky, watches, and penicillin — into southern Spain, Gibraltar, Italy, or the Mediterranean islands. As for the diplomatic corps, a standard Tangier joke was that the initials C.D. stood not for "Corps Diplomatique" but "Contrabandier Distingué."

The town even used to advertise in the *Paris Herald Tribune*. "Tangier is waiting for you. Tangier knows no restrictions of any kind." The city buzzed with haphazard construction. The *New York Times* called it a "building contractor's nightmare."

But if it was a building contractor's nightmare, it was a financier's paradise. Jewish and Hindu entrepreneurs made fortunes. Men like Jacob Alster, who arrived in Tangier in 1935 possessing only the clothes he wore on his back, had, within fifteen years, accumulated more than £3 million worth of real estate. *Fortune* magazine in 1949 described it as "a completely uninhibited dream . . . everybody's no man's land . . . that has no national anthem other than the sweet melody of hard cash."

In Tangier, everyone lived by his wits. There was an anecdote about a wealthy Jewish businessman who, because he was an American protégé, put up an office building two storeys higher than the city laws allowed. When the authorities tried to indict him, the owner pointed out that American protégés did not come within the province of local laws. But when his tenants refused to pay their rent and he applied to the Tangier courts for assistance, the latter reminded him sarcastically that, by the gentleman's own definition, the building did not exist for them. The businessman nevertheless had the last word, for when Tangier tax officials presented him with an accounting, he piously expressed surprise that they would expect to tax property that the courts claimed did not exist!

Samuel Reichmann achieved the difficult task of insulating his family from the corrupting influences of the city while taking full advantage of its commercial potential. Renowned for his mental agility, he kept literally hundreds of constantly changing cross-exchange rates in his head. He could translate American dollars into French francs, or Dutch guldens into Spanish pesetas quicker than it would take to punch the numbers into the most modern computer. His sons would later say that his word was as good as gold, and in Tangier, you could do wonderful things with gold. Following the 1944 Bretton Woods Conference in the United States — at which the International Monetary Fund was set up — the world price of gold was fixed at $35 an ounce, but Tangier was exempted from this restriction. Gold brought up to $100 an ounce in the International Zone, and Samuel Reichmann dealt in it.

A Wave of Fear

This halcyon era ended abruptly on March 30, 1952, when without warning an enormous crowd of native Tanjawis gathered in the medina, the oldest part of Tangier, and marched through the city demanding Moroccan independence and an end to the International Zone. The police fired on the mob and a wave of fear ran through the city's foreign communities. The riots marked a turning point in Tangier's history. Big money began moving out to Geneva, Montreal, Caracas, and Montevideo, and the Tangier boom began perceptibly to deflate. Samuel and Renee Reichmann, realizing that their family's fugitive life was not at an end, started to consider where their next move might take them.

In August, 1953, the French Resident General in Rabat ordered Sultan Mohamed V out of the country in order to prevent civil war. Then the French actually kidnapped him and flew him off to Corsica. It was considered an enormous outrage. Two years later, on August 1, 1955, on a typically hot, bright summer day a Tanjawi pastry vendor ran amok in the city, killing four people and seriously wounding five. This was followed by city-wide demonstrations on behalf of the deposed Sultan. In French Morocco, the Foreign Legion was brutally repressing any sign of revolt. An attempt was made on the life of Sultan Ben Arafa, the French puppet ruler. In September, 1955, French Premier Edgar Faure bowed to world opinion and Moroccan realities and announced that Morocco would have her independence. On November 16, Sultan Mohamed V returned from exile to Rabat. The new Moroccan minister of state announced that Morocco's status as an International Zone would be abolished. It was reported that more than forty tons of gold were moved from Tangier bank vaults to Geneva toward the end of 1955. The city disintegrated. The property market fell apart. Anti-foreign sentiments grew. Burglaries and assaults increased. A bomb was placed in the old Jewish cemetery that lay on the eastern wall of the medina. On October 29, 1956, the International Zone of Tangier dissolved, but Samuel Reichmann had already sent family emissaries across the Atlantic to find a new home.

The Reichmann children had all been brought up in strictly Orthodox fashion. After the war, Albert had joined his father's business, and Paul had gone off to England, where he spent five years at Orthodox *yeshivas*. In 1954, Edward, the eldest son, was sent to explore the possibilities of transferring the family's activities to North America. He was later joined in the reconnaissance by the second brother Louis, but neither of these elder brothers played a part in the development of the family's North American empire.

For the future of the empire, the significant arrival was that in Toronto via New York in 1956 of young Ralph, and, a year later, of his brother Paul. On Densley Avenue, not far from the present Lawrence Avenue tile headquarters, Ralph set up an import business based on contacts the family had with Spanish tile manufacturers, including Azuvi. The business was located in a 4,000-square-foot warehouse, and Ralph Reichmann, then aged twenty-two, says that he employed two and a half employees: a shipper, a receiver, and a bookkeeper who worked half-days. The business flourished and after Paul's arrival the brothers realized that they needed more space. They bought some land on nearby Colville Road and invited tenders to build a warehouse based on architectural plans drawn up by a young architect who was moonlighting from his main job in the Bank of Commerce's building department.

They decided, however, that all the tenders were too expensive, and, with some transatlantic encouragement from their father, they undertook to build the warehouse themselves. They put it up for $70,000 versus the lowest outside bid of $125,000.

The tile business soon outgrew the Colville Road property and moved to its present site. Today, that facility is the nerve centre of a tile and carpet operation that occupies 3 million square feet in both Canada and the United States. It not only imports tiles from all over the world, but also has a number of manufacturing subsidiaries that produce everything from terrazzo flooring moulds to soap dishes. Olympia Floor & Wall Tile and its satellites employ around fifteen hundred people. This part of the empire is still overseen by the youngest brother Ralph.

The business today generates several hundred million dollars of sales annually, but it was the building of that little warehouse that would take the Reichmanns to billionairedom. A more pivotal warehouse cannot be imagined. It was the little building on which an enormous real estate empire would grow.

2

GOLD ON THE TABLE

"There's gold on the table and no one wants to pick it up. Are we making a mistake somewhere? Am I missing something?"

— Paul Reichmann

They are a special breed but they are not easily distinguished by their appearance. They stretch from the guy in the white shoes and the cigar all the way to the most refined, well-spoken patrons of the arts. They come from all races, colours, and stripes. They are the property developers, the real estate men — and their ilk embraces both the slum landlord and the visionary who creates or remodels entire cities.

They are not usually architects or construction engineers or financiers, but their skill lies in bringing these specialities together to satisfy the demands of those who want buildings. They do not draw up blueprints or erect steel or pour concrete, but they cause these things to happen. They are often controversial figures. Those of them who work at the urban core must often tear down the old in order to make way for the new. Such disruptions are rarely popular. Some of their breed are in such a hurry that they send in the bulldozers a little too quickly. Publicity surrounding such activities has given them a less than pristine image as a group. Yet it was in the fiercely competitive world of real estate development that the Reichmanns made their name.

Paul Reichmann's supervision of the warehouse's construction and his relentlessly probing mind taught him that there was no mystery in the art of building. You needed land, money, a plan, a builder, local authority permission, and a client. But if there was no mystery, Paul Reichmann found that there was lots of something else: profit. The Reichmanns' architect had told them it would cost them $100,000 to put up the warehouse for the tile business. The lowest tender was $125,000. Paul built it for $70,000. If he had been building for a third party, he could have undercut the lowest tender by $20,000 and still pulled in a net profit of 50 percent. Paul Reichmann decided that he would leave the tile business to Ralph and move into property development full time.

He started buying industrial properties in the northwest suburbs of the city, where the tile warehouse was located, and began putting up simple, single-storey industrial buildings for lease or sale. Although he quickly mastered the art of real estate deal-making and construction, one obvious constraint was finance. A quantum leap was possible in 1959 with the arrival of the patriarch, Samuel, and Paul's elder brother Albert, who had been working in the father's business in Tangier. The tile importing business was named Olympia, after Ralph's love of the Greek classics. Another business, York Developments, named after the county surrounding Toronto, was set up to take care of the budding real estate program. These two companies would form the nucleus of Olympia & York.

Samuel brought the bulk of the family's fortune to the New World, and, in Paul's own words, multiplied the business's capital tenfold. But Samuel brought more than just money; he also brought access to money.

The source of the Reichmanns' outside backing in those early years is shrouded in mystery. Samuel's bank was rumoured to have been a depository in Tangier for the funds of wealthy Jewish families in Nazi-persecuted Europe. He was said to have access to British Rothschild money and also that of the Gestetners. His wife, Renee, was a cousin of David Gestetner, the Hungarian-born British industrialist who invented the modern stencil duplicating process.

Albert joined Paul in real estate, and the brothers began to pyramid an empire on the low-rise base of factories and warehouses in the suburbs of Toronto. The roots of their success were remarkably simple: the Reichmanns simply pursued excellence in all they did. They worked hard. They listened attentively to their clients, and they custom-built. They emphasized quality; they laid out attractive landscaping and built with brick instead of aluminum siding. Their rationale was that clients would pay for quality and satisfied clients would produce more business and spread the good word about the Reichmanns. By the mid-1960s, there were Reichmann-built warehouses and factories all over the Toronto suburbs.

With their impeccable manners and their sober dress, the Reichmanns cut strangely conservative figures amid the rough and tumble, concrete and dust atmosphere of the building sites. They would often converse in one of the half-dozen or more European languages that they spoke in addition to Yiddish. This speaking in foreign tongues was more than just a sentimental harking back to their European past, however. It was also a way of speaking freely in front of tradesmen and contractors without letting them know what you were saying. The Reichmanns knew that business advantage lay in cornering the market in knowledge as much as in quality control or tight scheduling of projects. Speaking Hungarian was a way of being secret in public.

The Great Zeckendorf

Part of the genius of successful real estate operation is to see values where others miss them. The successful real estate developer must also be at least part predator, part scavenger. As success contains the seeds of failure, so failure contains the seeds of success. The Reichmanns' first quantum leap in the real estate field took place in 1965, when they snapped up part of the crumbling empire of one of the most colourful of North America's developers, Bill Zeckendorf.

The Reichmanns would be Zeckendorf's heirs in a number of ways. They would purchase some of his empire's most valuable lands in Canada. As well, thirteen years later they would acquire a large chunk of Trizec Corporation Ltd., the property company that he had set up to build his greatest Canadian project. They would also inherit many of the real estate techniques that he used.

Bill Zeckendorf's life also had another object lesson to teach. In the late sixties and early seventies, New Yorkers, thinking that a friend, colleague, or member of the family was trying to take on too much, would say, ''What are you, the Zeckendorf of the Bronx?''

Bill Zeckendorf's lesson was that a great builder's reach often exceeds his grasp.

William Zeckendorf first burst into the headlines in Canada in September, 1956. While young Paul and Ralph Reichmann were establishing their little tile importing business up in the Toronto hinterland, and Paul was thinking about the warehouse, Zeckendorf unveiled his plan to transform the face of downtown Montreal. The centrepiece of his plan would be the forty-storey, 1.5-million-square-foot Place Ville Marie. The scheme to develop the twenty-three acres around the Canadian National Railway's terminal would, claimed Zeckendorf, turn Montreal from a merely big city into a great city.

Zeckendorf was a 250-pound bear of a man who had risen from building salesman to the world's number-one real estate operator. Born in Paris, Illinois, in 1905, where his father operated a general store, he had managed to get to New York University, but never got a degree. For thirteen years he stayed in New York as a real estate and rental agent. Then, in 1938, he went to work for Webb & Knapp, a conservative real estate firm. The turning point in Zeckendorf's career was his skill in managing Vincent Astor's U.S.$50 million estate while Astor was in the navy. Zeckendorf added U.S.$5 million to the assets and Astor rewarded Zeckendorf's success with a U.S.$350,000 commission cheque and instructions to "send him a bunch of flowers." Zeckendorf subsequently bought control of Webb & Knapp and took it through a period of dynamic growth.

His reputation was further boosted when, in 1946, he sold seventeen acres of development land on the East River to John D. Rockefeller, Jr., as a site for the United Nations building. Zeckendorf could have made much more money from the parcel, but what he lost in cash he made up in prestige. "We have just moved the capital of the world," he rather grandiosely told his wife after hearing that his proposal for the UN headquarters had been accepted. The great French architect Le Corbusier sat in Zeckendorf's apartment and sketched a prototype design for the UN building on the back of an envelope.

Zeckendorf was as flamboyant as the Reichmanns were reclusive, a showman as well as a salesman. He and his wife would occasionally turn up at Manhattan social occasions with their toy Doberman pinscher sporting a leather wing collar and a silk bow tie. Zeckendorf had played championship bridge, but his girth gave away his favourite hobby, and he once claimed that he got all his good ideas from indigestion. He was also superstitious. Each new Webb & Knapp subsidiary was numbered either to contain thirteen or be a multiple of thirteen.

Through his control of Webb & Knapp, Zeckendorf was the mastermind behind a U.S.$300 million empire that included not only real estate but also shipping and oil. After the railroads and the utilities, he was reckoned to be New York's largest taxpayer. He controlled his empire from a strange, windowless, circular hatbox of an office — designed by the famous architect I.M. Pei, who also designed Toronto's Commerce Court West — atop Webb & Knapp's Madison Avenue headquarters. The room was equipped with a variable lighting system, reputedly to induce specific moods in his business visitors.

Zeckendorf's greatest asset, and ultimately his heaviest liability, was his vision. His mind, like that of all great developers and entrepreneurs, lived always in the future, in the what-could-be. "If I'm a maverick in my business," he once said, "it's because other people work only with money. I employ imagination."

He was a dealer as well as a developer. In 1953, he bought a package of buildings that included the Chrysler Building, the Art Deco fantasy on Lexington Avenue, topped by its six levels of stainless steel arches and its radiator-ornament gargoyles. At U.S.$53 million, it was the biggest real estate transaction in New York history. The negotiations involved more than seventy bankers and lawyers in a three-day session that produced almost a ton of documentation.

The 1950s were William Zeckendorf's glory years. He shook up downtown Denver and left his development mark on Washington, Chicago, and Philadelphia. He was also, for a time, Manhattan's most spectacularly successful developer. With his "Wall Street Manoeuvre" he played a game of musical buildings with the country's largest and most powerful banks. To move clients into new buildings, he would take over their old leases, "like second-hand cars," he said. Thirty years later, Olympia & York would use the same technique to fill its mammoth World Financial Center in lower Manhattan. There was another strange echo in the very structure of the Reichmanns' World Financial Center, with its four towers named for their occupants. Bill Zeckendorf had hatched an ambitious scheme to redevelop the approach to the United Nations buildings. In his autobiography, he wrote, "My plan was that the four southern office buildings were to be occupied by four large corporations, and that each building bear the name of its tenant.''

In Montreal, Zeckendorf's Place Ville Marie would sit on the cellar dug thirty years before by Sir Henry Thornton, the CNR's first president, whose dreams for a similarly bold scheme were shattered by the Depression. Thornton's plans for the CNR terminal site had cratered in the most literal way. When the Depression put a stop to work in 1932, all that the project had to show was the results of removing 4 million cubic feet of earth. It was described as ''the world's most expensive hole.''

Donald Gordon, the six-foot-four tall Scotsman who headed the CNR (and was the only man that Zeckendorf admitted could drink him under the table) had been searching since 1952 for private interests to finance the development of the land around the Montreal terminal, but no Canadian firm had the resources. Zeckendorf realized that the completion of the Queen Elizabeth Hotel would draw other activity to the area. In February, 1955, the New York real estate wizard flew over Montreal to inspect the site and then met with the city's mayor, Jean Drapeau. Besides Gordon and Drapeau, two other men played a critical part in Place Ville Marie: Jimmy Muir, the autocratic head of the Royal Bank, and Lazarus Phillips, the wise and brilliant Jewish lawyer to the Bronfmans and leader of Montreal's Jewish community who later became a senator.

Zeckendorf saw Place Ville Marie as a Rockefeller Center-cum-Grand Central Station. In December, 1957, he signed the lease for the $100 million project. He raised an initial $25 million for the project and, typically, immediately spent this on other Canadian ventures, such as the purchase of 277 Petrofina gas stations.

Zeckendorf found himself caught up in the intricacies of Anglo-French politics in Montreal. He also had enormous problems finding tenants. But in the end he persuaded the Royal's Muir to move in. Muir was a renowned bully, and Zeckendorf became the butt of his bigotry. Muir called Zeckendorf's architect Pei ''that damned Chinaman,'' and sometimes addressed Zeckendorf as ''you * * * Jew.''

Zeckendorf's successful completion of the deal fulfilled Sir Henry Thornton's dream, and by the early sixties not only had Place Ville Marie transformed downtown Montreal, but Zeckendorf had changed the face of Canadian retailing with his huge suburban shopping centres. In May, 1964, the opening of the Yorkdale Plaza north of Toronto caused traffic jams on the Trans-Canada Highway. Housewives were chartering buses to come from as much as one hundred miles away to walk the centre's spacious malls.

But although Yorkdale might be booming, the Zeckendorf empire was by then crumbling. In 1965, Webb & Knapp, Inc. was put into reorganization under the U.S. Bankruptcy Act. The trustees discovered a situation of enormous complexity, reflecting Zeckendorf's pinball mind and grandiose vision. He had built a huge and spectacular empire, but he had built it too fast and without strong enough financial foundations. The moves he had made into hotels and urban-renewal schemes had been costly failures. Overrapid expansion had left the company short of cash and collapsing under the weight of its debt. But still Zeckendorf kept pushing into new projects, borrowing money at higher and higher rates. His crucial mistake was a 150-acre amusement park in the Bronx called Freedomland, part of a 400-acre tract for which Zeckendorf had paid U.S.$4.5 million.

Freedomland's bankruptcy was the last straw. The rides would eventually be torn down to make way for a huge co-operative housing project. Zeckendorf's empire had already effectively been torn down. Between 1959 and 1965, Webb & Knapp's assets had plummeted from U.S.$300 million to U.S.$22 million. The company's losses in that period totalled a crippling U.S.$70 million. By May, 1965, Webb & Knapp had U.S.$100,000 in ready cash and claims from creditors totalling U.S.$84 million.

Flemingdon Park: Gold on the Table

In Canada, Zeckendorf's company sought to stay afloat by selling off property. Corporate decay, like other forms, often provides the fertilizer for new ventures, and one part of Webb & Knapp's Canadian empire proved to be a critical building block for the Reichmanns, whose empire would one day far surpass that of Zeckendorf. The piece of land, to the northeast of Toronto, was called Flemingdon Park.

Webb & Knapp (Canada) and the Rubin brothers, a well-known pair of local Toronto developers, had originally bought the Fleming Estate adjoining the Don Valley in 1958 in what was at the time Canada's largest single land transaction. The land was destined to become significant because of the building of the Don Valley Parkway, which linked the Trans-Canada Highway and the downtown core. Flemingdon Park had been planned as a mixed-use development, combining housing with industrial and office facilities. It was already partly developed and much of the infrastructure of roads and services was under way.

By the time the Reichmanns bought it in 1965, the ownership of Flemingdon Park had been transferred to Swiss investors who had put up the original $25 million down payment on Place Ville Marie. The money in fact had been spent everywhere *but* on Place Ville Marie. Webb & Knapp (Canada) retained the task of selling the site. The negotiations with the Reichmanns were carried out by Bill Hay, a dour, reticent Scots lawyer who had worked for Blake Cassels & Graydon. Hay developed a good rapport with the family. He went on to become president of Trizec, but, a decade later, after Edward and Peter Bronfman staged their successful assault on Trizec, he wound up as a senior executive for O&Y.

Typically, the sale to the Reichmanns was shrouded in secrecy. The final deal was supposedly signed in the vaults of the downtown office of the Bank of Nova Scotia. Present were the Reichmanns, Hay, Lazarus Phillips from Montreal, and representatives of the Oelbaums, another wealthy Toronto Jewish family who reportedly provided a good part of the financing for the deal.

For Paul Reichmann, the values of the land were more than abundant. In fact, he couldn't believe that nobody else could see them. At the time he said to Gil Newman, who was then the Reichmanns' accountant: "There's gold on the table and no one wants to pick it up. Are we making a mistake somewhere? Am I missing something?"

But Paul Reichmann wasn't missing anything. The Reichmanns bought the bulk of the 600-acre project for $25 million as part of a $200 million expansion program. They recouped their investment in six months by slicing the parcel up and selling a few of the lots. Then they began to put up a cluster of office buildings on the property that would forever change that corner of Toronto.

Flemingdon Park literally took the Reichmanns above the ground floor for the first time. The Mony Life Insurance building on the southeast corner of Don Mills Road and Eglinton Avenue East was their first multi-storey building. When the building was completed, they moved their offices there. The Reichmanns were on the way up.

Excellence and Efficiency

Over the next eight years, the Reichmanns expanded their operations enormously. At Flemingdon Park they participated in the development of several thousand rental and condominium apartment units. They created the largest suburban office centre in Canada. By 1974, they had completed thirteen office buildings in the area with a total of 3 million square feet. Among their largest projects were data centres for Bell Canada and Shell Canada and the head office of Texaco Canada. They had plans for an additional 2 million square feet of office space over the next five years. Meanwhile, they also acted as a developer-builder for others, either on the client's property or where they sold a total "package" including land, plans, and completed buildings. The Reichmanns greatly favoured this package method, which gave them higher margins in return for taking the burden of the whole real estate process from land assembly through custom-building off the client's shoulders. They avoided as far as possible the more traditional "tender" approach, where the client with a piece of land invites bids from a number of general contractors and the lowest bid usually wins. The Reichmanns noted that in that system, all the subcontractors held back with their own sub-tenders until the last moment, and that in general, in Albert's words, "the bidder who makes the biggest mistake gets the job."

The Reichmanns started from the opposite end of the equation, a form of real estate "supply side" economics. Instead of waiting for a customer to come to them, they would, if they had a good site, go looking for a customer. They would ask the customer his requirements and then put together a plan that would, at the end of the day, mean that the client could move into a custom-built and equipped building. Projects on this basis in and around Flemingdon Park included buildings for the Ontario Federation of Labour, the Ontario Hospital Association, the Independent Order of Foresters, and Xerox Canada Inc.

Once the package had been sold, it was a matter of providing the highest quality at the lowest cost. They would not put up anything but buildings of the best quality because premium buildings demanded a premium price. At the cost end of the equation, they emphasized efficiency, which meant squeezing the maximum possible rentable and usable square footage out of a building.

Gross space is all the square footage within a building's walls. Obviously, not all that space is rentable, and not all the rentable space is usable for business purposes. The space taken up by facilities such as elevators, service shafts, and mechanical rooms has to be deducted to arrive at rentable space. The Reichmanns soon noticed that architects and engineers did not necessarily share the priorities of the developer. Their top priority was not always space-saving. But beyond the mere elimination of wasted space, a great deal of time was spent with consultants looking for innovations in areas like elevator systems that would maximize service but take up the minimum floor space.

To these ends, the brothers always took a very close interest in blueprints and layouts. Paul would take home a floor plan, spend the evening mulling it over, and then return the following day having squeezed another couple of percent of efficient space out of it when it seemed that there was no more to squeeze. Then, once the rentable space had been maximized, they sought to maximize the efficiency of the square footage devoted to elevator lobbies, washrooms, and so forth, so that the client got the best use out of his rented space. The success of their approach was obvious. The projects they owned or managed had the highest occupancy rates in the business.

Flemingdon Park led them into major developments in downtown Toronto, Ottawa, and Calgary. Clients for whom they had built smaller facilities at Flemingdon Park, such as Bell Canada and Shell Canada, were so impressed with the Reichmanns' work that they asked them to undertake bigger projects elsewhere. They built the enormous Place Bell Canada for Bell in Ottawa, and, in the latter half of the seventies, the thirty-three-storey Shell Centre in Calgary. In downtown Toronto, their work included the Toronto Star Building at the foot of Yonge Street, the York Centre on King Street West, and Global House on University Avenue.

Despite the size and scope of the projects, the organization was kept extremely lean. In 1969, Olympia & York Developments Limited was incorporated in Ontario. O&Y resulted from extensive reorganizations of a number of the companies controlled by members of the family. The head office was moved to the Toronto Star Building.

By 1974, the real estate operations were throwing off a cash flow of around $15 million a year. The tile business, too, had expanded enormously, and now generated annual sales of more than $30 million. Olympia Floor & Wall Tile had moved beyond merely importing to manufacturing. It made ceramic tiles through a wholly owned subsidiary, Maple Leaf Ceramics Industries in St-Laurent, Quebec. It also manufactured terrazzo flooring materials and machinery under the trade name of Domus Engineering Co. in Toronto. It had distribution centres in Toronto, Montreal, Quebec City, Ottawa, Hamilton, London, Windsor, Halifax, Winnipeg, Calgary, Edmonton, and Vancouver.

O&Y had now developed more than one hundred twenty industrial and office buildings ranging in size from a 10,000-square-foot industrial building for a pharmaceutical company to the 1.5-million-square-foot Place Bell Canada. From a standing start, the achievement, in eight years, was remarkable. But the family was seen, whatever their reputation, as still essentially just another firm of real estate developers.

The little warehouse on Colville Road had led to the perfection of the art of building simple industrial structures; the acquisition of Flemingdon Park had led to high-rise development and the mastery of office buildings. The next step forward would be an office building, but an office building like no other in Canada and like few in the world.

3

FIRST CANADIAN PLACE:
THE FLAGSHIP

The brothers loved it. Said Albert: "Half the money in Ontario is within a few blocks of this building." That money was already begging the Reichmanns to take it and make it grow.

The topping off of First Canadian Place in 1975 marked another giant step in the Reichmanns' growth. Twice as tall as anything they had built before, and the tallest bank building in the world, it not only elevated them into the top class of property developers, it also established their skills as innovators. The building's construction techniques were nothing less than revolutionary.

The brothers would have considerable problems with the Toronto City Council, and there would be a bitter wrangle behind closed doors with their main client, the Bank of Montreal, but the development would in the end stand as the flagship of their Canadian real estate empire.

From the luxurious penthouse offices and dining rooms of Bill Mulholland — the Bank of Montreal's autocratic chairman — through the corporate, law, accounting, and investment offices in the middle, to the throb of retailing activity in the basement, First Canadian Place would become a microcosm of Canadian business life. Moreover, filled with its list of blue-chip tenants, it would also provide both the stage and the dramatis personae for the corporate soap operas that the brothers would help script more than a decade later.

The Reichmanns' principal tenant in the development's main building, the seventy-two-storey First Bank Tower, was to be the bluest of the blue chips, the oldest of Canada's big five chartered banks, the Bank of Montreal.

The Montreal had adopted a policy of having a major building in each of the cities across the country. Toronto, as the country's financial capital, obviously had to have something special. First Bank Tower had to be a suitably impressive headquarters for a bank with 1,250 offices throughout the world and assets of well over $10 billion.

The King and Bay intersection on which the development would stand was the ultimate focus of all Canadian financial activity. Like so many important intersections all across Canada, it had banks on all four corners. But this intersection was more than just the most important, it was the one on which the banks had chosen to build the ultimate architectural monuments to themselves. Two of its corners already had huge new tower developments on them. On the southeast corner rose I.M. Pei's great silver Commerce Court West, head office of the Canadian Imperial Bank of Commerce, and on the block southwest of the intersection were the black boxes of Miës van der Rohe's Toronto-Dominion Centre, built for the Toronto-Dominion Bank. When it had first been built, the Montreal's office on the northwest corner had been an imposing edifice. Now it was a dwarf. First Canadian Place would, in the minds of the bank's management, restore the Montreal to its rightful stature. It would tower over both its rivals.

First Canadian Place was conceived as an unprecedentedly massive project, planned to cover approximately 90 percent of the block bounded by King, Bay, Adelaide, and York streets. It was to have a mammoth 5 million square feet of gross building area, including a gross retail and park area of 1 million square feet and total rentable office and retail space of about 3.5 million square feet.

As their principal architects and planners, the Reichmanns chose Bregman & Hamann, with whose senior partner, George Hamann, they had long held a close relationship. During the previous decade, Bregman & Hamann had been responsible for many important Toronto buildings, either exclusively or as co-architects. Among these were the Mount Sinai teaching hospital, the Toronto-

Dominion Centre, and, more recently, the huge Eaton Centre. The firm had also designed a number of buildings for the Reichmanns, including their largest project to date, Place Bell Canada in Ottawa. Their style was firmly imprinted on the Reichmanns' developments in and around Flemingdon Park, where they had designed Foresters House, the Texaco building, and the offices for Nestlé and Blue Cross.

The Reichmanns had built their business and their reputation on providing exactly what their clients wanted, so their buildings were designed to reflect the aspirations of their tenants. First Canadian Place would project quality and prestige because these were what the Reichmanns perceived both their principal tenant and their other, as yet unknown, tenants would want.

The site for the First Canadian Place development was owned 50 percent by O&Y and 25 percent each by the Bank of Montreal and Naloy Properties Limited, a wholly owned subsidiary of North American Life Assurance Company. O&Y leased the 50 percent owned by the bank and Naloy until 2023. The project was to have two phases. The first, started in 1973, with the Bank of Montreal's First Bank Tower as its centrepiece, would be completed in 1978. The second phase, featuring another, smaller, office tower on the west side of the block, would begin following approval from the City of Toronto. But the City of Toronto was less enthused about the mammoth development than either the Reichmanns or the Bank of Montreal.

Trouble with the City

In the late sixties and early seventies, Toronto was a hotbed of turmoil about development and the construction of urban expressways. David Crombie swept into office in 1972 as the city's new "tiny, perfect" mayor. A key part of his platform was to preserve Toronto's neighbourhoods and halt the higgledy-piggledy growth of huge office blocks in the downtown core. The Crombie team began work on a comprehensive Central Area Plan that would reduce the densities of commercial development while providing an overall framework for the city's architectural future. To show they meant business, they introduced a maximum height by-law of forty-five feet for new buildings. Anyone who wanted to build higher had to come and negotiate with the city. A dedicated group of bright young professional planners gravitated to the city as Crombie's praetorian guard. They were all caught up in the idea that the city was establishing a new destiny for itself. One of them was a young South-African-born architect named Ron Soskolne.

Soskolne had come to Toronto in 1969 to study architecture and planning at the University of Toronto. Then he worked as an architect and for a management consultancy firm before joining the city in 1972. Soskolne took over responsibility for working on the downtown plan, and this soon brought him into conflict with the Reichmanns.

The Reichmanns already had approval for First Canadian Place when the Crombie crew arrived on the scene, but there was a lot of antipathy to their scheme. This planned behemoth was the very symbol of everything the new planners were rejecting. The building became a gigantic political lightning rod.

The early phase of Soskolne's relationship with the Reichmanns was rough. The brothers were applying to close Pearl Street, which led into the heart of the block. They also wanted to close the laneway between King and Adelaide streets in order to link up the two phases of the development. They were also beginning to demolish three historic buildings on the site: the Globe and Mail building, the Toronto Star building, and the Bank of Montreal. Soskolne soon became embattled with them and rapidly tied them down with guerrilla tactics. He made their closing of the street conditional on their not demolishing the buildings. They were upset because they had an agreement with the *Globe and Mail* under which they were legally obligated to demolish the old Globe building.

Paul Reichmann called for a meeting and explained his position. Soskolne found him charming. Reichmann seemed, unlike most developers, who were up in arms about the Crombie team's initiatives, genuinely sensitive to the concerns of the city. The young planner developed a much clearer understanding of the Reichmanns' position, and they quickly came up with compromise plans.

One key guiding principle of the city planners was that they didn't want to see a repeat of the Toronto-Dominion Centre. This group of buildings, which effectively forced people underground, was seen as having done damage to the "streetscape." The planners wanted First Canadian Place to be more "sympathetic" to the street.

The Reichmanns had wanted to extend the base of the building right across the block and put a park on top, but Soskolne felt strongly that people did not use parks "in the air." He said he would rather have a small park usable at the street level. Another demand was that there would be a public right of way between King and Adelaide during the hours that the transit system was open. The banking pavilion was also redesigned to take account of the planners' desire to keep the "canyon effect" on Bay Street. Soskolne and his colleagues also demanded that the design of the second phase office block be different from that of First Bank Tower.

Soskolne and the city planners were impressed with the way the Reichmanns listened to and weighed their recommendations. The Reichmanns did not fight City Hall. This may partly have been out of deference to the wishes of the democratically elected council, but there was also a reason for not being totally displeased with the planners' anti-development stance. If the city succeeded in its plan of reducing commercial office space densities downtown, First Canadian Place would be that much more in demand.

In the end, compromise plans were agreed upon, demolition went ahead, 250,000 cubic yards of earth were dug out of the ground, and construction began.

Reach for the Sky

The Reichmanns saw First Bank Tower as dominating Toronto's skyline for the foreseeable future. It would be the tallest office building in Canada and the Commonwealth, and one of the ten tallest in the world. At the base of, and surrounding, the tower was to be a two-storey podium, with a further four levels below ground. The concourse level would link with Toronto's downtown climate-controlled pedestrian network, and the development would bring retail activity to the street level for the first time.

The building was to be of steel construction using the "structural tube" system. This system resembled a rolled up piece of paper placed on its end. The building was supported from its outside walls, which were built with small perimeter columns. That meant the floor space to the core of the building was column-free, giving First Canadian Place the largest ratio of column-free total office space — around thirty thousand square feet per floor — of any tall building in Toronto.

The Reichmanns' reputation and wealth had been acquired through a combination of quality and efficiency. Now, in First Canadian Place, they would demonstrate mastery of another skill that is critical to a developer's profitability: speed.

For developers perhaps more than any other businessmen, time is money. The key to success is to shorten the time between the start of any development and its tenancy. The skyscraper grew from the evolution of building materials — in particular, structural steel and cement — and from the desire to optimize the use of precious urban space. The developer's desire is to get that steel and cement in place as quickly as possible so that he can reap the benefits of that urban space's value. In that respect, First Canadian Place was a path-breaking development.

The Reichmanns and their construction men, in particular their head of operations, Keith Roberts, an English public-school-trained engineer who had joined them before Flemingdon Park and was the linchpin of their building operations, spent a considerable amount of time researching construction methods and devising a plan to put up a huge building faster than had previously been achieved.

The kernel of the project's revolutionary nature lay in a visit by Paul Reichmann to the York Centre, which was just a block from the site of First Canadian Place. Keith Roberts was conducting Reichmann on the trip, and they found themselves waiting for an elevator behind a line of workers carrying tools and construction materials. It suddenly struck Roberts how much time was lost on a big project just waiting to travel up and down the building, and also how haphazard and piecemeal the movement of materials was. The taller the building, the greater were the potential problems.

During that same trip, Paul Reichmann wondered out loud why it would not be possible to finish the lobby of a building before construction was completed. It was difficult to paint a picture of prestigious office space on a mud floor surrounded by hard hats. A finished lobby would be a valuable tool in selling to future tenants.

Those two observations would be critical in the building of First Canadian Place. Paul and Albert enthusiastically supported Roberts' efforts to devise a better method of building and took an active part in evolving the plan. They set themselves the objective of saving at least 1 million man-hours. They also formulated a plan to cut out haphazard storage and multiple handling of the 500,000 tons of materials that would go into the building. The bottom line was the bottom line. Saved time meant saved money.

Also, not only would they finish the ground floor and lower level lobbies (dictated by the building's innovative system of double-banked elevators) before the building was completed; they also planned to start moving tenants into the lower floors before the upper floors were fitted out. Their target was occupation of the lower twenty-two floors and both lobbies in a period of sixteen months, six months before the building was finished. To do so, they evolved a system for moving men and materials that combined the logistics of a fair-sized war with the timing of clockwork.

At ground level, O&Y set up a forty-five-ton, heavy-duty truck elevator that would remain part of the building's permanent freight system. This elevator, which could handle one hundred vehicles a day, took trucks to basement level, where they drove onto a giant turntable. This turntable, the largest in the world, then aligned them with one of eleven unloading bays. From the bays, the pallets of goods were mechanically handled straight to the temporary elevator system, which moved them at once to a preassigned floor.

O&Y's elevator system included two "jumbo jump" elevators. They were called "jumbo" because of their unprecedented size and "jump" because their hoisting machinery was "jumped" up the inside of the elevator shafts as the building rose. With their four-ton capacity, they could help distribute 1,500 men through seventy-two floors with less than half an hour of lost time per man. O&Y also pioneered the use of "climbing" elevators. Like the jump elevators, they moved up the shaft with the building. However, in their case, not merely the hoisting mechanism but a complete twelve-floor, caged elevator system was pulled up by the giant cranes which sat on top of the rising building.

These sixty-ton-capacity kangaroo cranes could erect a tier of three floors of steel frame in six days. They also hauled up all the electric ducts, the mesh for the concrete floors, and the huge prefabricated pipe clusters that would carry all the main services through the building. No ladders were used and permanent metal stairs were put into place right up to the steel working level. Through the jumping cranes and the jumping elevators, the building effectively lifted itself up by its own bootstraps.

Again, the concrete transportation system, which handled 60,000 tons of concrete, was a logistic marvel. The ready-mix trucks would arrive at the site and feed their load into a vertical chute. This chute took the concrete down to a conveyor, which ferried the product to hoppers. These radio-controlled hoppers could deliver concrete at the rate of 130 tons an hour to the thirtieth floor and 80 tons an hour to the seventy-second floor.

Following up the outside of the building, meanwhile, was a double exterior scaffold. The upper scaffold installed the brackets for the Carrara marble that would cover the building, as well as the insulation and the tracks along which the building's auto-matic window-washing system would move. The lower scaffold installed the marble. This combination doubled the speed of enclosing the building. While structural core steel was being hauled up and installed at the top of the building, reinforcing steel was following up six floors below. Three floors farther down, con-crete was being poured. Another six floors down, the upper scaf-fold was climbing the building with the second scaffolding three floors below. Finally, twenty floors below the top, the glaziers were installing the windows.

From the computerized control room, all this activity was sched-uled and monitored to within minutes. Each truck that entered the project was assigned a time and a delivery route that fitted it in with the tightly scheduled elevator and crane programs. All labour movements were tightly controlled and directed.

When O&Y outlined its new program to the subcontractors, they were highly skeptical about this break from traditional methods. But O&Y developed a detailed construction manual and gave them frequent briefings. Most important, the company gave them a guarantee of its own performance. As a result, O&Y was able to negotiate more competitive contracts and earlier comple-tion for each trade.

In the end, lost labour time was reduced not by 1 million but by 1.3 million man-hours. Handling times were drastically reduced. The loads of marble, dry wall, insulation, glass, fixtures, ceiling tile, and carpeting were unloaded in between a third and a tenth of the time it had previously taken.

The only major problem was a five-month hold-up in marble supply when it was discovered, to the horror of the Reichmanns, that the shipments of marble were subtly changing colour, moving from greyish white to whitish grey. They were in danger of ending up with a two-tone building. Otto Blau, a purchasing wizard and another linchpin of the O&Y organization, was dispatched to Italy to find alternative sources of supply. Blau secured the marble, and the exterior cladding of the building was finished only a month behind schedule.

The building's 9,000 double-glazed, tinted, heat-absorbing windows and its white marble would be kept spotless by an automatic system that ran on rails down the side of the building. The first of its kind in Canada, the system had already been proved on the 110-storey Sears Tower in Chicago and the twin blocks of the World Trade Center in Manhattan. It would also have a double-banked system of fifty-eight elevators—again the first of its kind in Canada—to maximize the building's rentable space. There was a sophisticated energy conservation and recycling system by which heat given off by lights, machinery, and people was reclaimed and recirculated throughout the building. The system could provide enough heat for the building until the outside temperature dropped to minus nine degrees Centigrade, when supplementary heating switched on. The air in the offices was changed every ten minutes. The building was state of the art in every way. Indeed, to call it a mere building seemed short of the mark. It was a climate-controlled, super-sophisticated *environment*.

Tremors in the Tower

Building First Canadian Place, however, was less than half the real estate story. Much more important was finding new tenants. The first steel column of First Canadian Place was erected five floors below King Street on January 15, 1974. Just over a year later, on February 4, 1975, the Toronto Construction Association held its annual general meeting on the fifth floor, attended by over four hundred people. The structure by this time was up to the sixty-sixth floor. Shortly afterward the building was topped off and on May 18, 1975, on target, the first tenants occupied the finished office space in the lower twenty-two floors. The rest of the building took longer to fill than expected—in fact, twice as long as the brothers had anticipated. The first year's cash drain was estimated to be $20 million. Despite this, O&Y refused to slash rents to attract tenants. The Reichmanns were wise. The first lessees reportedly paid $12 a square foot, the last more than $40.

The development also took the brothers into the field of retail leasing in a big way for the first time. Retailing as a part of the real estate industry has its own idiosyncrasies. It depends on a subtle blend of knowledge and intuition about which shops should be where, about points of access and flows of people. First Canadian Place was planned to have 600,000 square feet of retailing space on three levels. Twenty thousand people would work in it. Once links were established to the underground tunnel system of the Toronto-Dominion Centre on the south side of the development and to the Richmond Adelaide Centre on the north side, a great many more people would pass through.

The key aspect of leasing space in the lower three levels would be to persuade retailers that these people would stop. People going to Yorkdale went there to shop, but the lower levels of First Canadian Place presented a different problem. A retailing focus had to be built up so that people would come there to shop, and passers-by would turn into shoppers. Despite hiring expert consultants, the brothers still had to feel their way in this new area. There was also a constant fight with the city over the city's share of the costs of making the underground links to the north and south of the building.

Once the first phase of the building was developed and many of these problems had been ironed out, a more serious problem emerged. It occurred with the Reichmanns' principal tenant. Although both parties typically tried to suppress information about the wrangle, a storm blew up between O&Y and the Bank of Montreal over the development of the second tower of the development.

During the demolition phase of the development, the National Bank of Canada had been given an option to rent space in the new development. However, the Bank of Montreal had understood that they were to be the only bank in the project, and objected strongly when the presence of a National Bank branch in the second tower was announced. A legal dispute arose based on whether the second tower of the development was technically linked to the first and whether the whole development thus represented one project.

Caught in the middle of this dispute was Sun Life Assurance Company of Canada, which was meant to be the second tower's principal tenant. Sun Life had planned to purchase a 45 percent interest in the land on which the tower would be built, and take

400,000 of the 1 million rentable square feet of office space within it. But then, when construction was under way, the Bank of Montreal filed an objection to the plans and work was halted.

There were reports that Paul Reichmann called Bill Mulholland and said that he was prepared to sit down with the original negotiators of the deal from O&Y and the bank, along with Mulholland, and sort out the problem. But Mulholland was reportedly infuriated and refused to meet with Reichmann. There was also said to be some damage done to the Reichmanns' financial relationship with the bank.

Sun Life, in the end, did not move into the building, which soon acquired a new identity. It became The Exchange Tower after the Toronto Stock Exchange agreed to transfer its operations there. The Reichmanns' financial interests meanwhile were little damaged by Sun Life's withdrawal. In fact, the market firmed and they wound up with higher rents.

Despite all these problems, First Canadian Place, and in particular First Bank Tower, with its acres of white marble, was now the Reichmanns' flagship and showpiece. The brothers loved it. Said Albert, "Half the money in Ontario is within a few blocks of this building." That money was already begging the Reichmanns to take it and make it grow.

The brothers hated personal publicity, but they loved it for their projects. The *Guinness Book of Records* was contacted and First Bank Tower was duly listed, at 935 feet, as the world's tallest bank building, replacing the Chase Manhattan Building in New York City. The stylized, illuminated symbol of the Bank of Montreal also became the highest advertising sign in the world, replacing the RCA sign in New York's Rockefeller Plaza. Other bankers poohpoohed the twenty-foot-high blue sign as a piece of crass bad taste on the part of the bank. The whole point about such gigantic structures was that they spoke for themselves. But that was what the bank wanted, so that was what it got.

The Reichmanns had built a landmark that they believed could hold its own in Manhattan. That was not inappropriate, for soon the brothers would take Manhattan by storm. They would take it with a real estate purchase that would later be dubbed "the deal of the century."

4

"THE DEAL OF THE CENTURY"

*"Manhattan is Manhattan
and will remain Manhattan."*

— Albert Reichmann

There is a subtle transition — but a huge gap — between skill and genius, between reputation and mystique. For the Reichmanns, that transition occurred, and that gap opened, as the result of a deal consummated in New York in 1977. The groundwork for a mystique had already been laid, not deliberately, but by a combination of natural reclusiveness, business skill, and management style.

The Reichmanns' natural reclusiveness was part and parcel of their devout religious beliefs. Despite, or perhaps because of, their strict adherence to Orthodox Jewish beliefs, they were not well known even in the local Toronto Jewish community. Their reclusiveness from the rest of the world, including the business community, also arose significantly from the strictness of their religion, which lent some unusual twists to their business practices. Although they accepted all races and creeds within their business empire, their religion dictated an absolute ban on any form of work on the Jewish Sabbath — from sunset on Friday to sunset on Saturday. Their organization also closed for all the Jewish holidays, which could lead to the loss of up to fourteen work days in some years. Not only did they not work on the Sabbath, but they would take no work from consultants that had been done on the Sabbath.

The Reichmanns' strict orthodoxy also led to many potential pitfalls in everyday social contacts. They would not, for example, touch a woman outside of their family. Therefore, if any woman executive offered to shake hands, their position became acutely embarrassing.

The Jewish dietary laws relating to food and drink did not permit them to enjoy business lunches. Adherence to these laws, however, did not mean ascetic abstention generally. (At one time, Paul Reichmann chain-smoked Lark cigarettes and enjoyed social drinking, but he now neither smokes nor drinks.) But they could never have lunch at a club just to shoot the breeze with the boys-in-the-know. Nor would you ever find the Reichmanns at the Cambridge Club, where the more athletically inclined members of the Bay Street crowd went to thwack the ball around the squash court.

The Reichmanns recognized the dangers inherent in their separateness. They had been witnesses to too much of history not to be all too painfully aware. Nevertheless, they saw no good reason why their business activities should lead to access to their private lives.

At the same time, Paul Reichmann affirmed that his religious studies had a profound influence on his business outlook. He claimed that he received the key to much of his business success from the Talmud, the compilation of Jewish law and tradition that was meant to provide guidance for every life situation. The Talmud had been the principal substance of the family's formal schooling. Paul Reichmann expressed puzzlement about the role and usefulness of business schools, but his assessment, not atypically, perhaps says too little about his own extraordinary talents and too much about the collection of rabbinical writings. The Talmud helps its students to think, but the business skills of the Reichmanns were being honed by hard work, experience, and what would soon begin to look like almost superhuman insight.

The Reichmanns' mystique also grew within their own company. Their management style was that of benevolent despots. Paul and Albert would always seek advice, but they did not share decision-making. When asked, employees would contribute their opinions or knowledge; the brothers, usually Paul, would make the final decision. These decisions were not to be questioned, nor did the Reichmanns feel any compulsion to explain them. They were good employers, and they were dealing with their own money. What explaining was there to do? After all, the principles on which they were building their empire seemed remarkably simple. Paul Reichmann would sum them up in aphorisms as arresting as they seemed obvious. For example: "You build on cost and you borrow on value."

But the point was that the Reichmanns took such simple principles, which had long been basic tenets of the real estate business, and developed them into a fine art. They had, from the beginning, paid close personal attention to maximizing the "efficiency" of their buildings, squeezing out the greatest possible rentable and usable space. This helped to cut costs, but at the same time they emphasized quality and service. Thus they could command top rents. These rentals determined the value of the building, and it was this value that they could take to the banker as collateral against loans for further ventures. The greater the gap between the cost of a building and the amount they could borrow against it, the more funds there were to fund growth. By adding the most value, the Reichmanns established the best collateral and thus had the most funds to expand. But it was not the availability of funds *per se* that made their next deal so remarkable. It was that it seemed to be such a gigantic risk. It was not a piece of development but a simple deal. In it, the brothers would buy on cost, and the subsequent increase in the value of their purchase would put at their disposal borrowings almost beyond the dreams of avarice.

A Bite of the Big Apple

In 1976, following the completion of First Bank Tower, and before the wrangle over the second phase of the development, Paul Reichmann was still involved in meetings with Bank of Montreal executives on leasing and other details. One of the bankers remembers that Paul on one occasion apologized for having to cancel a meeting. "I'm sorry I couldn't see you last week," said Reichmann apologetically, "but I had to go to New York. We're just picking up a few buildings."

Reichmann's portrayal of O&Y's New York deal was typically low-key. When the bank executive discovered the nature of the transaction, he and his colleagues were, in his own words, "slack-jawed." The Reichmanns were taking what looked like the risk of their lives. They were spending more than $300 million on Manhattan real estate at a time when most developers feared that the island was about to sink.

During the latter half of the 1970s, Canadian developers had made a rapid penetration of American real estate markets, but New York City was one area of which both they and their U.S. counterparts steered clear. The New York authorities had spent and borrowed themselves into a hole from which there seemed to be no escape route. Martin Mayer, author of the best seller *The Bankers*, summed up the problem plainly and devastatingly: "On the simplest level, the story of New York's financial collapse is the tale of a Ponzi game in municipal paper — the regular and inevitably increasing issuance of notes to be paid off not by the future taxes or revenue certified to be available for that purpose, but by the sale of future notes. Like the chain-letter swindles, Ponzi games self-destruct when the seller runs out of suckers, as New York did in the spring of 1975."

Manhattan-based corporations had found themselves paying more and more in local taxes to get less and less in city services. The municipal government was seen as bloated, self-serving, and anti-business; the city's unions as rapacious. Businesses responded to the deterioration in the environment by voting with their offices. Many moved to the green and pleasant suburban satellites of lower New York State, New Jersey, and Connecticut.

In 1975, it looked as if the unthinkable might happen and the city would go bankrupt. The possibility of a stop to welfare cheques brought visions of a city in flames. New York's financial decline was, according to some — such as former secretary of the U.S. treasury William Simon — a microcosm of the potential disaster awaiting the whole country unless it mended its fiscal ways. A federal bail-out package was eventually announced, but there was still considerable doubt that the city had learned any lessons or recognized what William Simon called its "intransigent irresponsibility."

It was into this cauldron of uncertainty that the Reichmann brothers stepped in 1976. The brothers had already undertaken real estate projects south of the border in Dallas and Los Angeles, and by this time had accumulated total real estate assets of close to $1 billion, which meant they were hardly small fry. But the New

York real estate pond was about as shark-infested as the business got.

A sharp-eyed New York real estate broker named Edward Minskoff brought to their attention a mammoth group of skyscrapers known, after their builders, as "the Uris Package." Harold and Percy Uris had been bankrupted in the 1930s but had returned to become among Manhattan's most active builder-owners. In 1973, the assets of the Uris Corporation had been sold to National Kinney Corporation, which had made its mark in funeral chapels, parking garages, and commercial cleaning services. Kinney in turn was 40 percent owned by Warner Communications. Warner chief Steve Ross had decided that he wanted out of real estate, in particular New York real estate. Most big investors felt the same way. In the words of Harold Grabino, the National Kinney executive who negotiated the deal with the Reichmanns: "Most of the institutional buyers who could afford this kind of deal had already drawn a big red line around Manhattan Island. They were afraid of it."

Edward Minskoff was an almost archetypal New York investment high flyer, from the solid gold Rolex on his wrist to the Steinberg cartoons on his wall. He was whip-smart, well connected, and, most important, he was hungry. With his slicked-back hair, lean good looks, and flashy suspenders, he couldn't have appeared more different from the sombrely clad Reichmanns. But he had known the brothers for half a dozen years and had developed an enormous respect for them. Minskoff had been a senior vice-president with investment bankers Lehman Brothers and had become involved in the financing of some of the Reichmanns' earlier projects. Then he had quit Wall Street and gone out on his own and begun to buy and develop for his own account.

The Uris package had never formally been offered as such, but the entire industry knew that it was on the market. Real estate investors from all over the world, from The Hague to Hong Kong, had looked at the parts of the package, which then consisted of nine buildings. Minskoff went to Paul Reichmann and pointed out that the price of the buildings was considerably less than their replacement cost, while their rental charges, averaging around $10 per square foot, were 40 percent less than market levels. There were also low-cost loans on 80 percent of the portfolio, mortgages of U.S.$288 million with interest rates ranging from 5⅛ percent to 8¾ percent.

The Uris brothers were not renowned for the quality of their work, but the buildings were situated on some of the best real estate in the city. The package consisted of two giant towers on Park Avenue, at 245 and 320, which housed, respectively, the head offices of American Brands and IT&T; 10 East 53rd Street, the head office of publishers Harper & Row; 850 Third Avenue; the Sperry Building on the Avenue of the Americas; and 1633 Broadway. Downtown, there was 2 Broadway and the RCA Global Communications building at 60 Broad Street.

There had been a ninth property in the Uris package, the J.C. Penney building at 1301 Avenue of the Americas. But Penney exercised its option to match any offer for the building. A half-interest in the Sperry Building was held by the Rockefeller real estate interests, but the Reichmanns closed on the Rockefellers' 50 percent before the deal was signed on the other seven and a half buildings in the Uris package.

No. 245 Park Avenue sat cheek by jowl with what had once been the headquarters of New York Central Railroad but was now the Helmsley Building, property of Harry Helmsley, one of New York's most spectacularly successful developers. Built in 1967, it was described by *New York Times* architecture critic Paul Goldberger as "ruthless" in its "disregard of the ideas that made Park Avenue such a remarkable lesson in urban design." Both 245 and 320 were "head and shoulders" buildings in the boxlike International Style. But the brothers were not primarily interested in aesthetics. Park Avenue was, and in their minds always would be, one of the world's prime addresses.

The same went for the downtown locations. Wall Street and its environs, the Reichmanns thought, would always be the financial capital of the world. No. 2 Broadway occupied an entire blockfront in the financial district and towered over one of the world's most famous streets. Almost all of its thirty-two floors, embracing a total of 1.6 million square feet, offered panoramic views of New York harbour and historic Bowling Green. The thirty-nine-storey tower at 60 Broad Street had more than 1 million square feet.

After the Reichmanns had been made aware of the Uris package, they had travelled to New York and toured the buildings, chatting to the concessionaires in the lobbies and approaching a number of the tenants. They quickly became convinced that the land on which the buildings stood was worth more than the U.S.$320 million asking price. Also, because of existing mortgages, the cash portion of the deal was only U.S.$50 million. Like many great business moves, the Uris purchase was based on a simple premise. The Reichmanns looked beyond the heated political debate over city finances that pitched fiscal conservatism against feckless "liberalism," (although the Reichmanns were clearly on the side of the conservatives). They saw through the panic and decided that New York had to come back. "A boom in New York rents wasn't a hope," said Paul, "it was a conviction."

Two weeks after first visiting the buildings, the brothers decided to buy. Warner-Kinney negotiator Grabino was a little taken aback when he first met the Reichmanns. He wondered whether these two guys from Toronto, with their skullcaps and their dark suits and their gentlemanly ways, were in a league to make a deal like this. Nor did the negotiations run entirely smoothly among Minskoff, the Reichmanns, and Grabino. They started talking at the end of October, 1976, and signed a contract in March, 1977, but it took until September to close the deal.

On Friday, September 19, 1977, the deal was signed in the Park Avenue law offices of Paul Weiss Rifkin Wharton & Garrison. In the afternoon, following confirmation of the wire transfer of U.S.$50 million cash from the buyer to the seller, the Reichmanns acquired the empire that had taken the Uris brothers a lifetime to build. At a stroke, they acquired 10 million square feet of office space and 1,200 tenants and leaped into the position of Manhattan's second-largest landlord after the Rockefeller interests. Soon they would be number one.

Had there been a delay in the deal that Friday afternoon, the Reichmanns would simply have left in order to be home by sunset, as their religion demanded. Deals could wait; the Sabbath could not.

The purchase was seen at first as a staggering gamble, but in fact the timing could not have been better. The outlook for the city changed almost overnight. Compromise was reached with Washington and the banks on the city's finances, and real estate developers began to realize that the Big Apple was coming back. Ronald Nicholson, a New York developer (and also the son-in-law of Bill Zeckendorf), said: "The Reichmanns bought these buildings like twenty minutes before the real estate market turned around. They had a great buy — whether they were brilliant or lucky or whatever. Every sharp guy in New York had looked at those buildings and turned the deal down. I can't believe the

Reichmanns were smart enough to anticipate what was going to happen. Rents went from ten bucks a square foot to twenty overnight. Nobody could have anticipated that."

The deal would soon look shrewd. In another couple of years, it would look brilliant. In four years, it would be called "the deal of the century," ranking in real estate mythology right up there with the Louisiana Purchase. It would be recounted in real estate circles in the same hushed tones that Peter Minuit's original purchase of Manhattan Island for U.S.$24 was told to wide-eyed schoolchildren.

The Reichmanns established their New York headquarters in the American Brands building at 245 Park Avenue in October, 1977, and proceeded to make a number of other deals. In particular, they bought a majority interest in a behemoth of a building at 55 Water Street, facing over the East River and dominating a four-acre "superblock" of the financial district two blocks from Wall Street. Again, *New York Times* critic Goldberger had some hard words for Water Street as a whole, describing the block on which the building sat as a "row of horrors." But for the Reichmanns, 55 Water Street was more important for its statistics than for its aesthetics. Its fifty-three-storey tower and fifteen-storey wing offered a mammoth 3.5 million square feet, as much as all the office space in both blocks of First Canadian Place.

The Reichmann brothers set about upgrading the Uris buildings and establishing the reputation for quality that they had acquired in Canada. Lobbies were refurbished, services were improved. As a showpiece, they also refurbished a site at the side of the Helmsley Building and named it Park Avenue Atrium. The building was gutted down to the structural steel, five floors were added, and it was given an interior atrium rising twenty-four storeys. Stainless steel and glass walls with terraces and balconies dripping with greenery and flowers rose 300 feet to the skylights above. Somehow, the building provided an inner calm from the Manhattan turmoil without. From a financial point of view, meanwhile, the atrium was far from a waste of space. It meant that inward-facing offices, with their pleasant prospects, could command rents as high as those on the outside of the building.

In the meantime, the value of the Uris package increased, and with it both the cash flow from rentals and the collateral value against which the brothers could borrow. The Reichmanns over the next few years became one of the most powerful forces in New

York real estate, but they were still not known personally. The Real Estate Board of New York, the exclusive group of top developers, waited for the brothers to turn up and present themselves for approval, but the Reichmanns did not want, or need, approval. This, of course, only increased their mystique. An article in the *Washington Post* called them "the Rothschilds of Canadian realty." They were now seen both by the business community and by the press as possessors of almost superhuman commercial wisdom. They had achieved the *ne plus ultra* of real estate speculation. For their next trick, they would pull off the world's biggest commercial real estate development.

5

GRAND DESIGNS

Paul and Albert had some problems at first with Pelli's design. . . . Why weren't the buildings more like First Canadian Place?

One day in the fall of 1980, Paul Reichmann was shown into the Manhattan office of Richard Kahan, the man appointed to bring to fruition the long-frustrated attempts to develop Battery Park City, a ninety-two-acre landfill on lower Manhattan. The location, on the Hudson River beneath the World Trade Center, had been viewed as a white elephant almost since New York State had created the Battery Park City Authority in 1968. Various developers had broken ground in the 1970s but had always abandoned their plans. In 1979, the authority had been absorbed by the New York State Urban Development Corporation, of which Kahan was the chairman and chief executive officer, and he had received the thorny mandate from Governor Hugh Carey to get the project off the ground.

One of the main problems was, literally, the source of the ground. Much of the Battery Park landfill had come from excavations for the World Trade Center, whose huge twin towers had been the most spectacular example of an intensive building boom in lower Manhattan between 1969 and 1973 that had flooded the market with an additional 28 million square feet of office space. The World Trade Center had cast a 110-storey shadow over lower

Manhattan and an even bigger shadow over the real estate market. Downtown vacancy rates had soared to around 13 percent, with a corresponding softness in rents. It had taken the balance of the 1970s to absorb the space.

Kahan's job had been made somewhat easier by the improved economic environment. By 1980, New York had survived its crisis and there had been a resurgence in Wall-Street-centred finance and financial service industries. Kahan announced a new competition to develop Battery Park and a dozen top developers, including O&Y, presented proposals. Paul Reichmann came that autumn day to make his pitch. He lobbed up a slow ball that offered Kahan the opportunity to hit a homer.

While other contenders had come to Kahan with grandiose architectural visions for the site, Paul Reichmann came with a single, folded, blue sheet of paper in his pocket. The sheet contained not an architectural outline but a series of numbers. The numbers were the repayment schedule on the $200 million of bonds that the authority had floated some years before. "If I were to guarantee these bond repayments," asked Reichmann, "would I be on the right track?"

Kahan reportedly felt an urge to plant a kiss on the Toronto developer's hirsute cheek. Here, at last, was a man who understood. Reichmann had gone straight to the heart of the official's most pressing problem: the threat of default on the bonds.

Kahan had introduced a novel method of competition for the project. Usually in such circumstances, public agencies announce a "Request for Proposal" under which they invite developers to submit both a design and a financial plan. Then the agencies have to juggle with the relative merits of the two parts of the various plans, although the money side usually wins. In this case, Kahan had called in a prominent firm of designers, Cooper, Eckstut Associates, to draw up a detailed set of planning and architectural guidelines to which the bidders had to adhere. Kahan thus hoped to accelerate the process in order to generate income with which to pay off the bonds.

While other developers were still treating the project as a normal development, Paul Reichmann had seen that the required solution was not architectural but financial. He offered an ironclad set of guarantees. If there was a delay in construction, letters of credit ensured that O&Y would still pay the $50 million in ground rent and taxes it would owe if the buildings were finished. He also undertook to build the project much faster than any of the other contestants, in five years. Again, the attraction to the city of that approach was the speedier generation of municipal revenue.

Of course, by taking the pressure off Kahan, Paul Reichmann was putting it onto O&Y. He was committing his organization to finance, build, and lease the world's largest commercial development in record time and in one of the world's toughest building environments. "New York," in the words of an O&Y construction supervisor who had worked there all his life, "is a snake pit."

When Olympia & York got the job, some who had been watching Battery Park's snail's-pace progress thought the Reichmanns would wind up abandoning the project as their predecessors had. Others saw the potential for the men who had made the deal of the century to experience the pratfall of the decade.

The Young Lions

The Reichmanns had always hired away talent that they came across in the course of their business. Although it had taken them almost fifteen years from the first time they met him, they now employed Bill Hay, the Scottish lawyer who had negotiated the Flemingdon Park deal with them and then gone on to be president of Trizec. They had picked up Malcolm Spankie, who had been the Bank of Montreal's day-to-day overseer of the progress of First Canadian Place, and in January, 1981, Ed Minskoff, the sharp ex-banker and real estate broker who had brought them the Uris package, joined O&Y. They had also hired some of their most radical opponents from Toronto. These men, Mayor David Crombie's young lions, would all play a critical role in the New York development.

Ron Soskolne, the good-looking young South African architect who had locked horns with the Reichmanns over the demolition for First Canadian Place, had developed a respect for them in the course of negotiations. After Toronto's Central Area Plan was completed in 1978, Soskolne decided to move back into the private sector. He went to Paul Reichmann to seek his advice and was immediately offered a job.

Initially, Soskolne was hired to gain approval for a Boston project with which O&Y was having a lot of trouble. Called Exchange Place, it had become bogged down in a dispute with the city authority about the demolition of historic buildings. With the combination of his planning experience and architectural skills, Soskolne was able to come up with a scheme that incorporated the best of the existing buildings into the new project. The Reichmanns were impressed and the young architect soon became influential as the in-house "taste-maker" for Olympia & York. He was also instrumental in bringing in other young lions, in particular one of his most radical former colleagues, Michael Dennis.

Dennis, a lawyer by training, had been an advisor to Mayor David Crombie, and had then been appointed the first head of the city's new Housing Commission. One of the Crombie group's priorities was the creation of affordable housing. The logical outcome of their desire to reduce downtown commercial densities was to put this new housing in the heart of the city. Dennis became the driving force behind the St. Lawrence Market development.

Although he in fact came from a family of developers, Dennis seemed an unlikely property developer. He was radical, cocky, and abrasive. He enjoyed shaking up the Establishment. When he went to visit a friend's newly purchased house in the heart of Toronto's posh Rosedale district, he came armed with, and blowing, a hunting horn.

Dennis had left the Housing Commissioner's office shortly before Soskolne had quit the planning department. When he heard that Soskolne had joined O&Y, he called and asked if the Reichmanns would have any use for him. In fact, they were looking for someone just like him who could combine legal expertise with that of planning and development.

Dennis was soon assigned to New York, where he became one of O&Y's most influential executives. Toronto's former champion of social housing would wind up virtually running the world's biggest property development for the men who would soon be acknowledged as the world's biggest property developers. Perhaps it wasn't so much a classic example of gamekeeper turned poacher as a belief that the Reichmanns really *were* different from other developers. Or perhaps it was that whereas the city of Toronto had been the place to work in the early 1970s, now the only place to work was for the Reichmanns.

The last of the Toronto group to join was Tony Coombes, whom Soskolne had succeeded as chief city planner. When O&Y won Battery Park, Soskolne was given the responsibility for finding an architect and supervising the design, which he did by organizing a competition. Coombes had gone off to form a consulting firm,

Coombes Kirkland Berridge, and Soskolne called him in to help with the competition. Coombes went on to play a vital role in working with the Battery Park City Authority to gain the myriad municipal approvals needed for the development. Then, when the detailed design development work began, Coombes was hired to play a full-time co-ordinating role.

This core of former city planners — whose convictions had been tempered fighting developers in the cauldron of city politics—now set out with similar conviction to demonstrate what enlightened developers could do. New York held no dread for them. In fact, they were convinced that they had a few things to teach the Big Apple.

The Tuxedo Design

Soskolne chose a number of leading architects to submit plans for the Battery Park site based on the Cooper, Eckstut guidelines. Some, like Hellmuth Obata & Kassanbaum, were enormous established concerns. Others, like Kohn Pederson Fox, were smaller firms picked by Soskolne for the promise of their recent work. He gave the seven firms just three weeks to produce a rough proposal. From the submissions, three finalists were chosen: the entries of Kohn Pederson Fox; Mitchell/Giurgola; and Cesar Pelli & Associates.

O&Y's original request to the architects was for a three tower design. However, after the first stage, the Reichmanns decided to change the massing of the buildings and come up with a fourth tower. They added the requirement for some form of gateway leading in from Liberty Street to the development so that it would better "address" the existing downtown area. Based on these new parameters, the three finalists were asked to make fuller submissions, complete with scale models.

When Cesar Pelli, the dean of Yale's School of Architecture, arrived at 245 Park Avenue to make his presentation — at which Albert Reichmann was present—he was dressed in a tuxedo, even though it was only four o'clock in the afternoon. In fact, he wasn't trying to be smooth; it was just that he had a function to attend that evening and wouldn't have time to change. From Soskolne's point of view, Pelli's attire was appropriate. His design stood out as the classiest.

Kohn Pederson had produced four identical towers with a rounded facade facing southwest. Mitchell/Giurgola had come up with a more sensitive treatment of the location, but their buildings looked a little boxy and dull. Pelli's four towers, by contrast, were arresting. Indeed, for Paul and Albert, they were at first too arresting. But Pelli was the architect for the times.

Born in Argentina, to which his family had immigrated from their native Italy more than a century before, Cesar Pelli had studied architecture at the Universidad Nacional de Tucumán and later taught design there. After a scholarship to the University of Illinois, in 1954 he had joined the firm of Eero Saarinen and Associates in Bloomfield Hills, Michigan.

Saarinen caused a professional uproar in 1956 with his eaglelike design for the TWA terminal at Idlewild Airport (now Kennedy). He was considered beyond the pale by the purist purveyors of the steel, concrete, and glass boxes of the International Style, which dominated corporate and civic architecture in the postwar period. But the Finnish architect had an enormous influence on Pelli, who spent ten years with Saarinen's firm. In 1964, Pelli moved on to the firm of Daniel, Mann, Johnson and Mendenhall in Los Angeles, where his craft was further honed by tight budgets and schedules. In 1968, he joined Gruen Associates in Los Angeles; there, he was responsible for the city's Pacific Design Center and for the U.S. Embassy in Tokyo. Under his leadership, Gruen's designers in 1969 won the competition for a new United Nations Organization Headquarters and Conference Center in Vienna. In 1977, Pelli was appointed dean of the School of Architecture at Yale, where his commissions included the expansion and renovation of New York's Museum of Modern Art.

Two of the requirements of the Cooper, Eckstut's Battery Park City master plan had been that the design integrate with the New York architectural "vernacular," and that the material of the buildings change colour as they rose. Pelli's reference to the New York vernacular was clear. His buildings were computer-age descendants of the great crowned skyscrapers of the 1930s and 1940s. His interpretation of the change-of-colour requirement was considered brilliant. As they rose, the buildings would "peel" back and the surface area would shift from predominantly granite to predominantly glass.

Pelli's design was at the crest of a new wave in architecture, which was undergoing a sea change. A backlash had developed against the boxes of the International Style, whose intellectual source lay in the teachings of guru Walter Gropius, founder of the German Bauhaus school. Even as the Battery Park competition was being held, the International Style was being satirically savaged by author Tom Wolfe in two articles in the June and July issues of *Harper's* magazine.

In these articles, subsequently published in book form under the title *From Bauhaus to Our House*, Wolfe maintained that American architectural clients had for decades been held in thrall by the intellectual bullying of the Bauhaus gang. America had been subjected to a sea of "functional" buildings and gigantic, ugly cubes based on "revolutionary" theories that had no place in the United States.

"Every child," he wrote, "goes to school in a building that looks like a duplicating-machine replacement-parts wholesale distribution warehouse . . . Every new $900,000 summer house in the north woods or on the shore of Long Island . . . looks like an insecticide factory . . . Every law firm in New York moves . . . into a glass box office building with concrete slab floors and seven-foot-ten-inch-high concrete slab ceilings and plasterboard walls and pygmy corridors — and then hires a decorator and gives him a budget of hundreds of thousands of dollars to turn these mean cubes and grids into a horizontal fantasy of a Restoration townhouse."

Although many architects rejected Wolfe's lacerating attack as simplistic, the fact was that almost everybody else agreed with him. Perhaps he failed to take sufficient note of corporate and developer complicity in the International Style — after all, it had also been dubbed "balance sheet architecture": boxes were the most efficient way of putting useful space within walls — but the worm of taste was turning. In fact, a good part of the impetus was now coming from corporations who realized that they could hardly be strongly identified with their head office monuments if they all looked like cornflake boxes. The age of the cornflake box was drawing to an end.

"Postmodernism" was the catch-all for the new architectural styles. One branch went off in almost bizarre pictorial directions such as the Philip Johnson's Chippendale AT&T headquarters on Lexington Avenue. Another main branch harked back to the great New York and Chicago skyscrapers of the 1930s. That latter direction was the one taken by Pelli. His buildings had the subtle stepping of the best traditional skyscrapers, such as the Woolworth Building, not the huge, ugly steps of postwar Park Avenue, which gave buildings what looked like long, skinny heads on massive padded shoulders. Pelli's granite-to-glass transition was also both subtle and effective. And, although they did not have the fabulous spires that had made structures like the Chrysler Building world-famous, his towers were crowned with four different geometric shapes. If you wanted to be irreverent, you could call them "hats." But the whole point was that the mood of the time *was* irreverent.

Taken by themselves, Pelli's buildings were elegant and grace-ful. But standing so close to the World Trade Center they were almost *fun*. They would look like cute, expensively dressed, preppie kids standing beside strait-laced, pitchfork-toting parents straight out of *American Gothic*. Compared with Pelli's design, the World Trade Center looked square in every sense.

The Reichmanns had set up a committee consisting of Soskolne, Dennis, Coombes, and O&Y's construction chief Keith Roberts to oversee the choice of design. The committee soon sold itself on Pelli's plans. Its next task was to sell the Reichmanns.

Anticipating the Trend

One Sunday morning at eight o'clock, Ron Soskolne got a call at home in Toronto. Paul Reichmann was calling from New York: he and Albert had some time free and they would like the committee to come down and run them through the Battery Park plans. Rob-erts, Coombes, and Dennis were called. By noon the whole group was in the Park Avenue office.

At first, Paul and Albert had some problems with Pelli's design. It seemed less than revolutionary to them. In fact, they thought it looked a little old-fashioned. Their concern with building design, as ever, was not so much with aesthetics as with image. They looked at buildings from a marketing standpoint and tried to see them through the eyes of their clients. How would the head of a large corporation view the building? Would he want it for his head office? The Reichmanns' experience over many years had given them a clear idea of a prestige office building: it was an elegant tower with clean lines and high-quality materials. They were already experimenting with the new styles — for example, the pyramid-topped Fountain Plaza they were building in Portland, Oregon—but Battery Park was no place for experimentation. Why, they asked, were they going back to the past? Why weren't the buildings more like First Canadian Place?

Soskolne had his case well prepared. His argument was that, taking a long-term view of the architecture of office buildings, the ones that had best stood the test of time were those built in the 1930s. Lever House or the Seagram building, although excellent examples of the International Style, would ultimately appear — indeed already were appearing — more dated. He sold his bosses on the basis that O&Y was anticipating a trend. But the buildings were more than just a trend. Their architecture would prove timeless. Moreover, they would cater to the growing corporate demand for more individualistic and identifiable headquarters. By six that Sunday evening, the Reichmanns had been convinced. Pelli's design was given the nod.

The two brothers soon had evidence that their choice was a wise one. Pelli's concept drew rave reviews from critics, those of the *New York Times* in particular. Ada Louise Huxtable, the *Times*'s architecture correspondent, described it as "a co-ordinated and architecturally first-rate urban complex of the standard, significance and size of Rockefeller, Center, that will add a spectacular new beauty to the New York skyline. There has been no large scale development of comparable quality since the 1930's."

In his book, *The Skyscraper*, the *Times*'s architecture critic Paul Goldberger declared, ". . . this complex seems destined to become the major keeper of the New York skyscraper tradition in our time."

There was one slight problem with Pelli. As part of the second stage of the competition, Soskolne had quizzed the architects about their capacity to take on such a project. Pelli had said that he could. After he was picked, however, he had started to back-pedal. O&Y was not sure whether his concern was genuine, whether he had submitted the proposal without thinking that the project would go ahead, or whether he was just establishing a bargaining position. In the end, Pelli took overall responsibility for the exterior parts of the design and two other firms of architects — Haines Lundberg Waehler, and Adamson Associates — were brought in to design the "guts" of the buildings.

Pelli's main contribution, however, had now been made. He had given his clients a design that promised them a place alongside the builders of the world's great pieces of architecture. But the Reichmanns had more immediate concerns than posterity. They had to get the project built, and, even before that, they had to begin finding tenants.

6

BELL COWS AND
BRASS KNUCKLES

*"My faith in this project comes
from Paul . . . The biggest crapshooter
this town has ever seen."*

— *Richard Kahan*

Real estate development is, at the best of times, a business of frustrations. Even at Battery Park City, where there was a financially strapped state authority eager to push the development, progress still faced a vast array of obstacles. There were city authorities, who, although they wanted the revenues that the new complex would generate, also wanted to give away as little as possible in tax incentives; there were other developers, who, fearing Battery Park as a rival, put roadblocks in its way; and finally, there were the New York building unions, which many reckoned were the toughest in the world. Then, of course, there were the prospective tenants. Naturally, a developer could hardly refer to them as obstacles, since their leases would provide the collateral for financing the project. But the wooing process was long and difficult, and they often demanded handsome dowries.

Both Paul and Albert Reichmann, as always, were very closely involved every step of the way, from making design modifications to courting the lessees. One of the city authority's requirements was a "Winter Garden" as a public showpiece for the site. The interpretation was up to the developer and, as with all aspects of the development, the two brothers made the final choice: a

120-foot-high crystal palace of vaulted glass that would provide the focus for the site's retail, restaurant, and entertainment facilities.

Paul also introduced a number of modifications to the overall plan, based, once again, not primarily on aesthetics but on image and leasability. For example, the site was designed like a compound, with the buildings grouped around gardens facing the Hudson. Architecturally, the "entrance" was to be the twin octagonal towers of the gateway, but in fact almost everybody would enter the area via two pedestrian overpasses spanning the busy West Side Highway. Paul Reichmann was concerned that people driving down the highway would think they were looking at the backsides of the buildings; therefore he had additional entrances placed on the highway side.

The West Side Highway, meanwhile, was itself a source of problems. For a number of years there had been debate over the construction of a new highway along the old West Side route to link midtown Manhattan with Wall Street. O&Y was concerned because the construction of the new road would cut Battery Park City off, at least temporarily, from the rest of the financial district. The West Side Highway was already a significant barrier. It was therefore essential that overpasses be built to carry pedestrian traffic, whether the new highway went ahead or not. But the main crosswalk was linked to the World Trade Center complex, whose owners saw the Battery Park complex as an obvious rival for their leasing space. Thus they were less than accommodating.

There was a year's delay between "winning" the deal and completing all the documentation. Negotiations with the city over "pilots" (payments in lieu of taxes) and ground rents were very complicated. There was also controversy over tax abatements that O&Y wanted from the city. Abatements had been one of the methods used to lure real estate investment back into New York after its near collapse. Now, however, many critics were saying that, in the healthier real estate environment, abatement was no longer necessary.

Richard Kahan's regard for Paul Reichmann increased during the course of the negotiations. Opposition lawyers constantly tried to pick holes in the verbal agreement between them. But if Kahan said that something had been agreed, Paul Reichmann went along with it. Later Kahan said, "My faith in this project comes from Paul." Kahan joked that if Reichmann would stop chain-smoking, the project would require less security. He was, said Kahan, "The biggest crapshooter this town has ever seen."

Leasing: "No Problem"

While they were still struggling with final approvals for the deal, the Reichmanns and their staff had already begun an intensive search for tenants. The fourteen-acre section of the landfill site that O&Y had committed to develop would have a whopping 8 million square feet of space, of which 6 million would be office space. They needed not just tenants but big tenants.

The Battery Park site was off the beaten track. Even though it was only off by a few blocks, those few were important. The Reichmanns, Minskoff, and Dennis had to make Battery Park an "address." Lower Manhattan, the southern tip of the island, has within it an inverse "golden triangle" of property bounded on the north by Wall Street, on the west by Broadway, and on the east by Water Street. This area, the traditional financial heart of Manhattan, contains mainly buildings of 1930s vintage. Above it is the insurance district; to the east, along the East River, is a predominantly banking area; to the west, between the triangle and Battery Park City, lies the World Trade Center and the old shipping district, which had moved into decline along with its principal industry. North of the World Trade Center lay the "back offices" of the financial core.

A counterbalance to Battery Park City's location problem was that much of downtown Manhattan's space was unsuitable for the new demands of the financial industry. The older buildings didn't have enough power; they didn't have the ceiling heights to accommodate trading floors; and they didn't have the large floor spaces necessary to handle modern business. The 1930s buildings were obsolete when it came to coping with fiber optic cables and other modern communications developments. Also, the growth of many financial institutions had caused staff to be scattered among a number of buildings. Another selling point for Battery Park City was that the new tenants would be able to consolidate their space requirements in a single quality address.

Michael Dennis and Ed Minskoff drew up a "hit list" of dozens of potential tenants, then they began knocking on executive doors. Each of the four towers, ranging from thirty-three to fifty-five storeys, offered an average floor space of 40,000 square feet. "Look at the quality and size of these buildings," the O&Y executives said to clients. "Any financial institution worth its salt has to think seriously about taking a big piece of space in Battery Park."

If the executive replied that his company was quite happy where it was, the O&Y pitchman would change tack. "What would it cost you to move?" they would ask. "Three million dollars? Fine. We'll factor that in. You're moving at no cost. Now, what about the costs of fitting the space to your requirements? Do you want more elevator capacity, or underfloor ducting, or special security arrangements? Whatever the cost, we'll factor that in too. Any other problems?"

"Well," the prospect might say, "the fact is that we've already got a long-term lease." "So what's the cost?" O&Y would ask. "Well," the tenant might respond, "we're paying twenty dollars a square foot and we're signed up for ten years." "No problem," would come the reply. "We'll just take that lease back from you. All you have to do is just sign here on the dotted line."

The prospective tenant, faced with a free move, unburdened of his old lease, and offered the prospect of state-of-the-art, custom-fitted premises, would have to think pretty fast for reasons *not* to sign on the dotted line. But of course there was a price to pay: Battery Park rents reflected the quality and cost of the buildings. O&Y was the IBM of property developers, but as with IBM, top service meant top dollar.

Securing a first tenant to sign a big lease was very important. O&Y needed to attract a "name" into the development as a "bell cow" that would lead other tenants in. To do so, they were prepared to provide additional accommodations. The bell cow was brought to them by a well-known Manhattan real estate broker named John C. Cushman III.

When Cushman came to see Minskoff in the summer of 1981, he was trying to sell O&Y a skyscraper at 59 Maiden Lane, three blocks north of Wall Street, owned by City Investing — a conglomerate with $8 billion of assets whose interests ranged from air conditioning equipment and insurance to printing and budget motels. The asking price was $175 million. The insurance giants Prudential Assurance and Equitable Life — both mammoth holders of real estate — had already turned him down. O&Y also rejected a straight purchase. But then Minskoff and Cushman came up with a deal based on the old "used car" technique, of which Bill

Zeckendorf had made such good use during his "Wall Street Manoeuvre" twenty years before. It was really a variation on relieving tenants of old leases as an inducement to move, only in this case O&Y would buy the building if City Investing would sign a long-term lease on a big enough chunk of Battery Park.

The first face-to-face meeting between Paul Reichmann and George T. Scharffenberger, chairman and chief executive of City Investing, was reportedly a less than scintillating occasion. Neither man specialized in small talk. Seeking to break the ice, Scharffenberger asked what plans Reichmann had for the building's lobby. Reichmann suggested that it would be lined with shops. Scharffenberger was less than impressed; that didn't sound very good for the company's image at all. "Oh, don't worry," Reichmann said. "It will be very, very dignified."

The negotiations proved tough, but they also had a natural time limit imposed on them: the proposed enactment of a new city sales tax on real estate purchases that would have added $15 million to the cost of the sale. Racing to beat the clock, O&Y and the City Investing negotiators worked virtually round the clock for six weeks. Nevertheless, Cushman was both astonished and impressed that the Reichmanns would not work, or allow anyone to work on their behalf, on Rosh Hashanah and Yom Kippur, which fell on September 29–30 and October 8 respectively, right in the middle of the negotiations.

In November, 1981, just a week after the final agreement had been concluded with the Battery Park City Authority, a deal was announced under which City Investing would take nearly seven hundred thousand square feet of space. According to a rare O&Y press release, it represented "one of the largest tenancies, in dollar volume, in New York City's history." The release made no mention of the actual dollars, but the lease was reportedly for thirty-five years at $35 a square foot, which fitted in with reports of an "$850 million deal." But of course that sum referred to the total stream of lease income, which was a very different thing from the deal's present value. Discounted at 10 percent per annum over its thirty-five-year life, it was worth about $240 million. No mention was made in the release of O&Y's purchase of Maiden Lane. O&Y announced that construction of the "City Investing Building" at Battery Park would begin almost immediately. It was to be finished by 1984. In fact, City Investing never did move into Battery Park City, and wound up, with some irony, having to negotiate an expensive lease to stay in the building at 59 Maiden Lane, which now belonged to the Reichmanns. There were no press releases about that development.

At the time, however, O&Y seemed to have its bell cow, but it was really just a bell calf. City Investing's lease took only 11 percent of the Battery Park space. Minskoff and Dennis continued to make the rounds of financial giants with offices scattered throughout Manhattan, firms that might want to consolidate in one building. As it happened, the financial giant they wanted came to them as a result of a chance meeting.

Minskoff was walking home one evening up Park Avenue when he ran into Sandford "Sandy" Weill, chairman of the newly merged Shearson/American Express financial conglomerate. Minskoff had known Weill for many years, and as they chatted, he said, on the spur of the moment: "Why don't we buy your headquarters? You can take the capital gain [as City Investing had done] and consolidate all your operations in the Battery Park." Weill said he would think about it. A month later, serious negotiations began.

For American Express, the idea of realizing the capital gain on their headquarters was particularly attractive as it would help them solve another business problem. They had a bond portfolio that had declined considerably in value. If it were sold, large write-offs would hit profits. But if O&Y bought Amex's office block, the real estate write-up would more than offset the portfolio write-off.

O&Y's proposal was outlined in a simple two-page letter from Paul Reichmann to Weill. O&Y was helping Amex solve its particular problem, but Weill was also well aware that he was helping Reichmann solve his: once Amex had taken a big chunk of Battery Park, the place was "made." The Reichmanns could lure future tenants at higher rents on the basis of the Amex name. Just as you were not meant to leave home without Amex, so a lot of big companies would feel a lot more inclined to *change* home if they saw that the prestigious financial company had moved into Battery Park.

O&Y agreed to pay $240 million for Amex's building, giving the credit card and investment giant a $180 million capital gain to cope with its portfolio loss. In return, and after some hard bargaining between Reichmann and Weill over rent, American Express signed a lease on the biggest of the buildings, the planned fifty-one-storey structure on the northeast corner of the site, the one with the pyramid-shaped "hat." The thirty-five-year lease on the American Express building, when it was announced in March, 1982, was touted as "the largest real estate transaction in history," worth $2.4 billion in as-spent dollars.

With its second major tenant, and half its office space let, Olympia & York renamed its Battery Park development the World Financial Center. Many sage voices had said — privately of course — that the Battery Park development would depress the Wall Street real estate market for many years and that the Reichmanns were tying themselves to a white elephant. But now, with the City Investing and American Express leases signed, doubts were muted.

Said Henri Alster, one of Manhattan's leading real estate consultants: "They not only have confirmed what many said a year ago would be impossible: that is, to fill half of the office space at the $1 billion mixed-use complex in six months. They have done what William Zeckendorf did when he established the United Nations building on the East Side in the early 1950s — created an address and wound up with all the land surrounding it. An extremely intelligent move."

However, the project was still some way from being totally sewn up. Half the planned space still had to be leased. And the project had to be built. In record time.

Brass Knuckle Chess

Buildings have many meanings for those involved with them. Architects view them aesthetically; steel erectors see them as a place of macho camaraderie; corporate chieftains look at them in terms of prestige and costs; developers regard them as so much collateral and cash flow.

For most people, a building really comes into existence only when it is completed. For the people who put them up, by contrast, interest often ceases when the process of creation is at an end. For those in charge on the site, buildings aren't so much physical entities as a series of struggles against the forces of obstruction and chaos, against Murphy's law writ large.

By the time Governor Carey "broke ground" for the project in December, 1981, the logistics of the enormous development were already, under the supervision of construction chief Keith Roberts, well into the planning stage. The blueprints had to be transformed, via the organization of thousands of men and hundreds of thousands of tons of materials, into a huge, granite-clad, concrete-and-steel reality. Roberts would, over the next four years, spend an average of two or three days a week in Manhattan. But the man who held the hands-on responsibility for the physical construction of the project was John Norris, another Englishman who had been with the Reichmanns for a dozen years.

Norris was a British bulldog. Short and stocky, with a square, pugilistic face and a jutting jaw, he looked like the rugby player that he still was. Norris had joined O&Y in 1968, the year he came to Canada. In England, he had been an area manager for British property magnate Charlie Clore. When he joined O&Y, its construction side pretty much consisted of two men, Keith Roberts and purchasing wizard Otto Blau. The company had been mainly involved in the Flemingdon Park development and was just beginning to move to larger downtown projects in Ottawa, Toronto, and later Calgary. Norris took over the site management at many of these major projects, such as Place Bell Canada and the Esplanade Laurier in Ottawa, and also at the Shell and Esso buildings in booming Calgary. Norris had developed with the company and had been closely involved with the innovations for First Canadian Place, in particular the computer control system.

Norris had at first found the building styles in North America very different from those in the United Kingdom. The Reichmanns demanded as much from their staff as they demanded from themselves, and that in particular meant both quality *and* speed. Norris soon learned what "fast-tracking" meant, that is, literally designing a building as it was being put up. This method — to generate rentals as quickly as possible — put a lot of pressure on supervision and quality control, and it put a lot of pressure on people. John Norris was appointed as the source of that pressure. That, in turn, put a lot of pressure on him.

Norris was a hard man: he knew how to make subcontractors jump, and he was not above using an expletive or two to get his point across. But his style inevitably led to some problems with the New York unions. They could be pretty tough, too.

Manhattan's bustling character and the sheer cost of its real estate had created a peculiarly hothouse environment for the construction industry. Buildings had to be put up fast because of the potentially crippling carrying costs of real estate financed with large amounts of borrowed money. The implications were not lost on the building unions. They were renowned for driving hard bargains and for securing the maximum overtime. (During a later New York State inquiry into construction industry work rules, it was revealed that one of the union representatives on the Battery Park site pulled in an annual salary of $570,000, much of it while on holiday, and partly through the supernatural feat of working twenty-six-hour days!)

At first, Norris's uncompromising style did not sit well with the unions. Both sides were used to giving ulcers rather than getting them. Dealing with the unions, said Norris diplomatically, was "like a game of chess." About as much like a game of chess as a pool hall brawl in Harlem. It was also a rare game of chess where you had your life threatened, but that, on several occasions, happened to Norris. Nevertheless, an accommodation was eventually reached and the local unions developed a grudging respect for the O&Y vice-president.

Norris was hardly easier on his own construction staff, whom he used to gather for six o'clock breakfast meetings to plan the day's campaign. They were sometimes on the receiving end of his short fuse, but they suspected that there was really a heart of gold under that crusty exterior. Somewhere. You always had to have a sense of humour. One staff member found a magazine picture of a 2,300-pound great white shark, printed "John Norris" on it, and duly sent it on the rounds of the in-trays.

To supervise the nuts-and-bolts construction of the building, a more diplomatic approach was needed. That was where local experience came in, particularly in the form of men like Dan Mernit.

Dan Mernit, a bespectacled, avuncular figure with a bald head, tinted glasses, and a trimmed moustache, looked more like a friendly storekeeper than a builder. But he had spent the best part of forty years erecting skyscrapers in New York City. He had put up twenty-storey buildings with the help of just a timekeeper and a labour foreman. There had been no electrical or mechanical engineers in those days, none of the "brain surgeons," as he called them, on the sites. But the increasing specialization of the building industry had made men like Mernit, who could take in the big picture, all the more important.

Ironically, Mernit had spent many years working for the Uris brothers. When he turned up at the Toronto offices of O&Y to be interviewed for the Battery Park job, he was taken aback because all over the walls were pictures of *his* buildings, like 245 Park Avenue. It was only then that he found out that the Reichmanns had, with a small flourish of the pen and a gigantic leap of faith, acquired a thousand times his lifework and much more besides.

After his Uris years, Mernit had worked on such major projects as Detroit's Renaissance Center and Walt Disney's Epcot Center in Florida. He had seen enormous advances in equipment and materials, from the kangaroo crane to sheetrock. The technology within the buildings had also evolved beyond recognition. They still consisted of walls and floors, but those walls and floors were now alive with a multitude of sensitive systems that made the buildings "smart." They could automatically turn lights on and off; they could regulate heating and air conditioning; they could put you in touch with the rest of the world.

Looked at another way however, the building business had not changed at all. It was still all about human nature. Each building presented new problems, but essentially they were variations on a theme. Whatever happened, Dan Mernit had been there before. Now he was given the job of superintending the biggest commercial development in the world in record time. He, too, discovered what O&Y's "fast-tracking" meant.

The first employee on the Battery Park site, Mernit began to put in the roads and infrastructure on the flat barren ground. Rapidly, Norris hired people to take over specific site tasks, such as security and transport supervision. At the height of activity, 3,000 people worked on the site. Within Mernit's trailer, with its metal stacking chairs and its Styrofoam coffee cups, the walls were covered with notices, memos, and blueprints interspersed with those cute signs saying things like "It's tough to soar with eagles when you work with turkeys." There, Mernit received a constant stream of calls and visits about problems and progress on the site: an area needed the electricians to put in more light; a group of tradesmen had not turned up; part of one the buildings had a structural problem.

Often he would sally forth, Motorola walkie-talkie holstered at the ready, like some tough but kindly local sheriff, to deal with the workers and subcontractors. Everybody loved Dan. He had a comforting cliché for every situation. One of his favourites was "We have met the enemy and it is us." He even had it pinned up on his wall. Each morning at five-thirty he would be on the site, ready to take on the problems one by one, and each day, as the Circle Line Tour ferry ploughed past between the site and the Statue of Liberty, progress was made.

Many of the techniques introduced in First Canadian Place were refined for the World Financial Center. In particular, a more advanced system of computerized control for the movement and monitoring of men and materials was introduced and put under the supervision of Torontonian Dan Frank, one of O&Y's "Romanian Mafia," whose charter member was Otto Blau.

The system, designed by former NBC man Joe Weinstein, president of Autocomp Systems Corp., still required three full-time staff to spend most of their time on the phones to suppliers and subcontractors, but the program allowed them to co-ordinate schedules for deliveries and use of hoists very rapidly, and the computer's ability to spit out paper saved huge amounts of time.

For Mernit and those who worked with him, the Reichmanns were a mystery. Just as his vision embraced the work of literally thousands of individuals, from the labourers to the "brain surgeon" specialist engineers, so Mernit realized that, somewhere up there, the Reichmanns' vision embraced his. They were, he would say with a shake of his head, *swift*. He would see them at ceremonies, such as the groundbreaking, or he would get a call from their office or from John Norris telling him that one or both were coming for a site inspection. Then he would be waiting for them at the gate when they turned up in their limo, with their undertakers' suits and their homburgs, and he would take them around. He had little doubt that their basic questions had deep meanings. Compared with them, he felt that he was a simple man. He daydreamed about scuba diving or flying. He couldn't begin to guess what weird and wonderful things went on in Paul Reichmann's mind. Dan Frank had his own capsule commentary on the Reichmanns' knowability: "They make their deals in the clouds."

Even as the four towers of the World Financial Center were beginning to rise from the mists of the Hudson, Paul Reichmann was plotting deals that would make the heads not merely of ordinary men but of the most financially sophisticated observers spin. The World Financial Center was not built and it was only half leased, but in Paul Reichmann's mind it was already a *fait accompli*. His restless ambitions moved on to new challenges. There were few if any left in real estate.

In 1980, O&Y not only won the Battery Park contract, but also outbid rival Toronto-based Cadillac Fairview, North America's largest publicly owned real estate company, to redevelop twenty-five acres in the heart of downtown San Francisco. O&Y was building all over North America, from Calgary to Miami, from Los Angeles to Dallas. It was time to lay the groundwork for building of a different variety: that of a diversified commercial empire.

7

BUMPING INTO THE BRONFMANS

Between them, the Reichmanns and the Edper-
controlled Brascan would account for a very
large portion of the business news in the
1980s. Jimmy Connacher was always somewhere
behind the headlines.

The Reichmanns' apparent lack of concern about being part of any establishment only increased their fascination for the business community. When Peter Newman's *The Canadian Establishment* appeared in 1975, the family had scarcely rated a mention, being consigned to the mere listing of "the $50 million group." They also received a footnote for having capitalized on executives' desire for corner offices by building the York Centre in Toronto with eight corners per floor. Their lack of coverage was more than a little due to their aversion to publicity. However, they were still considered merely a reclusive family of property developers. But in the space of half a dozen years, their corporate profile rose dramatically.

Newman defined the business establishment by its associations and its trappings, but the Reichmanns were almost impossible to pigeonhole in such terms. They didn't buy hockey or baseball teams; they didn't belong to clubs; they didn't play golf or ski or fish. In fact, all they did, when they weren't with their families or studying the Talmud, was work. And the results of all that work were phenomenal.

Their real estate business was like a giant cash register, relentlessly ringing up millions of dollars each week in revenues. Equally important, the empire, in particular the Uris properties in New York, had become a growing collateral base against which the bankers and the other financial institutions were virtually begging the Reichmanns to borrow.

As for their wealth, their refusal to comment upon it merely whetted the appetites of the press and the business community. In a 1978 interview with the Toronto-based *Executive* magazine, the following exchange took place between the magazine's Dean Walker and Albert Reichmann:

> Question: As a private company you do not have to reveal any figures but I would like to give some indications of the size of this enterprise. Are there any sorts of figures you are prepared to give me?
> Answer: No.
> Question: I have seen one published guess, putting the assets at $1.3 billion. Do you care to comment on that?
> Answer: We'll leave it at a guess.

Those who had seen O&Y's financial statements were reported to have come away open-mouthed. In the course of the bidding for the San Francisco development, the city governors dispatched a Touche Ross accountant to examine O&Y's books in order to make sure they had the wherewithal to fund the project. The accountant returned with the astonishing news that O&Y could build its U.S. $300 million to U.S. $400 million share of the project without borrowing a cent.

Such financial strength made them all the more attractive to bankers and institutions with funds to invest. In the 1970s, "asset growth" had become the name of the bankers' game. A bank's assets are its loans, and success was increasingly measured by how much you could persuade your clients to borrow. The rapid expansion of Canadian developers into the United States in the 1970s had been made possible by their Canadian bankers. They could lend their individual clients far more than most American banks, whose exposure was restricted by law. As the value of the Reichmanns' property portfolio moved into the billions, so the funds available to them multiplied. The brothers were held in awe, even in Manhattan, because they could pick up the phone and arrange a $300 million credit in less time than it took to order a pizza.

The availability of funds supported accelerated expansion within real estate and diversification outside it. That expansion and diversification inevitably led the Reichmanns to run up against other empire builders in Canada's tight-knit business elite. In 1979, they collided with the junior branch of Canada's then most famous Jewish business family, the Bronfmans, just as that branch was finally casting off its junior status.

Trizec and the Growth of Edper

Real estate means, literally, building from the ground up. One obvious means of starting several floors up is to acquire the real estate operations of others. In the latter half of the 1970s, with a number of major developments such as the Shell Centre and Esso Plaza in the oil boomtown of Calgary, the Reichmanns began looking beyond Alberta for an acquisition on the West Coast. They held talks with Jack Poole at Vancouver-based Daon Development, one of the real estate companies that had led the Canadian charge into the U.S. market. However, there was considerable resistance to a Reichmann takeover from Daon's middle management and the deal fell through. Then they drew a bead on the more receptive Vancouver-based real estate development and brokerage firm of Block Bros. Industries, the creation of Arthur and Henry Block. Block Brothers had a large residential real estate portfolio in British Columbia and a smaller presence in Alberta. The attraction to the Reichmanns was that it gave them a ready-made presence on the West Coast. They eventually took the company private, but essentially left it to run itself.

They then began looking for real estate acquisitions farther afield. In 1979, they had their attention drawn to English Property, Great Britain's third largest developer, with considerable real estate holdings in France and Belgium. They were introduced to English Property's management by Bill Hay, the man who had negotiated the seminal Flemingdon Park deal with them fourteen years earlier. Hay had joined O&Y from Trizec after Edward and Peter Bronfman had taken control of the company in 1976 via their investment holding company Edper Investments. Because of the complex relationship between English Property and Trizec, the Reichmanns' interest in the London-based company put them, at least temporarily, on a collision course with the Bronfmans.

Edward and Peter were the sons of Allan Bronfman, the youngest brother of Sam Bronfman, founder of the mighty Seagram empire. The main Seagram inheritance had passed on to Sam's sons, Edgar and Charles, but Edward and Peter had made a shrewd move in acquiring two brilliant advisors to nurture and expand their investment interests. The men were Trevor Eyton, a large, gregarious, and slightly rumpled partner in the Toronto law firm of Tory, Tory, DesLauriers & Binnington, and Jack Cockwell, a whip-smart South-African-born chartered accountant who joined the Edper organization in 1969 from Touche Ross.

The keystone to the success of the Edper group was generally reckoned to be its 1976 acquisition of control of Trizec, the company founded in 1960 to complete William Zeckendorf's Place Ville Marie. Trizec had been formed by Webb & Knapp (Canada) Limited in partnership with the British company Eagle Star Insurance and Eagle Star's real estate subsidiary Second Covent Garden Property. The name was based on "Tri" for three, "Z" for Zeckendorf, "E" for Eagle Star, and "C" for Covent Garden. Zeckendorf originally held half of the company's equity, but in 1963, when Webb & Knapp found itself unable to meet its financial commitments to the Montreal project, Eagle Star bailed out Zeckendorf in return for a larger share of Trizec. Although the development still hadn't shown a profit, Place Ville Marie was viewed as having enormous potential.

Zeckendorf was succeeded as head of Trizec by James Soden, a tough Montreal lawyer, and under his guidance and that of Bill Hay, Trizec grew rapidly through both the acquisition and construction of properties. The company played a leading role in the development of suburban shopping centres, such as Toronto's Yorkdale Plaza, at one time the largest such facility in Canada. By 1968, with assets of $241 million, Trizec ranked as the largest publicly owned Canadian real estate company.

In 1970, it acquired the Montreal-based family-controlled Cummings Properties Limited, which had assets of $115 million, and also began to expand its operations into the United States via a 51-percent-owned subsidiary, Tristar Developments, Inc. The Cummings brothers had some joint ventures with a company called

Great West International Equities Ltd., the creation of flamboyant Calgarian Sam Hashman, so a merger with his company was seen as another logical move. Hashman, who was cut from the cloth of real estate giants like Zeckendorf, relished large, luxuriously equipped aircraft and ninety-foot yachts. Edward and Peter Bronfman had a large interest in Hashman's venture. Trizec's merger with Great West thus brought the Bronfmans onto the Trizec board and gave them 9 percent of its equity. By 1972, Trizec was the largest publicly owned real estate company in North America.

Toward the end of 1975, Peter Bronfman approached Trizec's Soden and asked if he would be sympathetic to a move by the Bronfmans to "Canadianize" Trizec. Canada had witnessed an increase in economic nationalism in the early 1970s, most clearly demonstrated in the creation of the Foreign Investment Review Agency (FIRA). The majority of Trizec's equity was still controlled by Eagle Star Insurance through its minority-owned property arm English Property Corporation, the management of which felt that the new Canadian climate was "inimical" to foreign investment and would make the raising of new capital difficult. A complex plan was worked out under which English Property would continue to hold the majority of Trizec shares, but control of Trizec for FIRA purposes would pass, via a new holding company, Carena Properties Inc., into the hands of the Bronfmans.

Once the deal was done, the Bronfmans moved quickly and ruthlessly to shake up Trizec, which they claimed had been badly managed. There was no doubt that its rapid expansion had left it financially overextended. But the changes were handled less than diplomatically. Bill Hay left to join the Reichmanns. From a story in the Toronto *Globe and Mail*, Jim Soden discovered that there was to be a shakeup in the executive suite; he then found himself frozen out of operations. Eventually he was terminated on terms he believed less generous than those dictated by his employment contract. The Bronfmans' seizure of Trizec thus left some ill feelings.

Edper pumped money into Trizec and installed Harold Milavsky, a hard-nosed and brilliant accountant who had been a protégé of Sam Hashman, as president and chief executive in Soden's place. Under Milavsky's guidance, Trizec became both larger and financially stronger. By 1979, its assets hit the magic $1 billion mark. But then the Reichmanns suddenly appeared on the scene. The Bronfmans thought that Paul and Albert wanted to steal Trizec from them.

"Corporate Poker and Bluff"

In the middle of January, 1979, Paul and Albert Reichmann travelled to London to visit English Property executive Stanley Honeyman. They told him that they were interested in buying control of his company. Honeyman was receptive to a bid, at the right price, and the Reichmanns went on a tour of English Property's European holdings.

The Edper side believed that it had a commitment from English Property to allow Edper to increase its holdings in, and thus cement its control of, Trizec. As far as they were concerned, it was their financial commitment and the managerial expertise they had installed that had turned the company around, and they were concerned that the fruits of that success would now be plucked from under their noses if there were new controllers of English Property who felt they owed the Bronfmans nothing.

English Property became the subject of a many-sided bidding war. The Netherlands' largest quoted real estate company, NV Beleggingsmaatschappij Wereldhave, made a bid, while Eagle Star Insurance, which now controlled just 21 percent of English Property, offered to buy all the shares it did not already own.

The Reichmanns initially said nothing to the Bronfmans about their intentions, and the Bronfmans clearly thought that it was Trizec that the Reichmanns were after. Edper executives claimed that Olympia & York would not be an acceptable partner for publicly owned Trizec because of potential conflicts of interest with O&Y's privately controlled real estate empire.

By February 21, 1979, the Reichmanns, through the British-based merchant bank of Rothschild, had bought 7.6 million common shares plus some convertible securities of English Property. That day they launched a 50-pence-per-share offer for its remaining shares. They had already persuaded Eagle Star to tender its 21 percent stake to their offer. The Toronto *Globe and Mail*, in a report on February 22, noted, "Edper has repeatedly stated that it views Olympia & York's actions as unfriendly and that it would regard the company as an uninvited and unfriendly partner in Trizec."

An analyst was quoted as saying, "It strikes me that there is going to be one terrible fight."

On Friday, February 23, the Reichmanns, who had now been dubbed "the shy Canadians" by the British press, sweetened their offer to 54 pence. English Property's management announced that it had accepted. Its deputy chief executive officer, Gerald Rothman, was quoted as saying that the situation between the Reichmanns and Bronfmans was now "a game of corporate poker and bluff." The battle was being billed as one to determine the ultimate domination of the Canadian development industry.

Over the weekend of February 24, the Dutch group, reportedly encouraged and supported by Edper, who had made a deal with them on English Property's Trizec stake, raised its offer to 56 pence. On Monday, February 26, the Reichmanns, with typical lightning speed, responded by raising their bid to 60 pence, valued at $157.3 million.

Paul Reichmann, breaking the family's silence to the newspapers if not to the Bronfmans, was quoted as saying: "There has been a very mistaken notion in the press that we are unfriendly bidders. It is not Trizec we are bidding for but English Property. Before we entered, the bid was 37 pence a share. I would say that at 60 pence ours is a very welcome bid. It was made in full co-operation with the management of English Property."

But if there was a "mistaken notion," it certainly hadn't arisen in the press. It was firmly implanted in the minds of Edward and Peter Bronfman and their management, despite public statements by Paul Reichmann that he was prepared to let existing arrangements between English Property and Trizec stand. If they won control of English Property, the Reichmanns would have the right to appoint four directors to Trizec's board and one executive officer, and could demand representation on the company's executive committee. Another senior Edper executive, Timothy Price, declared that he "regretted" the Reichmanns' actions. "Edper is prepared to vigorously assert its ownership and control position in Trizec under its shareholder agreements," he said. "If the Reichmann brothers were successful with their offer, they would consistently be in a conflict of interest position between Trizec and their private real estate holdings."

Paul Reichmann took up the debate in the press but still did not take it to the Bronfmans. He disputed Edper's assertions of conflict of interest. "We are both large companies in real estate and it

just happens our paths do not cross too often,'' he was quoted as
saying. ''Our operations are in different markets, but there are
some activities in common markets . . . Reasonable people can
find a way to insulate any transactions if there is a possible conflict
of interest.''

Asked what he would do if the Bronfmans started a fight, he
said: ''I am not worried about any battle, because I don't see the
potential of a fight in the future. I can think of many reasons why
they would not want us to be in English Property, but I don't see
any problem if we acquire it.'' Clearly, Reichmann did not consider
the Bronfmans' problems his problems, although he said, ''Trizec
is a very well run company and if our offer is accepted for English
Property we anticipate doing nothing to change its management
structure.'' The London stock market was banking on a fight.
English Property shares were trading above the Reichmanns'
offer price of 60 pence. Meanwhile, Reichmann's calming words
seemed to have the opposite effect on the Bronfmans.

In March, Edper, in order to protect its Trizec investment,
decided to enter the bidding war. A team of six financiers and
lawyers, headed by Harold Milavsky, Trevor Eyton, and Jack
Cockwell, was dispatched to Europe to evaluate English Property
and work out a defensive strategy. They had to make their offer by
March 23, when the Reichmanns' bid expired.

Then, somewhat anticlimactically, as the result of a chance meeting, the battle ended before it had started. The day before they
were due to launch their rival bid on the London Stock Exchange,
Harold Milavsky and Trevor Eyton were sitting in the lobby of
their London hotel when Paul Reichmann suddenly appeared.
Eyton and Milavsky watched him check in and go up to his room;
less than five minutes later they saw him come down and check
out again. Says Eyton, ''I guess he got to his room and found out
he was in the wrong hotel.''

Eyton and Milavsky watched him go to the front door to take a
cab. Milavsky suggested they should pay their respects. Recalls
Eyton, ''It's the Canadian way at the very least to be courteous, so
we went over to shake his hand. He obviously liked that and he
obviously didn't want a public fuss, so he said, 'why don't we go
inside and talk.' And so Paul Reichmann and Harold and myself
and Jack Cockwell sat in the lobby and in a period of ten minutes
we came to a general understanding which we translated into
agreements about a week later in Montreal, which is the basis for

our agreements and our understanding and our association in Trizec today."

At those subsequent meetings in Montreal, Eyton was impressed because Paul and Albert did not have a lawyer. He admired the Reichmanns' speed and facility of decision-making. Whenever they reached a difficult point, Paul and Albert would excuse themselves and step outside the door. Sometimes they would return in less than a minute, declaring with a smile that they had just had a board meeting, and here was their answer or their proposal. The talks continued through March 14 and 15, the day of Trizec's annual meeting, and were concluded just before midnight. The Bronfmans agreed not to challenge the Reichmanns' bid for English Property. The Reichmanns in turn gave the Bronfmans an option to increase their ownership of Trizec, and postponed the buy-sell arrangement that would have been triggered in July. They approved existing Trizec policies and management, and also gave an undertaking to avoid conflicts of interest in partnership dealings with Trizec.

The new agreements provided the Bronfmans with an option to obtain equal ownership with English Property of their mutual investment in Trizec and more of the profit. With regards to potential conflict of interest, O&Y was to assume the role of Caesar's wife, and just to make sure, part of the agreement was that Olympia & York would not begin a major development in a city in which Trizec had a partially leased property. Said Toronto analyst Ira Gluskin, "I always thought those Bronfmans were smart, but it turns out the Reichmanns were smarter."

In fact, both sides were smart.

Moving in on the Business Establishment

The accommodation over Trizec was of great importance in establishing links between the Reichmanns and the Edper empire. The critical link was not between the Reichmanns and the Bronfmans, but between the Reichmanns and Trevor Eyton and Jack Cockwell, who would go on to guide the Edper holdings through a dazzling array of acquisitions.

One of the first moves that Eyton and Cockwell made following the resolution of the Trizec affair was an assault on Brascan, a sprawling Toronto-based company with an exotic history but an uninspired management record. Brascan's origins were as the Brazilian Traction, Light and Power Company. The company had started with mule-drawn tram services in São Paulo and wound up electrifying, and then owning, large parts of Brazil. Under the controversial direction of Jake Moore, Brascan diversified both inside and outside Brazil. In 1978, it sold its main Brazilian electric utility for $447 million. That cash began to attract a lot of predators.

Eyton and Cockwell drew a bead on the treasure chest, and, despite an abortive attempt by Moore to acquire F.W. Woolworth — a move that would have made Brascan too big to swallow — Edper won control of the company after a bitter battle. During the fight, Edper's open-market purchases of Brascan's stock were directed by Gordon Securities, an ultra-aggressive Bay Street investment house headed by the ultra-aggressive Jimmy Connacher. Just as Eyton and Cockwell would become important contacts for the Reichmanns, so would Connacher.

Connacher was a hyperactive broker who had joined Gordon from Wood Gundy, the staid establishment doyen of Canadian investment dealers. He had taken control of Gordon and, under his leadership, the company had developed the speciality of ''block-trading,'' that is, buying and selling large chunks of corporate stock. This specialization put Gordon centre stage during takeovers, when the speedy, secret acquisition of a large position in a company could prove the critical factor in victory. The Gordon men made a point of knowing where all the shares were buried.

But Connacher played more than the passive role of middleman. Sometimes he would accumulate blocks in anticipation of a takeover, and even act as a financial *agent provocateur*, precipitating the battle by peddling the block. Paul Reichmann admired people who shot from the hip and were prepared to back up their words with actions. Jimmy Connacher — whose nicknames included ''the Piranha'' and ''the Barracuda'' — ranked very high on both counts.

When they first began to take positions in other companies, the Reichmanns had dealt with Jeff Green, a trader at investment house Bell Gouinlock. Bell Gouinlock's Bob Canning had done a lot of their real estate financing. When Green moved to Gordon, he took the Reichmann account with him. Jimmy Connacher was more than pleased to have their business.

In almost all of the Reichmanns' subsequent diversifications, Connacher would play the role of *éminence grise*, as he would also for the Edper Bronfmans. Between them, the Reichmanns and the Edper-controlled Brascan would account for a very large portion of the business news in the 1980s. Jimmy Connacher was always somewhere behind the headlines.

In 1979, Eyton left his partnership at Tory, Tory and joined the Edper organization full-time. After masterminding its acquisition, he shook up Brascan and, in the fall of 1979, he directed Brascan's bid for control of Toronto-based mining giant Noranda, once again using Gordon to accumulate shares. The battle dragged on for almost two years, and saw some highly controversial defence tactics by Noranda's head, the hard-driving Alf Powis, but Brascan won. One of Powis's defensive manoeuvres had been a $626.5 million purchase of 49 percent of MacMillan Bloedel Limited, Canada's largest forest products company, so Brascan wound up controlling that too.

The Royal Trust Affair

Another link between the Reichmann and Edper/Brascan empires was forged as a result of a controversial episode that went into Canadian corporate history as "the Royal Trust Affair."

In August, 1980, property developer Robert Campeau approached Ken White, the crusty, establishment chairman of Royal Trust, Canada's largest trust company, to sound him out on acquisition. Like many other shrewd businessmen, Campeau believed that Royal was too staid and conservative, and that it was not utilizing its business assets to the best advantage. White expressed indignant displeasure at Campeau's suggestion (the proposal was made at White's farm and White immediately marched Campeau off the property) and subsequently lined up a who's who of business establishment support to fight off the bid. His team included the Bank of Montreal, which already owned 10 percent of Royal Trust's shares, and the Toronto-Dominion Bank, which bought 10 percent.

Looking for further support against Campeau, White's defensive strategist Austin Taylor, the gargantuan head of McLeod Young Weir, decided to approach Paul Reichmann. The ironies of the Toronto establishment turning to Orthodox Jews to fight off upstart French Canadians were duly noted. Reichmann responded, not out of any desire to save, or to become part of, the financial establishment, but because he saw Royal Trust as an attractive investment. In fact, he responded more enthusiastically than the establishment wanted, saying that he was prepared to come in for 50 percent of Royal Trust. When his suggestion was politely rebuffed, he countered by committing to buy 10 percent of the institution with a view to increasing that stake over time to 20 percent. As a condition, however, Reichmann demanded seats on the Royal Trust board, plus a commitment that the trust company's dividend increases would continue. Olympia & York then purchased about 9 percent of the trust company's equity. Albert later was invited onto the board.

Campeau's bid foundered, although he sold out the stake he had accumulated to the Reichmanns for a $2 million profit. But the whole affair provided a somewhat embarrassing example of the business establishment's clubbiness. It became the subject of an inquiry by the Ontario Securities Commission, which looked into allegations that Royal Trust's executives had placed their control before the interests of their shareholders, while some of Royal Trust's corporate shareholders had placed the interests of the establishment above those of *their* shareholders.

The Reichmanns' role was not seen as reprehensible. Rather it turned out to be the ironic source of Ken White's comeuppance. Says Trevor Eyton: "Quite clearly change was needed at Royal Trust and Campeau may well have been able to bring about that change. . . . I think Ken White lost control of all of the fences. He appointed Austin Taylor and others and they went running around and said, 'OK, we've protected you from the big bad wolf,' but Ken White probably never thought to ask, 'What about the big bad bear?' "

By bringing in Paul Reichmann as part of the defence, the "big bad bear" was now loose in the Royal Trust compound. The consequences were inevitable. But before the *coup de grâce*, Royal Trust's management received the public humiliation of a few painful nips from the OSC watchdog. In March, 1981, the OSC called for sanctions against White and Royal Trust's chief operating officer John Scholes for actions "that fall far below the standards of conduct expected of senior officers and directors of a corporation whose shares are publicly held."

Says Eyton, "Once you start that game it's impossible. You recognize that the kind of activity that was going on was strained and questionable." Trevor Eyton was chosen by Paul Reichmann to be the final instrument of retribution for the Royal Trust management. He turned up at Eyton's office and suggested that Edper match the Reichmanns' stake in the trust company (which they had continued building), and that Eyton and Cockwell should "manage" the investment for both parties. Says Eyton: "He came to us and said, 'I would like you to be a partner in the Royal Trustco investment and I'd be happy for you to manage the investment. We're a separate investor but we'd be happy for you to take the initiative and speak to management,' because basically he knew us and trusted us. We took it as a great compliment. We always knew they liked us so our immediate reaction was to try to do what he asked. So we bought stock up to their position."

The brothers subsequently brought their stake up to 23.3 percent, and shortly afterward, Brascan started snapping up blocks of the trust company. By June, 1981, the Eyton-managed empire held 17.4 percent.

Eyton and Cockwell also had the support of the Toronto-Dominion Bank's chairman and CEO Dick Thomson to "manage" the TD's stake in Royal Trust, which basically meant once again to shake up and reorganize the company.

Says Eyton: "We took the leadership position for more than half the shares of Royal Trustco but on a very informal basis. We had nothing in writing except the handshake of Paul and Albert and the handshake of Dick Thomson. Both saw the need for change at Royal Trustco and we were effectively the instrument. . . We were anointed to speak to John Scholes and Ken White on a regular basis to effect change and to ask for the kinds of things we adhere to in our business principles: a coherent and plausible business plan with the means of doing it, and accountability. Things that the Royal Trust just didn't have. They were a fine company with a fine reputation but they really weren't ready for the kind of competition they were facing and the kind of change that was coming day by day."

Obviously, no management appreciates being told that it's not running the company properly, but Eyton and Cockwell didn't flinch from the task, although, says Eyton, "It wasn't very pleasant. Ken White had had a wonderful career and we always said that our troubles would be over if Ken White had been forty-five years old. He is exactly the kind of guy that could have given the ginger and the impetus for change. John Scholes was a first-rate investment fellow, but he was clearly not comfortable as the chief executive officer of Royal Trustco, and really was incapable of making the change. He really quit of his own volition.''

"And so it was," wrote Rod McQueen in his book *The Money-spinners*, "that Ken White gained his Pyrrhic victory. Less than ten months after he marched Campeau off his property, Royal Trust had gone from a widely held company with 6,600 shareholders to one owned 40 percent by the Reichmanns and the Bronfmans."

The Reichmanns' financial bonds with the Edper-Brascan empire were further cemented when, in 1983, they exchanged their Royal Trustco shares for cash and a stake in Trilon Financial Corporation, an insurance and financial services company set up by Brascan the year before.

Brascan had a controlling interest in London Life Insurance, the largest insurance business in Canada, and it seemed clear to Eyton and Cockwell merely from looking across the U.S. border and seeing the financial conglomeration at companies like Sears and American Express, that the same development was bound to happen in Canada.

"I think it's fair to say," says Eyton, "that the initiative for the financial conglomerate was obvious, but the first call was made by ourselves. Jack proposed the first terms for a Trilon but there was a lot of discussion out of that, so there was a joint consensus . . . You had to be some kind of a dimbo not to say, 'Well, we're starting off awfully lucky. We have two of the best pieces in the country.' So we went to the Reichmanns and we went to the TD Bank [which was also an investor in London Life] and we said, 'Look, we think we should pool this investment.' In financial terms, they've done very well, and so have we."

Trilon's formation, as Patricia Best and Ann Shortell pointed out in their book *A Matter of Trust*, "gave the Bronfmans a running start in the race to create financial conglomerates in Canada." Their action did not please the banking establishment, but it seemed like the wave of the future. And the Reichmanns had a piece.

In return for their 23 percent of Royal Trust, the Reichmanns received approximately $40 million in cash, an immediate 12.5 percent share in Trilon's common stock, and warrants and convertible shares that could ultimately bring O&Y's voting interest in Trilon to more than 20 percent.

The Reichmanns' enormous money power and reputation made it inevitable that the business establishment would wish to embrace them, but that desire seemed inversely proportional to the Reichmanns' desire to belong. It wasn't that they were echoing Groucho Marx's comic assertion that he didn't want to be a member of any club that would have him. It was just that they didn't join clubs.

In *The Acquisitors*, Peter Newman related an anecdote that made the point forcefully:

> Once a year, when the NHL playoffs are at full tilt, Monty Black, the president of Argus Corporation, sponsors a dinner at the Toronto Club as part of his philanthropic endeavours on behalf of the Ontario Foundation for Diseases of the Liver.
>
> It's a black-tie affair for thirty-eight men, and all the Establishment Heavies are there: a bundle of gleaming Eatons, a sparkle of Bassetts, guys like that. For the first time, in the spring of 1981, they invited Paul and Albert.
>
> Holy Bud McDougald, Reichmanns in the Toronto Club!
>
> But they didn't show. Finally somebody spoke up: "Do you think they'll come?"
>
> And somebody else answered, "Listen. There's about as much chance of the Reichmanns coming here as one of the Rothschilds going to a stag for Harold Ballard. . . ."

Although the Reichmanns had little desire to be embraced by the social side of the Canadian establishment, their low-key, behind-the-scenes approach was the very essence of the Canadian business way. You didn't get involved in knock-em-down, drag-em-out fights. You didn't get involved in formal agreements. You just had a word in the right ear. And things got done.

The Reichmanns weren't interested in establishments. They were interested in making money with money. Their real estate was so successful, generating so much cash, that they were now almost *forced* to diversify. The joint holdings with the Edper group in Trizec and Trilon were just part of the Reichmanns' plans — masterminded by Paul — for diversification.

In Canadian business at the turn of the 1980s, there was one industry that reigned supreme. In the course of the previous decade, it had led to a massive shift not merely in the financial but also in the political balance of Canada. For a family of devout Orthodox Jews, the role seemed a little unusual; but for a family bound by their wealth and relentless drive to be where the business action was, it was almost inevitable. The Reichmanns had to join the ranks of Canada's Blue-Eyed Sheiks.

8

DIVERSIFICATIONS: PETROLEUM AND PAPER

*Paul Reichmann loved free advice, and nobody
had more available to him than a billionaire
who wanted to spend money.*

While the Reichmanns had been quietly and inexorably building their empire in the 1970s, the province of Alberta had been turning out a virtual stampede of Canadian corporate success stories. The focus of that success had been boomtown Calgary.

Calgary's boom could be traced directly to the OPEC crisis of 1973 and the subsequent surge in oil and natural gas prices. Although there had been a bitter and protracted fight about petroleum revenues between the federal Liberal government of Pierre Trudeau and the provincial Alberta Tories under their iron-willed premier Peter Lougheed, the benefits of the petroleum price surge had inevitably found their way through to the industry. A whole new pantheon of Canadian business heroes had emerged virtually overnight. Men like "Smilin' Jack" Gallagher, the silver-tongued chairman of stock market darling Dome Petroleum; Bob Blair, the dour and aggressive head of Alberta Gas Trunk Line; and Daryl K. "Doc" Seaman, the soft-talking head of Bow Valley Industries, appeared to be rewriting Canadian corporate history and shifting the whole focus of financial power in the country.

Before the boom, Western oilmen had found their visits to the bastions of Toronto's Bay Street exercises in frustration and sometimes humiliation. They had had much more luck selling their investment dreams south of the border, where generous tax incentives for petroleum exploration had created a more receptive market. But the OPEC crisis had bestowed wondrous new charms on the West and its oil producers. Now the Eastern bankers came like supplicants begging the oilmen to take extended lines of credit; Bay Street's investment dealers and financial carpetbaggers flew in with briefcases bursting with a cornucopia of fancy financing schemes.

Calgary was not shy about its good fortune. Rob Peters, the golden-haired and golden-touched head of investment house Peters & Co. Limited, bought and mounted a bell outside his Fourth Avenue office in 1977. Whenever the company did a block trade, someone would be sent out to ring the bell. By the end of 1977, that bell was clanging at least half a dozen times a day. Peters's bell became a powerful symbol.

In the latter half of the decade, the most obvious sign of the boom was the city itself. Between 1973 and 1978, the value of building permits quadrupled to the magic $1 billion mark. Within this total, the permits for offices rose even more spectacularly, from $16 million in 1973 to $338 million in 1978, an increase of more than 2,000 percent. By the beginning of 1979 the value of office buildings either under construction or planned for Calgary passed $1 billion. The golden crescent of the city's downtown core — bounded on the south by the railroad tracks below Ninth Avenue and on the north by the slow curve of the Bow River — was sprouting skyscrapers like weeds. Fittingly, O&Y was deeply involved. It had built the thirty-three-storey Shell Centre and had a huge twin-tower development planned for Fifth Avenue that would house the headquarters of Esso Resources, the exploration arm of Canada's largest oil company, Imperial Oil.

Although the Toronto-based Reichmanns would have been appalled at the thought of literally ringing out the news of their wealth, they had a lot in common with Calgary's businessmen and their aggressive mentality. Like the Reichmanns, the biggest crap-shooters in Calgary had in most cases founded the companies they headed, and many were still the largest shareholders. And like the Reichmanns, they rejoiced in the flexibility and speed that only proprietorship gave. Oil was a business based on good faith and handshakes, and that approach, too, had always been pursued by the Reichmanns.

Finally, there were strong similarities between oil and gas and real estate. The Reichmanns, particularly in the light of the Uris deal, knew all about the impact on a company's growth potential of a dramatic increase in its underlying asset base. That, thanks to a combination of tight markets and Saudi Arabia's Sheikh Yamani, was what Calgary's boom was all about. It was only natural that the Reichmanns, seeking business diversification, should look West. There was certainly no shortage of deals.

Now, whenever Toronto's big time financial merchants had a deal to pitch, Paul Reichmann was at the top of their list. They clamoured to get into his Toronto office to peddle blocks of stock, or whole companies, or tax angles, or financings. And Paul Reichmann made a point of speaking to all of those he thought had something worthwhile to sell—or from whom he could learn. Paul Reichmann loved free advice, and nobody had more available to him than a billionaire who wanted to spend money.

Within a couple of years of the Uris deal, O&Y was taking its first tentative steps in the oil business, steps that would eventually lead to phenomenal stock market leaps. The first venture into the oil and gas market was in 1979, when the Reichmanns took a 10 percent stake in Canada Northwest Land Ltd., an oil company with producing wells in Western Canada, the United States, and offshore Spain, as well as exploration interests in Australia.

The following year, they took a bigger step through the acquisition of Brinco, a company with a famous name and a famous past, but a rather uncertain future. Brinco's origins lay in a meeting in 1953 at which Joey Smallwood, the premier of Newfoundland, had been introduced to merchant banker Edmund de Rothschild by Sir Winston Churchill. The purpose of the meeting was to finance a company that would develop the natural resource potential of Newfoundland. Brinco was formed that same year by a special act of the Newfoundland legislature, and went on to develop the giant Churchill Falls hydroelectric project on Labrador's Hamilton River. The man who brought the project to fruition was Bill Mulholland, the Wall Street investment banker who subsequently became head of the Bank of Montreal.

When the government of Newfoundland acquired the hydro project in 1974, Brinco's corporate rationale seemed to disappear. It went through a difficult transition period from a large public utility to a small company concentrating on natural resources. In

1979, the company was transformed when it merged with a junior oil company, Conuco, to form Brinco Oil & Gas. The merger gave Brinco a direct operating position in the oil and gas industry, increased its Canadian content, and enlarged its share "float," making it more attractive to the investment community.

Nevertheless, Brinco was still overwhelmingly foreign-owned. British mining giant Rio Tinto-Zinc still held 54 percent of its shares, while Bethlehem, Pa.-based Bethlehem Steel held 13 percent. The Japanese, in the shape of Marubeni Corporation and Fuji Bank, also held substantial minority chunks. Such heavyweight foreign ownership inevitably led Brinco to come under the disconcerting gaze of the Foreign Investment Review Agency.

Brinco's potential problems with foreign ownership and the Reichmanns' desire to diversify into resources seemed to dovetail nicely. In November, 1980, O&Y bought out Bethlehem Steel, Marubeni, Fuji, and a substantial part of Rio Tinto's interests — and also purchased 7.3 million Brinco preferred shares — to take a 50.1 percent stake in the company. Brinco was in the process of acquiring asbestos company Cassiar Resources Limited. Brinco bought 59 percent of Cassiar's shares from British, American, and Australian interests and made an $89 million bid for the remainder on the Canadian market.

The negotiations to buy Brinco were protracted. One potentially contentious point was that the Reichmanns did not want to have to make an offer to Brinco's minority shareholders. Their argument was that these minority shareholders could only benefit from their ownership. Also, they were Canadianizing both Brinco and Cassiar. The Reichmanns won their point.

The Brinco negotiations marked the beginning of an incredibly hectic period for the Reichmanns. Not only was Paul Reichmann preparing his pitch to build the world's largest commercial development at Battery Park City, but he also became involved in the Royal Trust affair. Then, early in 1981, he found himself in the middle of one of the biggest takeover battles in Canadian history, not in oil and gas, but in paper.

Paper Empire

Abitibi-Price Inc., although it only took that name in 1979, had effectively come into being early in 1975 when the Abitibi Paper Company had completed its $130 million acquisition of the Price

Company to form the largest newsprint manufacturer in the world.

In 1978, Andy Sarlos, the Hungarian-born Bay Street guru, and Maurice Strong, a fascinating hybrid whose career had embraced the presidency of Power Corporation, chairmanship of state-owned Petro-Canada, and high-level work for the United Nations, staged an assault on Abitibi.

The contention of Sarlos and Strong was that Abitibi's stock was undervalued, largely as a result of staid management. With financial backing from Peter Bronfman and Paul Nathanson, the very private heir of the Famous Players cinema fortune, they accumulated $31 million of Abitibi stock in a five-day spending spree in the summer of 1978.

Backed by institutions holding another 12 percent of Abitibi, Sarlos and Strong demanded management and financial reforms. They wanted higher dividends and representation on the board. Tom Bell, Abitibi's chairman, told them that board membership was out of the question. Canada's seventeenth-largest industrial corporation, with sales of well over $1 billion, did not take instructions from financial wheeler-dealers.

The aggressors sold out at a profit, and the Sarlos-Strong challenge went away, for the moment. Significantly, however, Tom Bell hoisted Abitibi's dividend from 95 cents to $1.50. But the sale of the Sarlos-Strong block created a potential loose cannon on Abitibi's deck. The block wound up in the hands of West-Coast-based West Fraser Timber. Also, during the summer of 1980, the Reichmanns started picking up Abitibi stock. By the beginning of 1981, they had accumulated almost 10 percent of its equity. In fact, they acquired the stock merely as an investment, but soon found themselves in the middle of a takeover battle.

Two other companies, Federal Commerce & Navigation Ltd. (Fednav), a little-known Montreal-based shipping company with U.S. petroleum interests, and Consolidated-Bathurst, a Montreal-based pulp and paper giant controlled by Power Corp., held stakes similar to that of the Reichmanns. West Fraser Timber still held 13 percent.

Federal Commerce made the first move with a bid to acquire 2.25 million Abitibi common shares at $27.50 a share to take its holdings to 20 percent. But then the Reichmanns jumped in with a $28 offer for 6.7 million shares. When combined with their existing stake, the $187 million offer would give the Reichmanns 40.6 percent of Abitibi.

Within a week, an alternative joint bid had been put together by Thomson Newspapers, whose chairman, Ken Thomson, sat on the Abitibi board, and property and petroleum group Nu-West, the creation of Calgarian Ralph Scurfield. They offered $31 a share for 8.5 million Abitibi shares. In the meantime, Fednav had withdrawn its first offer but upped its stake to 21 percent via purchases from Consolidated-Bathurst and the huge Quebec pension fund, the Caisse de dépôt et placement du Québec.

A full-scale bid for Abitibi was not part of the Reichmanns' plan, but they did not want to be left with their minority stake if either Fednav or the Thomson/Nu-West group gained control.

David Brown, a gentlemanly investment dealer with Burns Fry, who had earned the Reichmanns' regard in earlier financings, suggested that they should cut all the nickel-and-dime bid increases and just take the lot. They decided to follow his advice. The Canadian Imperial Bank of Commerce and the Bank of Montreal were only too pleased to put up the funds.

At the beginning of March, O&Y simply blew its competitors out of the water, bidding $32 for all Abitibi's shares in one of the largest takeovers in Canadian history. The Thomson/Nu-West group bowed out. Abitibi's conservative establishment management, which had been less than friendly to outsiders, now had to succumb to the one element that finally transcended all their activities: sheer, naked money.

On March 6, a news release went out on Canada News-Wire, announcing that 16.8 million shares had been tendered under the Reichmanns' offer, putting a price tag of $534 million on the purchase, excluding the cost of the shares they had accumulated already. Also, O&Y announced that they would extend their offer to March 13 to allow everybody to tender.

Paul Reichmann met with Abitibi's chief executive, Bob Gimlin, and assured him that O&Y wanted Abitibi to continue under its existing management. He also asked Tom Bell, the chairman, to convey to the directors that he wished the whole board to stay. He approached Ken Thomson and his chief lieutenant, John Tory, and after he outlined his good intentions, they, too, agreed to remain as directors.

Two of the losers in the battle appeared less than elated over its outcome. Fednav vice-president Harry Bell said that the company sold its 21 percent Abitibi stake "with regret. It's too bad that one more Canadian company has to disappear from the scene as a potential investment vehicle." West Fraser Timber's chairman

Henry Ketcham meanwhile declared, "It's disappointing to see a company like Abitibi come under single ownership." Richardson Securities of Canada produced a report headlined, dramatically, "Abitibi-Price is Gone," and declaring, "investors will have to look elsewhere."

However, both Fednav and West Fraser were private companies under family ownership. Also, they made profits of around $16 million and $26 million respectively by selling out to O&Y, so their posturings looked somewhat self-righteous. But they were also wrong, as was the Richardson report. Abitibi was very far from being taken out of the investment arena, although the Reichmanns did consider ways of putting Abitibi and Brinco together. In the end, the two companies were not linked, but the notion of linking Abitibi to expansion in the oil business remained in Paul Reichmann's mind.

Over the next four years, with the Reichmanns' encouragement, Abitibi undertook a massive investment program. From a stock market sense, however, the newsprint producer, with such a small float of public shares, lay rather dormant. But once Paul Reichmann found the key for it to help him with his oil ambitions, Abitibi, in the spring of 1985, bounced back into the headlines in the most controversial way.

Power Shift

From the point of view of the business establishment, the Reichmanns' Abitibi victory indicated a profound shift in the locus of Canadian corporate power. An article in *Maclean's* quoted a Bank of Montreal executive as saying: "In terms of traditional Canadian wealth and resources, it wasn't long ago that you'd expect Abitibi to be doing the take-over, not the other way around. That's how much things are changing."

Other establishment changes were afoot. The OSC inquiry into the Royal Trust affair had just taken place and revealed the establishment in a less than flattering light. Ironically, despite the machinations of the old financial élite, it was the new and increasingly powerful force of the Reichmanns that had wound up with 23 percent of the trust company. Meanwhile, their counterparts at Edper, who represented a new and highly innovative way of using old money, were busy accumulating their own Royal Trust stake.

The Abitibi takeover swelled the Reichmann myth. They had taken on the Thomson empire, which was not accustomed to losing corporate battles, and they had not merely outbid it, but co-opted it, making peace with Ken Thomson and persuading him to stay on the Abitibi board. There had been no master plan behind the Abitibi purchase. Paul Reichmann had looked at the fundamentals, looked at the management, and, when the moment came, borrowed the money and struck, confident that his proprietorship could only be good for the company.

The Abitibi acquisition did not satisfy the Reichmanns' appetite for diversification in any way, and later in 1981, they bought two other major corporate stakes, one in Bow Valley Industries, and the second, and ultimately much more significant, in Hiram Walker Resources.

Paul Reichmann had been introduced to Doc Seaman, the founder and head of Bow Valley Industries, early in 1981. Seaman, a farmboy from rural Saskatchewan and a wartime bomber pilot, had started working in the Alberta oilfields in 1949. He had bought a small seismic drilling rig and parlayed it, with the help of his two brothers, B.J. and Don, into not merely one of the most successful exploration drilling companies in Canada but also a petroleum explorer and producer with interests from the North Sea to Indonesia.

Reichmann took to Seaman, told him that he was interested in diversifying out of real estate, and said that he would like to pick up a chunk of his company as an investment. The main branch of the Bronfman family, through Cemp Investments, the holding company of Sam Bronfman's children, already had a sizable stake in Bow Valley. Reichmann made it clear that if he was not able to go above 20 percent of the stock over time, he would sell out. Doc Seaman declared himself amenable to a Reichmann share purchase, and O&Y began acquiring Bow Valley shares. By mid-year the company had accumulated just over 5 percent of Bow Valley's stock.

Similarly, Reichmann decided to buy a stake in Hiram Walker Resources, a Toronto-based liquor, petroleum, and gas pipeline conglomerate. His dubious welcome from Hiram Walker management would have a bearing on events five years later.

The Reichmanns started buying Hiram Walker stock in the spring of 1981. In the last three days of July, they laid out around $120 million to acquire 3.8 million shares of the company, bringing their holding to just over 4 million shares, or 5.9 percent of Walker's equity. By the fall, they had taken their stake up to 10 percent. Paul Reichmann believed that a holding of that magnitude should entitle the family to representation on the board. Intermediaries were sent to discuss the matter quietly with Hiram Walker's management. Paul Reichmann did not want to be seen to be asking for a seat, and he certainly did not want to be seen being turned down, but turned down he was. That made Paul Reichmann angry. Paul Reichmann is not a man to anger easily. Or to forget.

9

IMAGE AND REALITY
IN A CHANGING EMPIRE

*Getting to the heart of the Reichmann empire was
a little like reaching the end of the Yellow Brick
Road: when you drew back the O&Y curtain, it was
virtually a one-man show.*

Between 1979 and 1981, the Reichmann empire went through
a fundamental realignment. Since that first warehouse back
in 1956, the geometric progression of the family's business
growth had taken place in real estate. Low-rise industrial buildings had led to Flemingdon Park and multi-storey office blocks.
Multi-storey office blocks had provided the experience for the
building and financing of the O&Y flagship of First Canadian
Place. Buying and selling real estate had culminated in the 1977
New York "deal of the century." The next project at Battery Park
City provided both the greatest challenge, and the greatest
achievement, that real estate had to offer.

The Reichmanns' very success had created another challenge:
what to do with all the money thrown off by the property empire.
The answer, inevitably, had been diversification.

The Reichmanns' spending spree during 1980 and 1981 had cost
them at least $1 billion. They had gained control of Abitibi-Price
and Brinco, and they had snapped up chunks of Bow Valley,
Hiram Walker Resources, Royal Trust, and MacMillan Bloedel.
The master plan was simple: a commitment to diversify into natural resources and a search for "value." Most of the decisions were

made off the cuff. Paul Reichmann admitted that in the Abitibi battle he had "only reacted to the bidding." In the case of Brinco, advisors had told him that he was paying too much for the company. He had thanked them and told them he was not seeking such advice.

He explained his rationale simply: "Over time, we have accumulated shares in many Canadian companies, particularly natural resource companies. And when the opportunity to buy control is available, we have moved. We are not only interested in the company and its value, but in the quality of people who operate it. In Brinco and Abitibi, and any other investment we make, we depend on their existing management to run the business. . . If we did not have faith in their ability to handle crises, we would not have invested. But if we are wrong, other people can be found."

He freely admitted the opportunistic nature of his deals, and acknowledged that they were based on gut feelings rather than exhaustive calculations. In an interview with the *Globe and Mail* in 1981, he said, "It is a myth that corporations decide where they will go. They move where they will by being at the right place at the right time." At around the same time, he was quoted in the *Financial Times of Canada* as making the extraordinary statement, "You can go broke if you depend too much on numbers."

It all seemed so simple, and yet this very simplicity stirred a frenzy of adulation in the print media. The more candid the brothers were, the more mysterious they emerged in the press. As the influential U.S. business magazine *Fortune*, in a 1982 profile, declared, "As developers, Paul and his brother Albert are so colorless they're colorful."

Paul Reichmann could not have stated his motivations and goals more clearly; the nature of the brothers' wealth could not have been more obvious; their personal lives—although they refused to answer questions about them — could not have been more straightforward. They were devout, religious, family men who applied themselves relentlessly to business success. The intuitive genius behind their success was Paul.

The brothers were time and time again described as "reclusive" and "private," but an examination of the media files shows that they gave far more interviews than the average senior corporate executive. Yet they somehow managed to make each interviewer feel as if he or she was receiving some extraordinary boon. The brothers were in fact far less reclusive than any average multimillionaire. What they were was secretive. When they spoke to the press, they had a very clear idea of what they wanted to promote and what was off limits. Until it suited their corporate purposes, money had always been off limits.

In her 1981 book, *Men of Property*, Toronto-based writer Susan Goldenberg wrote: ''Publicity is rare for the Reichmanns who have become legendary not only because of their astute deals, but also because they are an enigma. In the real estate world, there are the Reichmanns and then there is everybody else . . . They are the deans of the real estate development world, possessed of infinite patience and down-to-earth common sense and practicality.''

They received this accolade despite the fact that when Goldenberg asked the very valid question of how acquisitions were financed, Albert Reichmann said that was an issue he ''would like to leave out. We work with banks and financial institutions and use leverage.''

Again, Paul, when granting an interview to *Maclean's* magazine shortly after the Abitibi takeover, said, ''We have always preferred to remain private in our affairs . . . That's always been our way, long before our company became big or we became rich. Surely no one can begrudge us that.''

Most pieces about the Reichmanns were not even so impolite as to address the crude question of money. A lengthy and breathless profile in the *Globe and Mail* in 1981 began:

From where they stand at the pinnacle of the Canadian development industry, the Reichmann brothers are in danger, their modesty and reticence notwithstanding, of becoming a legend . . . [they] have left the path behind them strewn with complex myths born of their passionate desire for privacy and the sense of awe they have inspired in people who watched them build their empire bloodlessly, calmly, systematically.

It is said that in an industry the public generally considers ruthless and disruptive, the Reichmanns offer stability and reliability.

It is said they consummate deals worth millions with a handshake and then keep their word even when, in time, the deal becomes less advantageous to them.

It is said their business acumen is second to none.

Those Reichmanns sure were well said of.

And if the Reichmanns were a little reticent about their business skills, there were plenty of those close to them who were prepared to sing their praises. Ron Soskolne, their architectural taste-maker, was quoted in *Maclean's* as saying, ''They're like grocery shop-keepers out at the market every morning at 6 a.m. squeezing and choosing the fruit and vegetables themselves personally.'' In another article, he called Paul Reichmann ''the Wayne Gretzky of money.''

Paul Reichmann, meanwhile, could pooh-pooh all the interest in him. In still another interview with the *Globe and Mail* in 1981, he said, ''I have never believed that anyone reads, remembers or cares about all that silliness that is published about where we come from or who we are. Your readers are not interested in that. As people, we are no different from any other of the three million people around this city.''

The article went on to say, ''Mr. Reichmann displays thinly veiled revulsion at the suggestion that there might well be an interest in personal material on a family with the accomplishments of the Reichmanns. 'If you're a movie star, I suppose there is some value in being bandied about, but frankly . . .' ''

Myth Under Strain

But mid-1981 marked the peak of both the resource and the real estate booms. Interest rates suddenly climbed through the strato-sphere and the bloom fell off the resource rose. Developers, too, were suddenly fighting for their lives and people began to realize how much damage the banks had done by lending money to all and sundry. By the spring of 1982, Canadian publicly quoted real estate companies had suffered a stock market bloodbath. While the Toronto Stock Exchange 300 Composite Index had fallen 34 percent from its high of November 30, 1980, the developers' and contractors' index was down 71 percent. The property manage-ment index (which included Cadillac Fairview and Trizec) was down 46 percent from its July, 1981, high.

The Reichmanns successfully promoted the view that they lived in another development world. According to *Maclean's* magazine of April 5, 1982: ''Olympia & York Developments Ltd., that market enigma, is seen as forging ahead against the common industry wisdom. It's expanding, analysts say, in spite of present conditions and the losses it has felt on major recent acquisitions such as Abitibi-Price . . . Yet it's also succeeding in leasing its large New York development in spite of a slowing Manhattan office market."

The deal referred to was that with American Express on the largest tower of the World Financial Center. But the climate soon led to a change in that deal. American Express agreed to buy the leasehold on the tower for about U.S.$600 million, while the price that O&Y paid for the Amex headquarters was hauled down from U.S.$240 million to U.S.$160 million. Amex's purchase of the tower led to a massive change of construction priorities on the World Financial Center site. General Superintendent Dan Mernit found his job suddenly complicated not merely by the accelerations of the Amex building but also because American Express brought in its own contractors to fit out the building. They inevitably clashed with O&Y's contractors. But the men on the site did not grumble too much. They just shrugged. They knew they were seeing the down-to-earth results of another deal done "in the clouds."

In 1981, Paul Reichmann had said in an interview with the *Financial Times of Canada*, "If we run short of money, we are luckier than an industrial company. It can't sell off a few machines. But we could always sell a building if necessary."

Now, a year later, O&Y quietly put parts of the Uris package on the market, but the Reichmanns reacted strongly to any suggestion that this had anything to do with their running short of money. They denied problems either with the state of the property market or with the more than $1 billion they had borrowed for their diversifications the year before.

The Reichmanns wanted to raise at least $500 million by selling or refinancing at least two of the Uris buildings, but they were also quoting a figure of U.S.$2.5 billion for anyone who wanted to buy the whole lot. Knowing the Reichmanns' penchant for tungsten-hard bargaining, U.S.$2.5 billion would obviously have been the top price. Nevertheless, suddenly the press started bandying about U.S.$2.5 billion as their value. It looked so good, so *mythical*, when set up against their U.S.$320 million cost.

Even as the renegotiations with American Express were going on at the World Financial Center, the costs of the project were undergoing a dramatic upward revision. Suddenly, without any explanation, the "U.S.$1 billion project" became the "U.S.$1.5 billion project."

O&Y found itself arranging long-term mortgages at high rates, and was also trying to get some U.S.$1.4 billion secured against the U.S. buildings then under construction, including the World Financial Center. Nevertheless, the company claimed that it still had considerable collateral left on the Uris buildings.

The empire had other problems. The building markets in Dallas, where it had completed a U.S.$100 million office tower, and in Calgary, where it had three huge developments either built or under way, were very soft. Paul Reichmann was obviously getting a little concerned about all these rumours of real estate problems and bad investments. In the spring of 1982, he gave a lengthy interview to *Fortune*.

In large part, he succeeded in persuading the magazine (which regurgitated the journalistic shibboleth that the Reichmanns had "a passion for privacy") that O&Y was somehow not subject to the economic laws that were laying waste to real estate and resource companies everywhere else. "O&Y," declared the article, "can afford to play the epic contrarian, but many of its rivals cannot . . . O&Y is an anomaly, a venturesome developer with the deep pockets of a big insurance company."

The question was, just how deep were the pockets? Paul Reichmann professed to come clean. "Disclosing key financial data for the first time, Paul Reichmann told *Fortune* that O&Y's assets, largely carried at cost, are valued on the books at U.S.$7 billion. That's more than double the assets of another big Canadian developer, Cadillac Fairview, which has the most of any publicly held real-estate company in North America."

The magazine estimated — although it is difficult to imagine where the estimates could have come from, either directly or indirectly, but O&Y — that the market value of O&Y's assets was U.S.$12 billion and that O&Y was "so conservatively leveraged" that it could sell off its assets, pay its debts, and still wind up with U.S.$5 billion, "a figure Paul Reichmann concedes is close to the mark. It is a safe bet that few families have ever had so grandiose a net worth. The company's cash flow, says Paul, is U.S.$233 million a year."

But if, with assets worth U.S.$12 billion, it could pay off its debts and still wind up with U.S.$5 billion, that meant its debts were U.S.$7 billion, a phenomenally high figure. Moreover, by Reichmann's own admission, the book value of O&Y's assets was U.S.$7 billion. Looked at as U.S.$7 billion of assets with U.S.$7 billion of debt, the empire took on quite another complexion, particularly at a time of high interest rates and jittery bankers.

As the director of one of Canada's major chartered banks pointed out to the author, it was getting "pretty hot in the kitchen" for the Reichmanns. There were heavy carrying costs attached to the diversifications, which were not doing well. O&Y's paper loss on Abitibi alone was around $200 million. On its other public company investments including Brinco, Hiram Walker Resources, and MacMillan Bloedel, it was losing more than $100 million on paper. Nevertheless, the Reichmanns shrugged off losses, claiming, as ever, that they were in for the long haul and that they were convinced of the value of their petroleum and newsprint holdings, whatever Wall Street or Bay Street said.

At the same time, for 1982 and a good part of 1983, the Reichmanns were concerned with putting the empire on a more solid financial basis. The two smallest of the Uris buildings — 850 Third Avenue and 10 East 53rd Street — were sold for U.S.$225 million. Also, O&Y remortgaged 245 Park Avenue, its headquarters, with Aetna Life for U.S.$308 million. In the middle of 1983, the brothers sold their 7 percent stake in Bow Valley at an after-tax profit of $14.5 million. Jimmy Connacher, the block-trading head of Gordon Capital, agreed to take a million Bow Valley shares off the Reichmanns at $29⅝, at what turned out to be the absolute top of the market. Gordon was only able to start selling off the block at $22 on the way down, and Connacher took a multi-million-dollar bath. But Connacher never whined. They were all big men, playing in a big man's world. Paul Reichmann liked that in a man.

Paul Reichmann obviously took umbrage at the notion that O&Y could ever be in real financial trouble. Nevertheless, the stories kept coming. In October, 1982, *Business Week*, in a long story entitled "End of the Office Boom," wrote: "Another episode that has distressed an increasingly skittish investment community involves Olympia & York Developments Ltd., the biggest — and reputedly indomitable — Canadian developer. Olympia recently sold off part of its interest in some big residential properties near New York City. The action set off rumors that even Olympia was strapped for cash and would soon be putting more properties on the block. Olympia asserts that the sale was misread and was in fact part of its plans, and it denies that there will be a wave of distress sales of any of its properties."

Paul Reichmann got visibly annoyed when he read such stories.

He vented his feelings to a *Globe* reporter at the end of 1982. The story said of Paul Reichmann, "Yesterday, he expressed noticeable exasperation about the latest reports that the company is being squeezed. He said he would put out a press release to correct the 'distortions,' if he can find the time." Paul Reichmann's concern for his public image was obviously greater than his "passion for privacy."

But O&Y was not, like other developers, merely retrenching from the excesses of the past, it was tidying up its financial condition for the next leap forward. In March, 1984, O&Y stunned the financial community with a highly original, and as usual unprecedentedly large, financing. It raised almost U.S.$1 billion through a unique issue of fifteen-year floating rate notes, secured by another three of its New York buildings, 2 Broadway, 1290 Avenue of the Americas, and Park Avenue Atrium. The U.S.$970 million deal, organized by the financial wizards at Salomon Brothers, was the first non-recourse, marketable security of its kind. It was also the largest mortgage of any kind. The money was raised via a private placement to more than forty institutional investors, mostly savings and loan associations. American Savings & Loan took U.S.$350 million of the issue.

The loan was also very original in terms of its interest rate structure. The notes carried an upper and lower level of interest, to protect O&Y against rates floating too high, and the lenders against their falling too low. They carried an interest rate of 1.75 percentage points above the rate on ninety-day U.S. Treasury bills, adjusted monthly, but the rate could not exceed 17 percent or fall below 7 percent.

With the U.S.$970 million Salomon mortgage, O&Y had not merely been put on a solid financial footing, it had the funds available for its next big move. *Business Week*, after getting yet another exclusive interview with the "private," "reclusive," Paul Reichmann, wrote in August, 1983: "According to Paul Reichmann, O&Y's long-term strategy for investment in other companies is to take a 'substantial position where we can have an influence on the affairs of the company.' As more of O&Y's real estate matures and is sold and surplus funds become available, the company plans to increase its corporate investments, either through its holding company or through subsidiaries. For example, as a buffer against the cycles of the forest-products industry, the Reichmanns might diversify Abitibi-Price into other natural-resource activities such as oil and gas.''

While other real estate companies were coming back from the traumas of 1982–83 licking their wounds, if they were coming back at all, O&Y was about to come back like a three-stage rocket.

Ready for Takeoff

The continuing ''reclusive'' image of the Reichmanns while they seemed in fact only too willing to talk about aspects of their business ventures pointed to one of the great difficulties of writing about businessmen. When entrepreneurs are written about, much of the lineage refers to their non-business activities. The Reichmanns had very few non-business activities. In the last resort, Paul Reichmann's guiding genius came down to the ability to say yes or no. The infinitely complex processes of intuition and genius on which those decisions were based were forever beyond analysis. All that could be seen, and judged, were the results.

To understand what happened after the retrenchments of the early 1980s, it is first necessary to step back and look at the nature and structure of the Reichmann empire, at its strengths and its weaknesses, at its philosophies and its attitudes.

The Reichmanns had developed an unparalleled reputation, but that reputation was based entirely on the quality of their real estate activities. The 1977 New York property deal had given them an almost superhuman aura of business wisdom. They were the men who took what seemed like great risks, but turned out to be no risks at all. Observers thought they just *had* to have a crystal ball.

The very success of the real estate operations, and the collateral provided by the New York properties, had made diversification almost inevitable. They had picked resources because they thought resources were like real estate: you held onto them and in time their value was bound to increase. Just as they were not making any more prime real estate (give or take a little landfill here and there), they were not making any more petroleum either. Forest products were renewable, but it took a long time to grow a forest. The value had to be there, too, whatever the short-term problems. The Reichmanns were seen as being the ultimate in ''patient money.''

But the Reichmanns were not superhuman, and they were not infallible. Moreover, the reality of their organization was almost frighteningly thin. Getting to the heart of the Reichmann empire was a little like reaching the end of the Yellow Brick Road: when you drew back the O&Y curtain, it was virtually a one-man show. That was not to say that it did not have talented executives, but these tended to be on the real estate side, and real estate was just where the money was made. The main emphasis now was on where that money was being spent.

The Reichmanns had proved adept at using the press to promote their projects or correct "misapprehensions" about their financial condition. Even if Paul Reichmann was not able to suppress the "silly" idea that they were in any way different from the other 3 million occupants of Metropolitan Toronto, he had successfully promulgated the notion that the three brothers were "equals" in business affairs and virtually interchangeable when it came to decision-making. Such assertions were based less on reality than on a sense of family loyalty. Albert tended to be more involved in land acquisition, financing, leasing, and building design, but Paul was always in on the major real estate decisions. Albert in turn was always closely involved in diversifications, but the strategic thrust always came from Paul.

The relationship between Paul and Albert was critical. The brothers' personalities and tastes were quite different. Albert was considered a lot "looser" than Paul, but he was also Paul's closest advisor and sounding board. The constant interplay between the two brothers was described by one of their executives as being almost like a process of osmosis. They interacted informally and frequently, and were always in each other's offices, tossing ideas back and forth. Their offices in fact clearly showed the contrast in their tastes. Paul's was more "classical," with traditional furniture and Persian carpets. His walls were decorated with paintings of Venice. His architectural tastes were also different. He liked simple, elegant, masonry buildings. First Canadian Place was very much a "Paul" building. Albert was more "modernist" in his leanings. His office sported contemporary furniture, and his walls had paintings by Marc Chagall. O&Y's Exchange Place in Boston — an irregular tower with glass curtain walls — was more his architectural preference.

Albert was more of an operating man, interested in the marketplace, the costs, and the structures. Paul was always mentally on the move, looking for the next step. He lived at a much more conceptual level. His obsession was how to increase yields, how to structure deals. Said Bernd Koken, who had now taken over as chief executive of Abitibi, of Paul: "He's lots more than a chief financial officer or a corporate developer or a treasurer. He's some super-version of all of these things combined. He's a deal creator. He is *always* thinking. He's an extremely intellectual guy. When Paul talks at a meeting, he's usually seven steps out in front."

One of the critical features about O&Y was that it was very much a family company controlled by a particularly tight-knit family. To work at Olympia & York was to be under no illusions about who the bosses of the company were. Some who had worked with the Reichmanns considered them insensitive to others' ego requirements. Employees were paid well but had to realize that they were essentially corporate servants whose expertise was there to be fed into the master equation that existed in Paul's head. Albert was one of the very few individuals who might suggest variations in the equation. Others were there merely to feed in the variables.

Said one senior employee: "They deal very sensitively with people in the organization, but they expect them to understand that it's their prerogative to exercise judgement and not have to explain it. The people who are successful in working with them are those who understand that they are here to support the Reichmanns in what they do, and that requires a degree of ego-subordination. On the other hand, it enables one to experience in an exhilarating way the sense of shared achievement when one's judgement is engaged as part of their process."

Another real estate consultant who worked for them said: "Their management style is based on accepting information from a number of sources and then acting. Once they have made a decision, they do not return to explain why any particular recommendation has been rejected." If the consultant ever questioned a decision and went to one of the brothers for an explanation, the brother would give him one — and inevitably one that made sense — but would seem surprised that the consultant's ego might have been bruised.

The Reichmanns paid, and paid well, for people's brains. They were not interested in egos. According to a former employee: "They ruffle lots of feathers because they are unaware that they're ruffling feathers. In Paul's case, it's almost a kind of naivety."

More than one O&Y employee compared Paul to a computer.

When a decision had to be made, he would draw on many sources. When an outside or inside advisor was summoned into Paul Reichmann's office, he never knew how long he would be there. Sometimes counsel was sought for ten minutes and then he was politely shown the door. Sometimes he would find himself still there four hours later as his mind was relentlessly probed for the key piece of information, the crucial insight, that Reichmann was seeking. And then, when all the input was in, Paul Reichmann would switch off the outside world.

Said one former senior employee: "You all feed your little bits in, then he takes it and churns it around and he comes out with an answer. And sometimes he tells you his conclusions and sometimes he doesn't. Sometimes you will tell him something very forcefully about what should or shouldn't be done and you'd think that he wasn't listening, but then you'd find out that he'd followed your advice."

Nevertheless, this view of Paul Reichmann as corporate automaton, as a great number-crunching brain, was also misleading. The essence of genius is the intuitive mental leap that is a mystery even to the brain that makes it. So many enormous deals start with boxcar numbers and feelings about a particular individual or management group. Paul Reichmann's intellectual churning was piggybacked on his intuition. Then, often to the wonder of those around him, the answer popped out, and everyone would marvel, "Why didn't I think of that?"

Olympia & York revolved around the mind of Paul Reichmann, and Paul Reichmann's mind revolved constantly, almost obsessively, on diversification, reinvestment, and growth.

Bill Zeckendorf had noted in his autobiography that "The secret of any great project is to keep it moving, keep it from losing momentum." Real estate was a business peculiarly susceptible to loss of momentum. Its most famous exponents always used their last building to help finance their next effort. This pyramiding process tended to make real estate companies rather like sharks, not in the predatory but in the purely physiological sense: once they stopped moving, they were in danger of sinking. The fate of Bill Zeckendorf's own empire had shown that.

The Reichmanns' momentum had now carried them beyond real estate. Bulging real estate funds had been used to buy minority positions in resource companies. These would in some cases be built into majority positions and control. The acquired companies in turn would be used to buy other companies. The only question was: Where would it all end?

Toward the end of 1983, Paul Reichmann began to think about the family's next quantum leap. They had tested the water with the acquisition of stakes in several small- and medium-sized oil companies. It was now time to consider a larger acquisition: the largest oil company acquisition in Canadian history.

10

GULF CANADA I: TROUBLED TARGET

*There was something symbolic about the
mists that wreathed the building's entrance.
Gulf still seemed to be trying to find
its way in a fog.*

To understand the way in which the Reichmanns seized control of Gulf Canada, it is necessary to understand something of both the oil company's troubled history and the peculiarly complex political and economic climate in which the takeover took place.

When the Reichmanns acquired it, Gulf Canada was Canada's second-largest oil company, the 60.2-percent-owned subsidiary of Gulf Corporation, the smallest of the Seven Sisters. The parent company traced its origins to Spindletop, Texas, a little hillock close to the Gulf of Mexico where, on January 10, 1901, an engineer and former officer in the Austrian navy, Anthony Lucas, drilled a prodigious 1,000-foot well and struck the biggest oil gusher to date. Spindletop soon dried up, but the company, under the control of the mighty Pittsburgh-based industrialist Mellon family, went on to make other major discoveries and expand all over the United States and then the world. Gulf opened the first drive-in gas station, in Pittsburgh in 1913, and made huge finds beneath the deserts of Kuwait and the swamps of Venezuela.

The 1970s and early 1980s were a time of turmoil for all the major oil companies, which were suspected of having manipulated the

OPEC crisis for their own corporate ends. For Gulf Corp. and its Canadian subsidiary, the political and business turmoil created by OPEC was greatly exacerbated by internal corporate problems. Scandals rocked the parent's pyramid-topped Pittsburgh headquarters, while muffled wranglings over managerial succession could be heard from behind the boardroom doors in Toronto.

In 1973, as part of the investigation of Watergate, Gulf Corp. was revealed to have made major illegal contributions to President Richard Nixon's Committee to Re-elect the President (or CREEP, as it was unaffectionately known). It was further discovered that Gulf had, between 1966 and 1972, paid U.S.$5 million to foreign politicians and parties, including U.S.$4 million to President Park in South Korea. These payments had come via a slush fund set up in 1958 by company president William Whiteford. Money was delivered by hand to a Bahamian subsidiary, whence it was returned in plain envelopes to Washington for distribution to domestic and foreign politicians. The Securities and Exchange Commission eventually charged Gulf with falsifying financial records relating to the slush fund. Gulf also became embroiled in a furor over an international cartel accused of attempting to fix world uranium prices.

Suspicion of Uncle Sam

These revelations of corporate skullduggery south of the border would have come as no surprise to Albert Leroy Ellsworth, the man who, in 1906, founded British American Oil Company Limited (BA), the company that would one day become Gulf Canada. Ellsworth had a profound distrust of Americans. His negative feelings were obviously not without foundation. He had spent ten years working for the granddaddy of them all, John D. Rockefeller's Standard Oil, in Buffalo.

With an initial investment of $135,000 put up with seven partners, Ellsworth, a native of Welland, Ontario, started a kerosene and lubricating oil business in Toronto. Following the spread of the automobile throughout Canada, the company rapidly developed gasoline refining capacity. In 1920, Ellsworth purchased Winnipeg Oil Company, giving it outlets in the Prairie Provinces. In 1931, he opened a refinery in Montreal, and, three years later, followed it with another in Moose Jaw, Saskatchewan. The Moose Jaw refinery developed a special significance for executive development at British American, and later Gulf Canada. The no-nonsense engineers who came out of the University of Saskatchewan and/or worked at Moose Jaw were considered the models of the "Gulf man." They were dubbed the "Moose Jaw Mafia."

Ellsworth had a bookkeeper's passion for detail reminiscent of Rockefeller himself; he would lean over the shoulders of junior clerks to check that they were affixing postage stamps neatly. But he also had corporate vision and in twenty years he had built British American into the largest Canadian-owned oil company, second only to Imperial Oil, the Canadian subsidiary of Standard Oil of New Jersey (later Exxon).

Despite Ellsworth's aversion to American business, connections with the United States inevitably increased as BA developed oil and gas production south of the border. It was through these American operations that William K. Whiteford, the man who would eventually plant the American flag on BA, came into the company.

Whiteford had joined BA as vice-president of its American subsidiary. In 1942, Ellsworth reluctantly brought him to Toronto as executive vice-president. Ellsworth left Whiteford in no doubt about his misgivings at having an American head the company. Upon his arrival, Whiteford was told by Ellsworth that to "ease the blow" of a Yankee's elevation within such a staunchly Canadian company, there would be no announcement of his appointment. Also, he would receive no salary but would live on an expense account. Whiteford was merely given an office where he was meant to "get acquainted" with the other employees. In time, by some strange process of corporate communication-by-insinuation, the staff would come to understand his position. Despite this chilly welcome, Whiteford soon became president of BA and oversaw a period of dynamic corporate growth during and after World War II. Soon BA's refining and marketing operations stretched from coast to coast.

Shortly after the war, the Pittsburgh-based Gulf Oil Corp. acquired a 20 percent interest in British American. At the same time, Gulf started its own Canadian exploration via a subsidiary, Canadian Gulf Oil Co. The links between British American and Gulf were further strengthened when, in 1951, Whiteford was invited to join Gulf in Pittsburgh. He eventually became president and chairman of Gulf, and Gulf took control of British American.

In 1956, BA issued 8.3 million of its shares to Gulf in return for Gulf's Canadian interests. Gulf thus swallowed British American as British American swallowed part of Gulf. This technique would be echoed thirty years later when Paul Reichmann "repatriated" the company. At the time of these high financial negotiations between Pittsburgh and Toronto, however, young Paul and Ralph Reichmann were concerned with the arrival of their next tile shipment from Spain.

The name of the company was not changed to Gulf Oil Canada until 1969. Shortly afterward, Jerry McAfee, a brilliant and articulate executive, was appointed head of the Canadian operations. McAfee was from Port Arthur, Texas, home of a large Gulf Corp. refinery and also of Gulf Corp.'s head, Bob Dorsey, who now found himself hemmed in by scandal on all sides. While the tough, uncompromising Dorsey attempted to ride out the corporate storm over the slush fund and the uranium cartel, Jerry McAfee — who had always been regarded internally as Dorsey's corporate rival — enjoyed a happier time north of the border.

Gulf Canada under McAfee produced the outstanding performance among the Canadian majors in the early 1970s. Between 1970 and 1974, the company quadrupled its earnings to $176 million and raised its return on capital — the critical measure of business success — from the lowest to the highest among the "Big Four." But the Pittsburgh scandals had an important ramification for Canada: they led to Dorsey's replacement by McAfee. The significance of McAfee's elevation was not lost on his colleagues at Gulf Canada's Bay Street headquarters. When he left for Pittsburgh, they presented him with a T-shirt. On it were emblazoned the words "Mr. Clean."

Succession Problems on Bay Street

McAfee's departure led to major problems north of the border. While the affable Texan struggled with Pittsburgh's difficulties — which now included the nationalization of the company's interests in both Kuwait and Venezuela — the Canadian subsidiary went into an identity crisis. It entered a period of uncertainty about managerial succession and became absorbed in soul-searching about its corporate direction.

McAfee left Gulf Canada without identifying a successor. John

Stoik, a big, heavy-set man who had been brought back to Canada after running Gulf Oil Corp.'s operations in Korea (where so much of the slush fund money had found its way) was a candidate for the top spot, but he was felt to be as yet too raw. Stoik was a solid citizen, and a charter member of the Moose Jaw Mafia, but he was no McAfee. He lacked charisma and looked uneasy in public. The decision was made to split top executive responsibilities. Stoik was made president and chief operating officer, but the title of chief executive officer was vested in Clarence Shepard, the company's tall, bald, avuncular chairman.

In 1977, the cat was thrown among the corporate pigeons when Bill Wilder was invited to become the company's executive vice-president. Wilder, educated at Upper Canada College, McGill, and Harvard, and a naval lieutenant during the war, had risen to be president of leading Toronto investment dealer Wood Gundy. Then he had moved to head the Arctic Gas consortium, the blue-chip group of Canadian companies that planned to build a natural gas pipeline from Prudhoe Bay, Alaska, where North America's largest petroleum find had been made in 1968. Arctic Gas, however, had been killed by politics, and Wilder had immediately been snapped up by McAfee, who obviously thought he would be a good candidate to head the company. But after a short time, and much internal politicking, Wilder left to become head of the large Toronto-based gas utility Consumers' Gas. He was fated to be a close observer of the Reichmanns' moves into the oil and gas business in the coming years.

At Gulf Canada, although Stoik had prevailed in the power struggle, the soul-searching continued. The company was beset with bureaucracy and inertia. A leading firm of management consultants was shown Gulf Canada's organization chart without being told what sort of organization it was. They came to the conclusion that, because of the huge number of committees, it had to be either a hospital or a university.

To improve efficiency, Gulf Canada was reorganized as a holding company with an upstream — that is, oil and gas exploration and production — arm, and a downstream — refining and marketing — division. The holding, or corporate management, company was to give strategic direction to the upstream and downstream arms, to set basic policies and performance objectives, and to provide effective controls. Or at least that was the theory.

The resources arm was housed in a giant, new, glass-faced building on Calgary's Ninth Avenue. The squat building, touted as "the biggest in the West," seemed somehow analogous to Gulf Canada as a whole: massive but not outstanding. It contained a supposedly state-of-the-art system of energy conservation. Part of the system was a sculptured concrete construction in front of the entrance which, in the depths of Calgary's winter, would belch forth plumes of white steam. It looked a little like the entrance to Hades. There was something symbolic about the mists that wreathed the building's entrance. Gulf still seemed to be trying to find its way in a fog. The company sorely lacked strategic direction.

Whereas companies like Imperial or Shell employed a "rifle" approach, identifying and taking aim at specific targets, Gulf was seen as a "shotgun" company that tried for a little bit of everything. Gulf was a follower rather than a leader, and the company that it followed most often was Imperial, Canada's oldest, largest, and at times most self-righteous oil giant. Imperial's management made little secret of their belief that they were the best. This galled Gulf's senior management. J.C. Phillips, who succeeded Shepard as chairman, was once quoted as saying: "If Imperial jumped off a cliff, the others would follow. And when they hit the bottom and were hurting real bad they'd still say 'it can't be all that bad because Imperial is down here with us.' "

Then, suddenly, Gulf's shotgun began hitting targets.

The Ugly Duckling Becomes a Swan

The first hit was made toward the end of 1979 at Hibernia, in the storm-tossed, iceberg-gouged Grand Banks, 200 miles northeast of St. John's, Newfoundland. The discovery of Hibernia followed twenty years of disappointment for explorers off Canada's East Coast. It had long been thought that a fifth or more of Canada's petroleum reserve potential lay beneath the seabed off Newfoundland and Nova Scotia, but until Hibernia, the search for the geophysical and geological keys that would unlock the hydrocarbon treasure chest had proved fruitless. During those two decades, $850 million had been spent on the search. The key was eventually found by Chevron Standard, the Calgary-based subsidiary of another of the Seven Sisters, Standard Oil Co. of California.

Chevron had already earned considerable kudos for its discovery of the important West Pembina field in Alberta in the mid-1970s. It came up with the Hibernia prospect by taking Mobil's seismic data — that is, analysis of soundwaves bounced off subterranean rock formations to spot likely hydrocarbon "traps" — and "working it over" with advanced, computerized techniques. Chevron's explorationists thought they had spotted the seismic ghost of a major find and decided to drill a well, Hibernia P-15, on Mobil's lands.

Gulf Canada too had, in the early 1970s, farmed-in (that is, put up exploration money in return for a portion of the finds) on Mobil's Grand Banks acreage, but had enjoyed little success. More than forty wells had been drilled in the area without a commercial find. Gulf Canada decided to have one last fling by participating in Hibernia P-15. Mobil had a 28.125 percent interest in the well, Gulf and Petro-Canada, the state oil company formed in 1976, had 25 percent each, and Chevron held 21.875 percent (part of which was taken under a previous agreement with Columbia Gas Development of Canada Ltd.).

The well was started, or "spudded," on May 27, 1979. By the time drilling and testing had finished seven months later, Hibernia was clearly the most significant find since Imperial Oil's discovery at Leduc, Alberta, thirty-two years before. Leduc had heralded the modern age of Canadian petroleum. Hibernia promised a new era in North American hydrocarbon development. Oil gushed from the well at over twelve thousand barrels a day. Chevron believed that it was capable of producing twenty thousand. Here was another potential North Sea. Meanwhile, to add to its exploration blessings, Gulf Canada was also involved with Dome Petroleum in the Beaufort Sea in what Dome claimed to be major finds. The ugly duckling among the Canadian majors was suddenly on the point of achieving swan status.

Once again, Gulf had played the "follower" in both exploration plays, but it was the only member of the Hibernia drilling consortium whose shares were publicly traded in Canada. The two pieces of news sent Gulf shares soaring. In less than a month, they doubled in value to $100. By early 1980, they had reached an astonishing $190. Gulf Canada made a five-for-one stock split (that is, giving shareholders five new shares for each existing one to bring the stock market price out of the stratosphere and allow the shares to be more easily traded).

In 1979, trading in Gulf shares on the Toronto, Montreal, Vancouver, and American stock exchanges reached $2.1 billion, second only to Dome Petroleum. In 1980, the desire for Gulf stock reached fever pitch. The value of Gulf trading reached $5.4 billion as the shares touched a post-split high of $38.63. But they would not see that level again. Just when it seemed that the oilman's greatest asset, luck, had at last come along to help the company out of its prolonged personality crisis, something far less pleasant arrived on Gulf Canada's business horizons: the National Energy Program.

Politics Rears its Ugly Head

The 1980 Canadian federal election was a matter of the Tories losing power rather than the Liberals gaining it. The Tories had been in power less than a year. Energy policy played a major part in their downfall. One key contributor to the fall was a Tory budget measure proposing an 18-cent-a-gallon excise tax on gasoline. The tax was introduced to fund the sharply increased costs of subsidizing more expensive oil imports. The Liberals, who after so many years in power seemed driven by cynicism rather than political objectives, succeeded in portraying the tax as a heartless move on the part of the Conservatives rather than as an economic necessity. The Tories' other big energy policy problem was with one of Gulf's partners in the Hibernia well, Petro-Canada.

The national oil company had been set up in 1976 in response to the uncertainties of OPEC-controlled oil. Its mandate was to promote petroleum self-sufficiency through frontier exploration and to provide a "window on the industry" so that the federal government could make better-informed energy policy. There was, inevitably, much heated political debate over its creation. The Clark Tories came to power in 1979 promising to dismember this interventionist instrument. But the policy was ill conceived because of its timing, because of the Canadian electorate's fondness for Petrocan, and because the Tories were a minority government.

Joe Clark had the misfortune to come to power at the same time as the Ayatollah Khomeini. The Ayatollah's accession, and its impact on oil supplies and prices, led to a resurgence of the fears that had provided public support for a national oil company in the first place. The Canadian populace reaffirmed its belief that Petro-Canada could in some way provide a security blanket against both the harsh realities of world oil and paranoia about foreign control of the Canadian oil industry. For Joe Clark's Tory government, Petro-Canada turned out to be like the tar-baby of Uncle Remus's fable: the more they tried to assault it, the more they found themselves stuck to it. The Clark government eventually staged a *volte face* on Petrocan, claiming that they had really meant to increase its size all along, but by then it was too late. Joe Clark's Tories found themselves in history's trashcan.

The Liberals returned to power promising lower energy prices, "Canadianization" of the oil business, and energy security through self-sufficiency. These promises were a mixture of long-stated objectives (self-sufficiency), impossible targets sold to a gullible electorate (lower energy prices), and motherhood (Canadianization). The buoyant oil industry at first paid them little heed. For the oilmen, things were looking good.

The return of Pierre Trudeau's Liberals coincided with unprecedented optimism about East Coast prospects in the wake of the Hibernia find. It was also thought that, just as after the first OPEC crisis, Canadian prices would inevitably follow world prices, Alberta would enjoy a further surge of revenues, and the oil companies would enjoy another leap in profits. But the Ottawa Liberals had other ideas. Not only were they determined to grab more of Alberta's revenues and the oil company's "windfall" profits, they also decided to stage an unprecedented attack on foreign-controlled oil in an attempt to make it loosen its supposedly pernicious grip on the Canadian economy.

Throughout the spring and summer of 1980, the policy was hatched in Ottawa's corridors of power with minimal industry consultation. John Stoik and his lieutenants, like the executives of the other major oil companies, developed an uneasy feeling. The feeling was justified. By the fall of 1980, the Liberals' vague election platform had been transformed, with the aid of a fiercely committed group of backroom policy advisors and public servants, into one of the most revolutionary policies in Canadian history.

On October 28, 1980, the National Energy Program was unveiled. It painted a threatening picture of foreign oil, in particular of companies like Gulf Canada. If the existing tax system was not changed, declared the policy, then, given that world oil prices were undoubtedly heading toward U.S. $80 a barrel, the foreign-controlled multinationals would wind up owning an inordinate amount of the national wealth. Finds like Hibernia, far from being a cause for congratulation, were a source of fear. Three-quarters of the field would be owned by foreign oil companies, who would use its proceeds to increase their stranglehold on the Canadian economy. Such companies had to be stopped in their tracks. They would be more heavily taxed and, in the place of the old tax-based exploration incentives, which were claimed to give the foreigners unfair advantage, a new, discriminatory grant system would be introduced. Meanwhile, a quarter of their frontier acreage — including Hibernia and the Beaufort — would simply be expropriated. The not-so-hidden agenda of this policy was that foreign oil, faced with this crippling array of taxes, discrimination, and expropriation, would sell out.

For Gulf Canada, which was not merely predominantly foreign-owned and controlled but also had its most attractive assets in the Canadian frontiers, the NEP was a disaster. Meanwhile, the East Coast waters had been further muddied by a jurisdictional dispute between Newfoundland and Ottawa. Once again, the oil companies were cast as the meat in the sandwich.

The NEP poisoned Canada-U.S. relations. The walls in Gulf Corp.'s executive suite down in Pittsburgh rang with denunciations of the Canadian federal government's perfidy. The Liberals' response to these denunciations was simple: if foreign oil companies didn't like it, they could sell out. Pittsburgh's reaction was that they'd be damned if they were going to be blackmailed into selling.

Although John Stoik and the Gulf Canada management and board despised the NEP, they realized that they had to cope with it. The prospect of "Canadianization" was not repugnant to them. After all, most of them were Canadians, and proud of it. More important, there was suddenly lots of money—in the form of the new discriminatory Petroleum Incentive Payments, or PIP grants — in being officially stamped with the Maple Leaf.

Gulf Canada's management decided to stop playing follow the leader. It was time to put away the shotgun and pull out the high-powered rifle. If they couldn't get their hands directly on the highest levels of PIP grants, which offered a mouth-watering 80 percent of frontier exploration expenditures, they could at least take a bold initiative that would indirectly benefit from the grants. They would build a massive drilling fleet to carry out PIP-funded drilling in the Beaufort Sea, and they would bring in as exploration partners Canadian companies that *did* have access to top-level PIPs. There was an additional rationale for building such a fleet: frustration with the Beaufort's existing offshore driller, Dome Petroleum.

Boldly into the Beaufort

The Beaufort Sea had first come into the exploration spotlight following North America's largest oil and gas find, at Prudhoe Bay in Alaska, in 1968. That single field, with over 10 billion barrels of oil (more than all of Canada's proven reserves), sparked a landrush in the Canadian onshore and offshore lands to the east: the Mackenzie Delta and the Beaufort. But the Beaufort presented unprecedented exploration difficulties. For most of the year the sea is a slow-moving sheet of ice, grinding clockwise with the polar ice pack at about three miles a day. As the twenty-four-hour dark of winter gives way to the twenty-four-hour light of summer, the ice melts, allowing a brief but hazardous three-month marine drilling season.

The history of Beaufort exploration had been more a case study in politics than geology. It all started with the ''northern dream'' of Dome Petroleum's uniquely persuasive chairman, ''Smilin' Jack'' Gallagher. Gallagher went to Ottawa in the mid-1970s and sold the Liberal government on the concept of ''superdepletion,'' that is, very high tax allowances, for drilling high-cost frontier wells.

The soft-spoken Manitoba native, who delivered his low-key Beaufort slide-show to the investment faithful, politicians, and bureaucrats almost like a holy rite, sold these write-offs to Ottawa by painting an alluring picture of huge Beaufort finds, massive tax revenues, insulation from uncertain world oil markets, and independence from Alberta's oil and its combative premier, Peter Lougheed. For Dome there was an additional, although inevitably less publicized, rationale: the company had already committed itself to a $225 million Beaufort drilling fleet, Canadian Marine Ltd (Canmar), consisting of three drill ships and four icebreaking supply vessels. Unless Beaufort exploration could be encouraged, Canmar would turn out to be a white elephant. It might even sink the company.

Gallagher's lobbying was a classic example of a private entrepreneur attempting to gain public funds to further his own corporate ambitions. This form of lobbying is not *per se* pernicious, and may, with a wise enough government, lead to positive benefits. Businessmen all over the world attempt to gain benefits from governments in the name of the national good, but Canada's particular fears about freezing in the dark, and its paranoia about foreign ownership of the oil industry, created a unique environment for exploiting the public purse. Paul Reichmann was well aware of this political background when he eventually moved on Gulf Canada.

The bottom line of Gallagher's highly successful piece of lobbying was that federal tax dollars wound up paying for virtually all Beaufort drilling. There was an inevitable surge in exploration activity, and Dome did not fail to take advantage of its monopoly position. Those forced to use Dome's facilities didn't see Gallagher and his belligerent president, Bill Richards, as visionaries; they saw them as pirates.

Gulf Canada was the operator for some 2 million acres of the Beaufort situated between the shallower inshore lands held largely by Imperial — which could be drilled from artificial islands — and the deeper offshore lands controlled by Dome. Gulf also had an interest in Dome's deeper lands, which it had acquired from the Hunt family of Texas. Gulf's explorationists were constantly frustrated either by Dome's attempts to drive hard bargains for the fleet's use, or simply by its unavailability. The NEP, somewhat ironically, by introducing incentives even more generous than superdepletion, offered the opportunity to Gulf Canada to build a rival fleet.

Within six months of the NEP, Gulf Canada had committed itself to the largest single investment in its history, $674 million for a giant "drilling system" for Beaufort exploration. The system consisted of two huge drilling units, the two most powerful privately owned icebreakers in the world, and two icebreaking supply vessels. The drilling units were a combination of brute engineering and high technology. The Conical Drilling Unit, or CDU, was a giant circular barge with a special ice-deflecting hull, held on location with twelve eighty-three-ton mooring winches. The other, the Mobile Arctic Caisson, or MAC, was a massive hollow steel structure rising 95 feet from its base to a deck 240 feet across.

Gulf executives bristled at the suggestion that the drilling fleet was built to take advantage of the hated NEP. It was, they declared righteously, predicated on the need to evaluate the company's Beaufort acreage *despite* the NEP. But the PIP program soon ran into financial and political problems. And so did Gulf.

In 1983, a number of Beaufort exploration agreements were announced. They called for the most expensive wells in world exploration history. The projected cost of one of Gulf's PIP-supported wells was a mind-boggling $214 million. Even if the government paid 80 percent of that mammoth cost, there was still a $43 million bill to foot. Gulf's Canadian partners, in particular Canterra Energy Ltd., began to kick and scream behind the exploration consortium's closed doors, while the nine-digit well costs also set off the alarm bells in Ottawa.

The bureaucrats who administered the PIPs suddenly found themselves under heavy pressure to reduce the politically embarrassing hemorrhage of public money into Beaufort drilling. They forced Gulf to pull down its charges. Meanwhile, Canterra withdrew from some of the most expensive wells, leaving Gulf to pick up the extra costs. To top off its woes, its 1983 Beaufort drilling season was filled with frustration. The worst summer ice in memory drove the CDU off two drilling locations and prevented it from starting a third well scheduled for that season.

The political controversy surrounding PIPs — whose multi-billion-dollar costs were far higher than those projected by a naive government — made it clear that the grants were a far from long-term proposition. Meanwhile, a pronounced weakening in world oil prices undermined the whole economics of the Beaufort Sea. Once again, Gulf Canada had blown it. Once again, a corporation had been encouraged to blow it by perverse government policies. And yet ironically, given the intentions of the NEP and the company's own managerial ineptitude, Gulf in 1983 seemed safer from takeover than ever.

The NEP had declared a holy war against foreign-controlled oil. It had led to an orgy of corporate acquisition in the name of "Canadianization." When the party was over, most of the Canadian acquisitors were left with terminal financial hangovers. Companies like Dome Petroleum — which, typically, had made the most ambitious and expensive acquisition — were put on life support systems by banks too scared to face the consequences of their death.

Besides damaging Canada-U.S. relations, this government-backed, bank-funded buyout had done severe damage to the Canadian dollar (via the outflow of dollars to pay for the foreign acquisitions), but it had still not been enough to dislodge any of the major, foreign-controlled oil companies. Indeed, in the wake of the disastrous consequences of the NEP, the majors — Imperial Oil, Gulf Canada, Shell Canada, and Texaco Canada — appeared more firmly entrenched than ever. They would have been difficult to swallow at the best of times. Now, it seemed, they had returned to their old position of invulnerability.

It certainly wasn't that Canadian companies hadn't looked long and hard at acquiring them. The investment community had quickly seen that there were big bucks to be made from Canadianization. Soon after the NEP, Gordon Securities Jimmy Connacher had gone to Gulf Canada and offered to help put the company under the Maple Leaf flag. Close to the top of his list of potential buyers was Paul Reichmann.

In 1981, Reichmann had gone to Bill Wilder, who was by then the president of Hiram Walker Resources, in which O&Y had just taken a significant stake, and suggested that the two companies might stage a joint assault on Gulf Canada. Reichmann had been impressed by the strategy used by Dome Petroleum to take control of Hudson's Bay Oil & Gas from its parent, Conoco. Dome had bought Conoco shares and then swapped these for Conoco's stake in HBOG. Reichmann suggested to Wilder that O&Y and Hiram Walker might jointly purchase Gulf Corp. shares with a view to swapping them for Gulf Corp.'s control of Gulf Canada. However, Hiram Walker's board had turned the idea down.

The concept of an assault on Gulf Canada was put on the back burner as the investment climate became increasingly uncertain in 1982 and 1983. Moreover, Pittsburgh retained its powerful objections to being blackmailed into a sale of one of its prize assets. As Alf Powis, head of mining giant Noranda and chairman of Gulf Canada's executive committee, told the author: "Once the NEP came along the Gulf Canada management was very keen to have the company Canadianized, particularly since we were so active in the frontiers. . . . But at the end of the day, the only way they could Canadianize was to get Gulf Pittsburgh out of there, and Gulf Pittsburgh was reluctant to get out."

In the end, change of control at Gulf Canada was brought about neither by its own managerial ineptitude nor political blackmail, although politics would still play a major role in the company changing hands. Canada's ill-advised post-NEP takeover spree was followed by an even more aggressive — and perhaps even more ill-advised — bout of acquisition fever south of the border. That, and the managerial incompetence of its Pittsburgh parent, was the reason Gulf Canada finally came on the auction block.

11

GULF CANADA II: GULF CORP. STUMBLES

Paul Reichmann's plan called for the use of
a great deal of other people's money. Because
of Petrocan's role and the Little Egypt Bump,
a lot of it belonged to the public.

The chain of events that led to Gulf Canada falling into the hands of the Reichmanns began in the fall of 1983 with T. Boone Pickens, Jr., the fitness fanatic and swashbuckling head of Mesa Petroleum. Pickens, who was also a Presbyterian elder, had made a career, and a lot of money for Mesa and himself, by picking fights with larger companies. In 1980, his before-tax income of U.S.$7.9 million made him the highest-paid executive on the continent.

Boone Pickens had established himself as an expert at "greenmail," a manoeuvre that involves buying blocks of a company's stock with the explicit or implicit threat of takeover and subsequent purge of the target's executive suite. Panicked executives usually either bought Pickens off or sought a "white knight" to rescue them with a more friendly takeover. Sometimes they were merely snapped up by a bigger predator. Whichever of the three happened, Pickens wound up richer, selling his stock at a hefty premium over his purchase price.

Pickens had bought into Superior Oil and it had been acquired by Mobil. Mesa made over U.S.$30 million. He had launched an attack on Cities Service Co., which had fled into the arms of Occidental Petroleum, leaving Pickens with U.S.$44 million. He had sparked the rescue of General American Oil by Phillips Petroleum, resulting in another U.S.$44 million for Mesa's kitty.

But there was more to Pickens than mere greenmail. He was also a corporate crusader, sharply critical of big oil's "waste" of shareholder funds in high-cost frontier exploration and diversification into unrelated businesses. If they had cash to burn, he said, then they should give it to the shareholders. Pickens had pioneered the concept of segregating all or part of an oil company's producing assets into a "royalty trust," the cash flow from which would flow directly, free of corporate tax, to shareholders. He had done it with Mesa, to the considerable benefit of his shareholders, and he claimed there was no reason why larger companies could not do the same. In the fall of 1983, his attention fell on the Gulf Oil Corporation. Gulf was ripe for the plucking.

The man who had taken over from Jerry McAfee as chairman of Gulf Oil Corporation in 1981 was James E. "Jimmy" Lee. Jimmy Lee was regarded as a true gentleman in the oil patch. He looked a little like Phil Silvers' Sergeant Bilko, but his attitude could not have been more different. He played it straight down the line. Some thought a little too straight. He was regarded as a good manager, but he had a blind spot: he did not understand the mysteries of Wall Street, in whose eyes he had also made a fatal mistake. Pickens had been involved in the misadventure. In the summer of 1982, when Pickens had launched his first David-and-Goliath greenmail bid by tendering for the stock of Cities Service, Cities Service had sought a white knight. The man who rode up on the charger was Jimmy Lee. But then Lee, when confronted by U.S. Federal Trade Commission antitrust concerns — which most considered no real barrier — suddenly, and with no warning, rode off again. His withdrawal left a lot of unhappy speculators. Wall Street's "arbitrageurs" — high-stake dealers who snap up blocks of stock during takeover fights — had accumulated large amounts of Cities Service stock. When Lee withdrew, Cities' stock price collapsed and the "arbs" were left holding the baby. The arbs didn't like stock market babies. Although Occidental Petroleum emerged as an alternative white knight, the arbs still lost around U.S.$400 million. Jimmy Lee had cost them. If anybody took a run at Gulf, then it was felt that they would participate with particular gusto. A run became increasingly likely because of the company's depressed share price, which reflected its management's performance.

Lee inherited the problems with which McAfee had struggled during his term — including the political instability of the company's remaining sources of overseas supply in Nigeria and Angola — at a time when the whole industry was coming under pressure to reorganize itself. Pickens was not the only critic claiming that the big, integrated oil companies were slow in adapting to the problems of both the upstream and the downstream ends of the business. In the upstream, most companies were failing to replace reserves as they produced them. Moreover, said the critics, they were going after high-cost replacements whose economics looked doubtful as a worldwide softening of oil prices was beginning to take hold. The frontier exploration of Gulf and its Canadian subsidiary was considered a perfect example. As for the downstream, there was chronic overcapacity as a result of a fall-off in demand. Refineries were running well below optimum capacity, and there were still too many gas stations.

Lee in fact had made valiant strides in his first two years as chairman to cut costs. He reduced Gulf's payroll by 14,000 and sold off most of its European refining and marketing operations. But the company's shares were still wallowing in the doldrums. Its price valued its oil reserves at barely U.S.$4 a barrel, versus an average finding cost for new reserves of U.S.$10 a barrel.

On August 11, 1983, news of unusually heavy trading in Gulf stock came to the company's Pittsburgh headquarters. When Jimmy Lee and his executives heard that Pickens was buying, they were annoyed rather than scared. By comparison with Gulf, Mesa was minuscule. Gulf's 1982 revenues had been U.S.$30 billion versus Mesa's measly U.S.$407 million. Its production that year had been 182 million barrels. Mesa's was a piddling 4.4 million. But Gulf executives had only to look at Pickens's record to realize that once he picked on a company, then that company usually wound up being taken over.

Pickens declared that Gulf should organize a royalty trust, as Mesa had done, in order to maximize value for its shareholders. Gulf rejected the suggestion out of hand, but Pickens succeeded in having the issue put to shareholders. After a very expensive proxy battle, in which both sides spent many millions of dollars lining up shareholders to support their point of view, Gulf won its bid to have Pickens's plan rejected. But it had far from won the war.

Gulf's defensive campaign was astonishingly inept, a combination of bravado and bumbling. One of Lee's field commanders for the battle, a Gulf executive named Harold Hammer, came across almost as a parody of the corporate heavy. During the fight to line up shareholders for the vote on the royalty trust plan, he told the press that he was going to "wear the black hat. We've got to kick him where it really smarts." "Who is Pickens anyway?" he challenged a *Fortune* reporter. "Everything he says is horse---- and hot air. You can take a high road or a low road, and I'm taking the low." Gulf also hired private detectives to dig up dirt on Pickens's past, which was, as an article in *Harper's* magazine pointed out, "hardly an inspired stroke of tactical genius."

Pickens and his supporting group of investors — which included the Vancouver-based Belzberg family — continued to pick up Gulf stock. Despite the proxy victory, the *de rigueur* battery of lawsuits, and the ritual beefing up of the company's credit line to U.S.$6 billion, Gulf's ineptitude piqued the interest of other, larger predators. Soon, several more suitors emerged from the corporate woodwork. The foremost of these was Atlantic Richfield Company, ARCO (for whom the Reichmanns had built a forty-nine-storey tower in Dallas). Lee began the inevitable search for white knights, and finally found one in George M. Keller, the chairman of Standard Oil Co. of California, Socal, also known by its gasoline brand as Chevron. In March, Socal won the battle for Gulf with a bid of U.S.$80 a share, a mind-numbing total of U.S.$13.2 billion, by far the world's largest takeover. The new merged company would bear the name of Chevron.

Wall Street's arbs made a fortune from the bidding war for Gulf. Pickens, too, had won. He and his group had acquired most of their shares below U.S.$50. They made a cool U.S.$760 million.

The arbs, not surprisingly, loved Pickens. On June 5, 1984, the stock brokerage firm of Spear Leeds & Kellogg threw a dinner in his honour at Park Avenue's Regency Hotel. At the dinner, New York Mayor Ed Koch presented Pickens with a crystal apple as a recognition of the huge volumes of money that Pickens's activities had generated for Wall Street, and, indirectly, for the city.

Pickens produced a live monkey. "I'd like you people," he said, "to meet Jimmy Lee."

Gulf Canada on the Block

The management of Gulf Canada were more appalled by their parent's inept performance than almost anybody else. Jimmy Lee, Harold Hammer, and the others down in Pittsburgh might claim that they had got the best deal for Gulf shareholders, but in Gulf Canada's mind they had blown it. Gulf Canada would either be absorbed into Chevron's Canadian subsidiary, Chevron Canada, or it would be sold. The former alternative held few attractions for Gulf Canada's management. Pittsburgh had always been a relatively passive major shareholder and had allowed Gulf Canada to go its own way. Chevron's head office in San Francisco was felt to have a much tighter grip on its Calgary-based Canadian operation. The Gulf exploration and production people feared that they would be decimated if they were rolled in with Chevron Canada. Also, there were great uncertainties about how Gulf's refining and marketing would fit in with Chevron's downstream interests in B.C. and the Maritimes. Gulf Canada management could see the Chevron guys in Calgary rubbing their hands at the thought of taking over Gulf's choice landholdings.

There was another, and as far as Gulf management was concerned preferable, alternative: they would be sold to a Canadian buyer. Chevron's debt load, because of the Gulf purchase, had grown to massive proportions. Chevron considered getting money out of Canada by having Gulf Canada buy Chevron's Canadian operations, but in the end, for tax and political reasons, they decided on a straight sale.

Paul Reichmann had already expressed his interest in the company. While Gulf's battle with Pickens had been in full swing in the final months of 1983, Paul Reichmann had several times had meetings with Gulf management in Pittsburgh with a view to buying its Canadian subsidiary. His plan had been to acquire Gulf Canada via Abitibi for a combination of cash and Abitibi shares. He had reportedly started with an offer of $15 a share and raised it to $17.50, but Gulf had told him that they wanted at least $19. Talks had broken off.

Following Standard's takeover, Reichmann had then spoken to Chevron's investment advisors, but they, too, had wanted more that Reichmann was, at the time, prepared to pay. Paul Reichmann, for the time being, left the field of play. There was much unfinished business within the family empire. The chief concern in 1984 was securing the final lessee for the World Financial Center.

Luring the Thundering Herd

The City Investing and Amex leases had accounted for half the space at the World Financial Center, but that still left almost 4 million square feet. The Reichmanns' New York staff had been working for over a year on the perfect candidate to take all that space. City Investing had been the bell calf, American Express the bell cow. Now came the "thundering herd," Merrill Lynch & Co. Inc.

Merrill Lynch, the world's largest investment company, with 40,000 employees worldwide, was an obvious candidate to consolidate its office space. It had eleven head office and administrative facilities scattered throughout Manhattan. Over many months of negotiations, the Reichmanns, Michael Dennis, and Ed Minskoff worked on Merrill Lynch management, and a complex deal was finally worked out where the investment company would occupy two of the World Financial Center's four buildings, which it would partly own as a joint venture with O&Y. The two buildings, one of thirty-four storeys and one of forty-four storeys, would have a combined space of 3.9 million square feet.

Once again, on the basis of the "used car" technique, O&Y agreed, in a separate transaction, to buy Merrill Lynch's existing headquarters, the 1.8-million-square-foot One Liberty Plaza, which was a mere stock certificate's flutter up Liberty Street away from its new offices.

The deal was announced, with much fanfare, on August 24, 1984. Press releases were issued containing the usual computer-generated executive remarks, only in this case, they came from some very high level sources. William Schreyer, Merrill Lynch's freshly appointed president and chief operating officer, stated, "This major undertaking will assure that Merrill Lynch remains a major corporate presence for years to come in New York City, which is truly the financial capital of the world."

Paul Reichmann declared, "We are delighted that Merrill Lynch, an industry leader, shares our great confidence in New York and its future."

New York state governor Mario Cuomo got to the real nitty-gritty of the transaction as far as the city was concerned. "Today's action," he said, "will result in the creation of thousands of construction, office and retail jobs, guarantee redemption of Battery Park City Authority bonds and repayment of State advances with interest from the 1979 financial rescue plan, and permit the Authority to proceed with development of another 12,000 housing units on the 92-acre landfill site."

Mayor Ed Koch, with a little more colour, noted, "Merrill Lynch's spectacular headquarters and operations project insures that the city of its birth and nurturing will remain the financial capital of the world. This is a real New York story."

No figures were released.

The realities of the deal were inevitably somewhat tougher than the sweetness and light of the announcement. At the end of the tenuous negotiations, a Merrill representative came to Paul Reichmann and said that he would have to pay a $6 million leasing commission to Merrill Lynch's in-house real estate brokerage arm. Landlords usually pay the brokerage commission. In this case Paul Reichmann felt, since Merrill Lynch was the principal, that it was inappropriate. He turned with a look of displeasure on the unfortunate emissary and said, "You take that message back to your principals and ask them if they really meant you to deliver it."

The brokerage fee was not mentioned again.

The leasing of the World Financial Center was now substantially completed. Elsewhere, the Reichmanns felt that real estate had plateaued for the time being. The oil industry slump had led to problems with leasing their buildings in Calgary and Houston, and they had decided to concentrate their real estate activities on just a few prime areas, in particular New York, Toronto, Los Angeles, and San Francisco.

Paul Reichmann could now turn his attention once more to acquisition. One of the candidates he was considering was Hiram Walker Resources, of which O&Y already held 10 percent, but then Gulf Canada was presented to him on a plate.

A Rare Prize

Whatever the criticisms of its management, Gulf Canada was still a rare prize in the Canadian oil industry. Its 1983 earnings of $218 million on net revenues of $5,163 million were well down from their 1980 peak of $380 million on sales of $3,843 million, but the company had excellent reserves and even more promising frontier prospects. With proven oil and natural gas liquid reserves of 412 million barrels, and proven natural gas holdings of 2.5 trillion cubic feet, it was Canada's fourth largest holder of petroleum resources, behind Imperial, the financially crippled Dome, and Shell Canada. Its 23 million net acres of exploration lands were second only to those of Dome. Most promising, 13.6 million of Gulf's acres were off Canada's East Coast, where the company held the largest overall exploration position.

These holdings made it an attractive company, but they also made it a very expensive one. Gulf Canada was estimated to be worth around $5 billion, so it would take some $3 billion to buy out Chevron's 60 percent. Within the Canadian private sector, there were few companies that could manage an acquisition of that magnitude.

Business Week, referring to a sale of Gulf Canada in the wake of the Chevron takeover, opined that "no Canadian buyers with the resources to take on such a deal are apparent, and foreign companies are likely to be no happier than Keller with the prospect of relying on Gulf Canada's modest dividends to pay off a massive investment." But *Business Week* was obviously unaware of the Reichmanns.

Paul Reichmann didn't like hostile takeovers, and he liked his targets to be standing still, so for him, Gulf Canada was perfect. The company, which would rather be taken over by almost anybody than rolled in with former rival Chevron Canada, provided the Reichmanns and their advisors with all the data they needed. Gulf had a sophisticated computer model through which it could run projections of what various petroleum price levels, tax changes, and other variables meant in terms of the company's future cash flow and value.

As usual all final decisions were made by Paul, but a number of advisors were crucial over the long and complex negotiations of the following year. Within O&Y, apart from Paul and Albert, much of the load was carried by Gil Newman, the bulky, bespectacled former chartered accountant who was their chief number-cruncher. Also, in November, 1984, Reichmann hired David Brown, the investment dealer from Burns Fry who had, over the years, done much business for the Reichmanns, including the Abitibi purchase.

Among Reichmann's important outside advisors were Howard Blauvelt, the former chairman of U.S. oil company Conoco, which had now been acquired by chemical giant Du Pont, and Garfield "Gar" Emerson of the Toronto law firm of Davies, Ward & Beck. Deeply involved too, although their presence was less obvious, were several of the financial hit men from Gordon Capital, including Jimmy Connacher, Bob Fung, and Neil Baker. Connacher and Fung had for several years been working on the potential sale of Gulf Canada.

The Chevron side was represented by Salomon Brothers and Wood Gundy. Salomon's Ron Freeman already knew the Reichmanns from earlier discussions about Gulf Canada, and also from their giant financings with his company, including the record U.S.$970 million mortgage that O&Y had raised on three of its Manhattan properties. Ted Medland, the white-haired head of Toronto's Wood Gundy, was also well acquainted with the Reichmanns since he was on the board of Abitibi.

Paul Reichmann's fundamental concern when looking at the Gulf Canada acquisition was the same as when he considered a real estate development: how could he minimize the cost and maximize the value of the investment?

Howard Blauvelt told him that he certainly didn't want Gulf's refining and marketing activities. These, like all such facilities, had suffered from overcapacity and offered a low return. When considering how to dispose of them, Paul Reichmann's immediate solution was to sell them to state-owned Petro-Canada. His advisors thought that this might be very difficult, given the arrival in power in September, 1984, of a new Tory government that had no love for the national oil company, and presumably little desire to see it expand. Nevertheless, Paul Reichmann felt that a deal could be worked out and, as usual, his instincts were good.

Another key part of his strategy was to take advantage of a potentially enormous tax loophole that had been brought to his attention to gain the biggest tax break of its kind in Canadian history. It would be worth almost $600 million.

Another key element of the deal was the role that Abitibi-Price would play. Since Reichmann had bought the newsprint giant in 1981, he had toyed with the idea of using it as part of his planned expansion into oil and gas. The deal he had originally proposed to Gulf Oil Corp. at the end of 1983 had been for Abitibi to be the purchaser of Gulf Canada, but now he hatched a new and even more inventive plan, a form of "leveraged buyout," under which the acquired company pays for its own acquisition. Reichmann decided that instead of having Abitibi buy Gulf, he would have Gulf buy Abitibi. Then he would use the funds to help pay for Gulf. It was a classic example of both having and keeping one's corporate cake. Not all his advisors thought that it was a good idea, and Abitibi's management was less than enthusiastic, but that was what Paul Reichmann wanted, and so that became part of the strategy.

The final critical issue that had to be addressed was the fate of Gulf Canada's minority shareholders. Securities Commissions and Stock Exchange watchdogs are always keen to ensure that minority shareholders received as good a deal as major block holders, but Paul Reichmann had no desire to pay cash to the holders of the 40 percent of Gulf Canada shares not owned by Chevron. That would have brought his outlay to $5 billion, which was more than even O&Y had available to it. He therefore hoped to gain an exemption from making a "follow-up" offer to minority shareholders at the same price as that to Chevron. In the end, the minority would receive a follow-up offer, but the burden of making it would fall not directly upon the Reichmanns, but on Gulf Canada.

The components of this plan, which were modified in the course of negotiations, had to be carefully orchestrated. But they were a good deal more than merely complex, they were also highly controversial. Paul Reichmann's plan called for the use of a great deal of other people's money. Because of Petrocan's role and the Little Egypt Bump, a lot of it belonged to the public. That inevitably caused problems for the Tory government. The Reichmanns' takeover of Gulf Canada would, in the end, prove a particularly telling example of the role of politics in Canadian business.

12

GULF CANADA III: PAUL AND BILL DO THE BUMP

*When O&Y's tax lawyers . . . turned up in Ottawa
to strut their stuff before Revenue Canada,
the Revenue Canada audience did not applaud.
In fact they booed.*

Foreign-controlled Canadian oil companies, which had been through a decade of adverse public sentiment culminating in the National Energy Program, knew that their every step came under political scrutiny. When Chevron began considering what to do with Gulf's Canadian subsidiary, it knew that its first stop had to be Ottawa.

The man who oversaw the fate of Gulf Canada from Chevron's head office was Thornton "Thorn" Savage, a personable executive close to retirement. Chevron's local head was the well-respected Gerry Henderson. Shortly after Gulf Corp. was acquired, Savage flew to Ottawa to visit Liberal industry, trade and commerce minister Ed Lumley and the director of the Foreign Investment Review Agency (FIRA) Bob Richardson. Lumley had little desire to make a big issue of the acquisition. There was an election coming and the Liberals had other things on their mind. The government allowed Chevron to take title to Gulf Canada in return for promising to offer the company for sale to Canadian-controlled entities.

When the Tories came to power, Henderson and Savage went to see Lumley's successor, Sinclair "Sinc" Stevens, an intense and tenacious former businessman who would later be caught in conflict-of-interest controversies. The men from Chevron expected a warmer reception from the new government, but the Tories were still struggling with the reins of power and Chevron's negotiators had problems getting answers. The Tories' position was complicated because they were facing several "indirect" takeovers in which the parents of Canadian companies had been acquired by other American companies. In addition to Chevron-Gulf, there was also the acquisition of Superior Oil Co. by Mobil Corp., and of Getty Oil Co. by Texaco Inc. Both Superior and Getty had Canadian subsidiaries but neither was as significant as Gulf Canada. Although they had declared themselves "open for business," and although the much-despised FIRA had been transmogrified after the election into the new, supposedly less xenophobic, Investment Canada, the Tories were wary of letting all three companies pass to their new American owners. The attractions of "helping" one of the indirect takeover targets into Canadian hands were great. The most attractive was Gulf Canada. The question was: who could afford it?

Bill Hopper, the pudgy, ebullient chairman of state-owned Petro-Canada, had long lusted after Gulf Canada. He had numerous times been down to Pittsburgh, window-shopping for the acquisition that would make his the largest oil company in Canada. But he had never been able to muster political support from his previous Liberal masters. It seemed less than likely that he would receive it from the new government.

The Tories had learned a bitter lesson from their ill-conceived 1979 assault on Petrocan, and despite their inevitable determination to treat it with caution, the antagonism obviously remained. John Crosbie, the feisty and funny Newfoundland finance minister in the doomed Clark government, asserted in the fall of 1983 that he would turn the Crown corporation's Calgary headquarters, nicknamed "Red Square," into "Black and Blue Square." In May, 1984, Michael Wilson, the arrow-straight former investment dealer who was Tory opposition finance critic, made a devastating attack on Petro-Canada's financial reporting during an appearance by Bill Hopper before the Standing Committee on National Resources and Public Works. Petrocan's results, said Wilson, although they appeared poor, were in fact much worse. They were only in the black at all, he said, because of "misleading" reporting practices.

The Tories returned to power determined to take a firm line with their old nemesis. They had learned from the Clark era that they should not threaten its existence, but they said that they would change its nature by privatizing it and selling shares to the public. They moved quickly to replace most of Petrocan's board, and dictated a new "mandate," which appeared in Petro-Canada's 1984 annual report. It spoke volumes about their ambiguity toward the Crown corporation.

"In the first nine years," it declared, "Petro-Canada was directed to work towards Canada's energy security effectively and efficiently, without overriding concern for profitability. The Corporation has now been given a new mandate by its shareholder — to operate in a commercial, private sector fashion, with emphasis on profitability and the need to maximize the return on the Government of Canada's investment. In this regard, Petro-Canada is not to be perceived in the future as an instrument in the pursuit of the Government's policy objectives. However, the Government maintains the right as a shareholder to formally direct Petro-Canada to carry out certain activities in the national interest."

The final two sentences of this new mandate were contradictory; the company was not to be a policy instrument, unless the government decided that it wanted to use it as such. The thorny issue of using Petro-Canada "in the national interest" was to arise almost immediately for the Tories. If they wanted to Canadianize Gulf, the only candidate was Paul Reichmann. But Paul Reichmann told the government that there would be a price to pay. Part of that price was "participation" by Petro-Canada. The other multinationals might be prepared to look at acquiring Gulf's downstream assets, but they were unlikely to pay as much as Petrocan. Moreover, the Tories were more scared of being seen to promote the multinationals' growth than that of Petro-Canada.

Take Your Partners

In February, 1985, the Tories announced that they had allowed Gulf Canada's control to pass into the hands of Chevron on the condition that the American company put its block on the market "for sale to Canadian-controlled purchasers." A deadline of April 30, 1985, was placed on such a sale, after which Chevron could dispose of Gulf Canada as it sought fit. Ideological opposition to

Petrocan's growth was about to take second place to the political attractions of bringing Gulf Canada under Canadian ownership. Paul Reichmann began discussions with Sinc Stevens.

Tory cabinet members like Pat Carney, the new minister of energy, mines and resources, who was suspected of being a closet economic nationalist, were particularly keen for the Reichmann acquisition. Taking an active role in encouraging this largest of all Canadianizations would deflect any suggestion that the Tories, although they had dismantled the NEP, disagreed with its motherhood principles. O&Y was given the nod to approach Petro-Canada. O&Y's David Brown, the former Burns Fry investment man, called Bill West, head of Petrocan's downstream operations, to sound out the Crown corporation's enthusiasm for acquiring Gulf's downstream. West, who had formerly headed Imperial Oil's downstream operations, said that Hopper was the man to talk to, and so a meeting was arranged between Paul Reichmann and Petrocan's chairman.

Toward the end of April, Reichmann went to Hopper's Ottawa office and asked if Petro-Canada would be interested in taking Gulf Canada's downstream off his hands. Hopper declared that he was primarily interested in Gulf Canada's refining and marketing operations west of Ontario, where Petrocan had a relatively small share of the market. Pat Carney, however, wanted Hopper to take more, not for commercial, but for political reasons. There was a concern among the Tories that Petro-Canada would be perceived as the cat's paw used by the Reichmanns to pick up the choice upstream assets of Gulf. Pat Carney wanted Petrocan to take part of Gulf's upstream assets off the Reichmanns, too. The rationale was that it would "play better" in the public arena.

After a few weeks of preliminary discussions, serious negotiations began. Bill Hopper and Petro-Canada senior vice-president David O'Brien camped out at the Royal York Hotel in Toronto and began rounds of almost daily discussions with Paul Reichmann and other O&Y representatives. Reichmann was reluctant to sell any of Gulf's upstream. After all, its oil and gas reserve potential were the reason he wanted the company. But Bill Hopper was particularly enthusiastic to get some of Gulf's prime East Coast offshore acreage. For years, he had been galled by what he saw as Mobil's foot-dragging on the development of the Hibernia field. But Mobil was the official "operator" of the exploration program, so it called the shots. If Hopper could gain part or all of Gulf's interest in Hibernia, then he could become the dominant partner in the development. Gulf's explorers, however, were strongly opposed to Petrocan walking off with their prize. Paul Reichmann told Hopper that the East Coast was not on the table. He would, however, let him take the Beaufort, where, although finds had been made, the prospects looked less certain.

Realizing that Carney wanted some upstream for cosmetic purposes, Reichmann of course drove a hard bargain. Petrocan finally settled on a package consisting of all the downstream — although Hopper was unenthusiastic about Quebec and particularly unenthusiastic about Ontario, where overcapacity had led to fierce price wars and bottom line losses for the refiners and marketers — and the Beaufort. The cost was a whopping $1.8 billion.

The Reichmanns in the meantime had, via Wood Gundy and Salomon, made an offer of $3 billion for Chevron's 60.2 percent of Gulf Canada, which Chevron had accepted. However, the offer was conditional, not on Petro-Canada's involvement, but on tax rulings from the federal government. Those tax rulings, again, were part of the price the people of Canada had to pay for Gulf's Canadianization.

Playing the Tax Angles

Every budget, governments tinker with the tax system in an attempt to encourage or discourage some form of economic or social activity, or in pursuit of "fairness," or merely to correct the faults of previous tinkerings. The result, over time, has become a jungle of fiscal complexity through which sharp-eyed tax lawyers and investment advisors prowl, looking for that juicy beast "the tax loophole." At least as much time, and possibly more brainpower, is spent on seeking ways to avoid taxes as on earning the taxable income in the first place.

The Reichmanns knew all about the tax angles. Property development financings were always structured with an eye to the tax system. In the proposed takeover of Gulf, the tax jungle had been thoroughly charted and an enormous loophole had been found. The Reichmanns and their advisors could see the enormous prize lying there in the undergrowth. The question was: would they be allowed to make off with it?

The so-called "partnership step-up" rules had been put on the law books in 1971 as an innocuous measure relating to the liquidation of business partnerships. Specifically, they were intended to eliminate the double taxation of capital gains when new partners had been brought into a partnership and the partnership was subsequently wound up.

Under the provision, when a partnership interest was sold, the partnership's assets were written up for tax purposes to the sale price. This was deemed reasonable because the selling partner would, theoretically, already have paid the capital gains tax on the difference between the assets' original value and their sale price to the new partner. If the partnership was then wound up, the value of the assets would be decided on what the partners had paid for them. Sharp legal brains had found how the law could be used to gain a double step-up, and in the process avoid lots of tax. The loophole was nicknamed "The Little Egypt Bump" after a famous Chicago striptease artist of the 1890s. In cases where there was a large difference between the book value of assets and their market value, the value of the bump became correspondingly large. Oil and gas assets were a prime example.

Gulf Canada's oil and gas assets were on the books at much less than their market value. Oil and gas assets, moreover, could be written off against income. So, if the assets' book value for tax purposes could be "bumped up" to their real value — or even more — then there would be correspondingly larger amounts of depreciation available to be set against future income. Assets depreciated once could be depreciated all over again, with potentially heavy tax savings. The Little Egypt Bump provided the complex route to this desirable goal.

There were three steps to the dance. First, Gulf had to roll its assets, tax-free, into a partnership. Second, a partner had to be found to buy a sufficient percentage of the partnership to make it look legitimate. And finally, the partnership had to be wound up and its assets distributed between the partners. Gulf would have virtually the same assets — less whatever had been sold to the partner — but these would now have a much higher value for tax purposes. This was clearly not the intention of the legislation, but it was the law.

The Department of Revenue regarded the move as little short of fiscal perversion. Although it was the law, the department's feelings were not irrelevant. They were required to give a ruling on the tax-free rollover, and they could make life very difficult for people they thought had just come to raid the federal treasury. In the meantime, Paul Reichmann needed a partner. The state oil company was not an inappropriate partner, for Bill Hopper had himself danced the Little Egypt Bump before.

Petrocan's chairman, advised by the company's Toronto-based lawyers, Tory, Tory, DesLauriers & Binnington — where a number of former Department of Finance whiz kids worked — had utilized the manoeuvre in the wake of its takeover of Belgian-controlled Petrofina back in 1981. Even Petrocan had been surprised that they had managed to get away with it. They had, in the words of one close to the deal, sent the proposal over to Revenue Canada and then "held their breath."

Although auditor-general Kenneth Dye had highlighted the loophole in his more general attack on the excessive costs of the Petrofina takeover, it had not been removed by the Liberals. When Paul Reichmann first went to see Bill Hopper to discuss Petrocan's role in the Gulf takeover in April, 1985, he brought up the bump because he knew that Hopper had experience of the fiscal side-step.

When O&Y's tax lawyers, from Davies, Ward & Beck, turned up in Ottawa to strut their stuff before Revenue Canada, the Revenue Canada audience did not applaud. In fact they booed. In their view, the Reichmanns had simply come to snatch the public purse.

Previously, Revenue Canada might have turned them down on the basis that their manoeuvre served no other purpose than avoiding tax. However, a landmark Supreme Court decision in 1984 had ruled that lack of business purpose alone could not invalidate a tax-oriented transaction.

A senior energy executive involved in the transaction, who spoke on condition that he not be identified, said: "The tax law is the root of the problem. The Conservatives campaigned on the notion that the law is the law and that they didn't like ministerial discretion; if you didn't like the law, change the law. But under the Liberal regime, they didn't want to change the law because there were some legitimate partnerships that came along . . . But they realized that it was bad tax policy if the partnership was only formed to provide the tax bump . . . The Liberals may have said in the Gulf thing, look, the intent of you doing this thing is to avoid taxes, so we're not going to change the law, but we're not going to give it to you. But in this case Reichmann said look we've got all this written up, and I'm sure that Wilson probably said: 'Look, that's an abortion. Can we allow this sort of thing?' "

The Revenue Department wasn't going to give up without a

fight. Officials brought in the lawyers from the Justice Department, which is usually a bad sign for those seeking a ruling. The guys from Davies, Ward & Beck decided to back off, just in case they were turned down.

The good news for the Reichmanns was that political momentum remained on their side. Pat Carney continued to think that Gulf Canada's Canadianization would be a particularly telling achievement if it could be pulled off through free enterprise. Somehow, she saw no contradiction in the fact that this "free enterprise" solution required enormous tax breaks and the participation of Petro-Canada to take unwanted assets off the Reichmanns' hands. "Free" enterprise had acquired a whole new meaning.

Sinc Stevens liked the idea of Canadianization, but didn't like the scale of Petrocan's planned involvement. Perrin Beatty, the young revenue minister, was as unenthusiastic about the Little Egypt Bump as his senior cabinet minister at Finance, Michael Wilson. They were both horrified at the thought of the Reichmann deal being used as a precedent and leading to a wholesale corporate raid on the Treasury. It was not clear where Prime Minister Brian Mulroney stood.

Pulling the Plug On O&Y

Chevron's negotiators were not party to these machinations. They knew that a tax ruling was involved, but they did not find out about Petrocan's role until late in the day. Their main concern was signing a deal and getting the money. But they knew that O&Y was having problems with the government because of Paul Reichmann's repeated requests for delays.

The deal was originally due to be signed in the middle of May, but failure to tie all the pieces together led the Reichmanns to ask for a month's extension. In the middle of June, they were forced to ask for another month. They had given Chevron a $10 million deposit on the transaction to indicate their good faith. Then, when they asked for the second delay, Paul Reichmann suggested that the deposit be increased to $25 million.

Meanwhile, Reichmann was negotiating with other parties besides the Revenue Department and Petro-Canada. His style had always been to play his cards close to his chest, but he also obvi-

ously realized that the best price could always be obtained in negotiations when there were several bidders. O&Y decided to look for
other possible partners for their tax dance. The company chosen
to say "Excuse me" to Petrocan — should O&Y and the state
oil company's fandango appear to be leading nowhere — was
Calgary-based Norcen Energy Resources. Norcen was particularly
interested in Gulf Canada's natural gas liquids subsidiary, Superior Propane, but Superior Propane's value was only estimated at
$120 million, and to be a "legitimate" partner, Norcen would have
to take a minimum 5 percent of the planned $5 billion Gulf
Resources partnership. Therefore it also negotiated a selection of
upstream assets to bring its total expenditure to $300 million. That
would give it 6 percent of the partnership and make it *really*
legitimate.

Lining up an alternative partner for the bump was a wise move,
indeed almost prescient, because suddenly the heat over Petrocan's proposed involvement in the deal began to increase, ironically just as it looked as if was to be put to bed. Western members
of the Tory caucus hit the roof when they discovered the size of
Petrocan's planned involvement. Pat Carney tried to explain that it
was really all part of "rounding out" Petrocan's interests in order
to make it a more attractive candidate for privatization, but the
Western members weren't buying it.

This wave of political outrage hit the prime minister's office just
as the Cabinet passed the Order in Council approving Petrocan's
expenditure of $1.8 billion to acquire all of Gulf Canada's down-
stream and most of its Beaufort interests. At a critical lunch in the
prime minister's office, Sinclair Stevens told the prime minister
that Petrocan's involvement in the deal would do major damage.
Astonishingly, only now, at the eleventh hour, did the political
implications of the deal hit the prime minister. Mulroney gave the
order to pull the plug on the deal. The plug was pulled in a particularly backhanded way. Instead of rescinding the Order in Council,
Mulroney gave instructions for Bill Hopper to call Paul Reichmann
and tell him that whatever their previous understandings, Petrocan would not now be participating. Hopper admitted that he
made the call to Reichmann, but refused to say who made the call
to him.

"Look," he said during an interview, "what happened was this.
We looked at the bundle and we said we'd rather not buy the
upstream, and some of the downstream is just too much for us, so

we said let's carve it down. This happened all within a four- o
five-day period that the thing went through Cabinet and Treasury
Board. It got the Order in Council. Then we started to look at the
whole thing and said you know, we *could* do this — and of course
I'm not sure that Paul *wanted* to sell the upstream — we said we
could do this but let's carve it back . . . We told Carney we don'
like the deal the way it was.''

Hopper admitted, however, that the primary motive for ''re
thinking'' the deal was political rather than economic. He was
plainly uneasy with the notion that the plug was pulled on the
Reichmanns. ''We had an understanding but it wasn't signed
sealed and delivered and we got ahead of ourselves and wen
back.''

A couple of days later, after flying to Washington to meet with
Chevron's chairman George Keller and explain what had hap
pened, Paul Reichmann apparently walked away from his $25
million deposit. The deal had foundered on the shoals of politics
and the prime minister's perfidy.

But it wasn't quite that simple.

In fact, it looked as if Reichmann had seen it coming all the time
and was quite prepared for it. Pulling the plug turned out to be less
a betrayal than a golden opportunity to negotiate a better deal.

Blowing the Whistle on Mulroney

Paul Reichmann had been growing increasingly worried about the
direction of oil prices in the course of the summer and was also still
unsure of the value that he was getting in the Gulf acquisition. He
had talked many times to Bill Hopper about the likely direction of
crude prices. Hopper, insofar as he was at the time trying to buy
upstream assets whose value was a function of the oil price out
look, had no compunction in painting a gloomy picture. But he
had his own concerns. Said Hopper, ''We were a little skittish and
he was getting a little skittish.''

But in any case, Reichmann had never been enthusiastic about
selling a large chunk of Gulf's upstream to Petrocan. He had also
been trying to gain further concessions from Sinclair Stevens to
sweeten the deal. Finally, if Petrocan were to be forced out of the

...ittle Egypt Bump partnership, as it now had been, then he had ...lready lined up its replacement in Norcen.

The story of Mulroney's vacillations was rapidly leaked to the ...ress, which reported that the duplicitous prime minister had ...ounted on Paul Reichmann being far too much of a gentleman to 'blow the whistle" on his conversations. It never occurred to the ...ress to ask themselves, if he were being so stiff-upper-lipped, ...ow they were getting the stories. The fact was that Reichmann's ...dvisors had no compunction about blowing whistles. They clev-...rly worked the press to paint Mulroney's behaviour in its worst ...ight. "Deep throats" close to the Reichmanns suggested to some ...ournalists that they might like to call former Liberal cabinet minis-...er Jean Chrétien to get his comments on the issue. Chrétien ...oured scorn on Brian Mulroney. He neglected to mention, how-...ver, that during the Gulf deal he had been working as a consul-...ant for Gordon Capital.

Whatever the impact of Reichmann's departure from the scene, ...nd of the adverse publicity, within just a couple of weeks the deal ...vas miraculously revived. An adjustment to the U.S. and Cana-...lian dollar elements of the Gulf Canada's purchase price enabled ...aul Reichmann to reduce the effective price he was paying Chev-...on by almost $200 million. Petrocan's participation was carved ...back in record time so that it now took none of the upstream and ...imited its downstream purchases to Gulf's refining and market-...ng assets in Ontario and the West. Hopper didn't want Ontario, ...and bought it apparently only because nobody else would. The ...purchase created unforeseen problems for the state oil company, ...since the structure of Gulf Canada's downstream management ...had been divided into East and West not at the Ontario-Manitoba ...border but at that between Ontario and Quebec. The split of the ...downstream was thus quite arbitrary.

Typically, all that the Gulf people got from the Reichmanns was ...a three-page letter, the chief contents of which were the price and ...the closing date of the sale. The valuation had been done on the ...back of an envelope, and was based primarily on what the ...Reichmanns wanted to pay. The rest, for them, was mere detail. ...Norcen meanwhile was installed as the partner in the Little Egypt ...Bump.

This still meant that buyers had to be found for Gulf's down-...stream assets east of Ontario, but it just so happened that the

Reichmanns had been negotiating with a number of prospective candidates for some time. The company that wound up buying them was Ultramar Canada, the Canadian subsidiary of the British company Ultramar PLC.

Ultramar had first approached the Reichmanns in May after seeing press reports that O&Y had a prospective deal with Chevron and that they wanted to sell the downstream. With a large, modern refinery near Quebec City, the British-controlled company was keen to take over Gulf's downstream assets in Quebec and the Atlantic provinces. They, like every other downstream operator, had no interest in Ontario.

Ultramar's executives found the negotiations difficult. Each time they came together with O&Y's Gil Newman, he seemed to want to start from square one. They attributed the slow negotiations partly to Newman's — and the Reichmanns' — lack of knowledge of the business, but they also realized that O&Y had many complex negotiations going on at once and that Ultramar was a relatively low priority.

The negotiations went on through June and July, and through the collapse of the original Petrocan deal. In August, Ultramar, partly out of frustration and partly because they were involved in other deals, made a take-it-or-leave it offer, with a deadline. When the Reichmanns did not meet it, the British company walked away. A month later talks were reopened, this time with Gulf Canada's people doing the negotiations for the Reichmann side. A deal was formally signed on December 2.

From the Tories' point of view, any kudos they might have received from Canadianizing Gulf had been damaged by public perceptions of Mulroney's vacillations. Two other aspects of the deal also caused them trouble. The oversupply of refinery capacity in Montreal had meant that Gulf Canada had planned to close down its refinery in the city. This closure, since the Tories were obviously so deeply involved in Gulf Canada's sale, became a political hot potato. Then, in October, the Little Egypt Bump hit the headlines.

Dancing Out of the Dark

The principal purpose of the Little Egypt Bump had been to regain tax write-offs from Gulf's oil and gas assets. But one of the most controversial aspects of the deal was that the Reichmanns had, at the last moment, caused Gulf's Edmonton refinery to be put into the partnership, although the facility was to be sold to Petro-Canada. The Crown corporation didn't even *know* that this was being done. The reason the refinery was put in was that its book value was so low relative to the price of $275 million that Petrocan was to pay for it. That meant that the tax advantages of "bumping it up" were correspondingly high.

The Edmonton refinery aspect of the tax bump was revealed in a story by *Globe and Mail* reporter Christopher Waddell on August 17. Waddell pointed out that the placing of the Edmonton refinery in the partnership had led to a $111 million loss in tax revenue. But the much greater loss on the oil and gas assets was not revealed. Yet.

On October 1, Liberal opposition leader John Turner made front-page headlines with allegations that Gulf Canada's manoeuvres had saved $1 billion in taxes. "That partnership device," he declared in the Commons, "allowed the assets to be revalued considerably and on the basis of that revaluation provide a shelter for taxes." He went on to say that it was "a very strange use of the partnership rules under the Income Tax Act." He called for submission of the whole affair to a parliamentary committee.

Then, following rumours throughout the summer, there was more controversy when it was announced that Marshall "Mickey" Cohen was joining Olympia & York, having been invited to do so by the Reichmanns the previous February. The controversy arose because Cohen had been deputy minister of finance during the whole period that the negotiations were going on over the Little Egypt Bump.

Cohen, a lawyer who had represented the Reichmanns before he moved to Ottawa in 1970, had been a powerful force in the nation's capital throughout the 1970s. In 1971, he had been appointed assistant deputy minister of tax policy at the Department of Finance. Following the first OPEC crisis, he had been at the centre of the Liberals' energy policy formulation. He had played an important backroom role in the difficult federal-provincial negotiations over oil pricing during 1974, and had rapidly moved to the heart of Liberal Pierre Trudeau's technocratic policy-making machine. He had held three deputy ministerships, the highest bureaucratic level in any department, the most controversial of which had been his stint as deputy minister of energy during the formulation of the NEP. Somehow, however, Cohen had managed to sidestep any responsibility for that disastrous policy and had moved on to be deputy minister of finance. In the words of one senior oil executive, "Mickey Cohen makes Houdini look like a piker."

Now, some more subtle sidestepping was required. Cohen explained to the press that he had had nothing whatsoever to do with the Little Egypt Bump. He said that as soon as Paul Reichmann had approached him, he had told both Brian Mulroney and his minister, Michael Wilson, of the offer.

Cohen told the *Globe and Mail* that it was Sinc Stevens who first informed him that the Reichmanns were going to make a bid for Gulf Canada. He said that the potential deal raised issues about the exchange rate, taxes, and the role of Petro-Canada.

"He started to talk to me about it," Cohen was reported as saying, "and I turned him off, went to Wilson and said, 'Look, I can't touch this deal,' and from that day forward I was out of it. . . . It was all kind of comical, because I kept saying to everybody in the place, 'Look, I'm busy' — it was right around the budget — 'I just haven't got the time, you guys look after this, leave me out of this.' "

Sinc Stevens said that he had no memory of talking to Cohen.

But given that Cohen did successfully stay away from the issue of Petro-Canada and the Little Egypt Bump, that still leaves another even more intriguing issue: Paul Reichmann's side of the deal. *He* obviously knew that he was going for one of the biggest tax breaks in Canadian history when he approached the deputy minister of finance to offer him a job.

For O&Y, a highly secretive company, these allegations about the Little Egypt Bump brought an unfamiliar and unwanted publicity. Suggestions of impropriety or special treatment caused Paul Reichmann to refute the charge publicly. "The tax rulings," declared a release from Gulf Canada, "which have not involved any special Government concessions, confirm the application of existing laws to the facts of the proposed transaction." Reichmann pointed out in another of his exclusive interviews with the *Globe and Mail* that Turner's $1 billion figure was way off. The deal would save only $500 million in taxes over five years, "with another $50 to $90 million saving after that time."

Reichmann said that the Little Egypt Bump ruling—which he of course did not refer to by that name—"is simply an interpretation of law. It is nothing given.'' Asked about concessions he had been seeking from the government, Paul Reichmann decided that that point, unlike rumours of the $1 billion tax giveaway, did not need clarification.

''I think I'll stay away from the details of those discussions because they'll only get me in hot water . . . these questions are irrelevant because they were rejected in the end.''

It was not clear what concessions Reichmann was referring to, or *could* have been referring to. He had already received about every concession imaginable.

He even got his $25 million deposit back.

13

GULF CANADA IV: THREE RING CIRCUS

. . . it had been a game of tax smoke and market mirrors, a masterful exercise in the art of corporate arm-twisting, political manipulation, and the exploitation of bad tax policy.

The Gulf Canada purchase negotiations were like a three ring circus, with Paul Reichmann as ringmaster. In one ring, tax lawyers and government officials jockeyed for position over Petrocan's participation and the Little Egypt Bump. They were like a cage full of lions and tigers, reluctantly snarling their way through the paces Reichmann had planned for them. The most sedate and straightforward activity was going on in the second ring, where Chevron waited, like an elephant, to receive its financial peanut. In the third ring was Gulf Canada. Gulf perched like an expectant, attentive, and slightly nervous performing seal, waiting for Paul Reichmann to teach it new tricks.

Traditionally in a takeover, the acquisitor makes an offer for the target company, and the target's management and board have to decide whether to accept or reject it. If they reject it, they usually have to come up with an alternative, or a defensive strategy. The Gulf Canada situation was quite different. The company knew that its fate was sealed. Paul Reichmann did not fail to squeeze the maximum advantage from that situation. He had two tricks in particular that he wanted his new acquisition to perform: the purchase from him of Abitibi-Price; and the buyout of its own minority.

Their many years as a privately owned family company had given the Reichmanns a natural secretiveness about their business dealings. For those who could see only part of the picture, the negotiations proved at times frustrating. Within Gulf Canada, the realization that the company was being sold and split up, and that many employees would finish up with Petro-Canada, or with no jobs at all, inevitably created severe morale problems. Nevertheless, anything was at first considered better than being rolled in with Chevron Canada. Moreover, the Reichmanns assured that at least the upstream side of the company would stay intact.

Keith McWalter, the hard-nosed executive who had taken over from John Stoik as president of Gulf in April, found himself immersed in a baptism of fire. For most of 1985, he worked seven-day weeks at the head of a key management group that he described, with some irony, as the "Happy Gang." McWalter, who, like his predecessor, was a member of the Moose Jaw Mafia (he had been born in the city) was also, like his predecessor, somewhat stone-faced. However, he privately gave vent to his frustrations. On one occasion he said to another executive: "They're like flies. They land, shit, and take off again."

The Reichmanns' demands put heavy pressure on Gulf's board of directors, in particular its so-called "independent" directors, who are in theory the overseers of good management and the guardians of shareholders' interests. Insofar as the Little Egypt Bump had increased the value of Gulf by reducing its future tax burden and increasing its present value, the fiscal dance met little opposition from Gulf's board. There were also more general advantages in a buyout by a Canadian-owned company. The PIP grants introduced under the NEP were still in place until at least the end of 1986. Due to Gulf's large frontier exploration program, a change to Canadian ownership would mean another $100 million in grants — good news for Gulf Canada and the Reichmanns, although once again arguably good news for the Department of Finance and the people of Canada.

Abitibi: Let's Make a Deal

The mechanics of the Reichmanns' proposals left some thorny problems for the Gulf board. In particular, they were concerned about the Reichmanns' plan to sell them Abitibi. The move had a single rationale for the Reichmanns: to help pay for their Gulf purchase. In the best traditions of modern-day, sophisticated finance, Gulf would be paying for its own acquisition. Of course, the deal could not be portrayed in such crude terms, and was declared to be a "diversification" for Gulf Canada in which it effectively swapped its downstream interests for a forest products company.

The Reichmanns had acquired Abitibi for $560 million. Now they wanted to sell out to Gulf for $1.2 billion. The proposal obviously placed a heavy burden on Gulf's negotiators. Keith McWalter realized that he could hardly negotiate the purchase with the men who would be his future bosses, so he asked Alf Powis, chairman of the independent committee of Gulf Canada directors, to deal with the Reichmanns.

The head of mining giant Noranda had never met Paul Reichmann until Reichmann turned up in Keith McWalter's Toronto office in the spring of 1985 to outline his takeover strategy for Gulf. Like the other directors at that meeting, Powis was concerned about Reichmann's suggestion that Gulf purchase Abitibi, but he had little objection to selling off Gulf's downstream assets, provided a good price could be obtained. As for the Little Egypt Bump, Alf Powis was so impressed with the plan that he went straight back to Noranda's lawyers and told them to look at the possibility of Noranda using the manoeuvre itself. But he couldn't get a deal moving in time. At the end of 1985, Michael Wilson announced two measures to amend the Income Tax Act, "designed to make the tax system fairer and safeguard federal revenue." One was the removal of the use of partnerships in corporate takeovers to increase tax deductions. Little Egypt had bumped her last bump.

Powis needed every form of imaginative financing he could get because he had his own problems back at Noranda, which was saddled with an enormous debt load as a result of a number of expensive diversifications. He was grateful for the fact that the Reichmanns worked on Sundays. That was the only way he was able to fit the negotiations over Abitibi among his other corporate burdens.

The key issue was putting a price on Abitibi. Some knowledgeable observers, such as Montreal investment counsellor Stephen Jarislowsky, thought that the issue of whether Gulf should be buying Abitibi at all should be put to the minority shareholders, but in the end it came down to one-on-one negotiations between

Paul Reichmann and Alf Powis. Powis found Reichmann a tough negotiator.

As always in such circumstances, the two sides brought in their respective investment advisors: Morgan Stanley for the Reichmanns and Burns Fry for Gulf. These advisors then set about producing an evaluation based on a set of suitably doctored assumptions. Morgan Stanley's, for the seller, were of course massaged to be high; Burns Fry's, for the buyer, were manipulated to be low.

Reichmann produced an opinion that said that Abitibi was worth at least $26 a share. Powis, for his part, got a fairness opinion that put an upper value on the newsprint giant of $21.50. But he didn't want to announce that opinion because then Reichmann would be justified in asking $21.50, which Powis thought was too high. So he asked the Morgan Stanley and Burns Fry analysts to get together to compare their methodology. When he saw the projected earnings assumptions on which Morgan Stanley's valuation was based, he thought they were far too optimistic. Not surprisingly, Reichmann thought those of Burns Fry understated.

For Powis, another worrying aspect of the deal was that Abitibi's share price had risen sharply in the early months of 1985 while Gordon Capital had been aggressively buying the stock. Gordon was deeply involved in the Gulf takeover. It was obviously in the Reichmanns' interest for the Abitibi share price to be close to the purchase price. Otherwise they would be accused of corporate rape. Gordon had started buying in February and the stock had moved in the first quarter from $11 to $19.

In the end, Powis was squeezed by Reichmann into paying $21 a share for 90 percent of Abitibi, just below the upper limit of Burns Fry's valuation. Compared with $11, that looked very expensive. Compared with $19 it didn't look too bad. Powis, with admirable candour, said, ''I wasn't particularly proud of my negotiating prowess.'' However, he felt that he could justify the price in terms of the other financial ''goodies'' that Reichmann was bringing to the takeover party.

''The price that we ended up paying for Abitibi had to be viewed in the context of the overall transaction,'' said Powis, ''because my personal view was that we were paying too much for it. But on the other hand, if Paul could realize a similar amount of money on the downstream, then it wasn't so bad. In my view, a reasonable price to pay for Abitibi would have been $17 or $18 a share. Paul wanted

$26. We finally settled on $21 and I was able to say to the Gulf directors that we could justify that in terms of the context of the overall transaction, including the tax deal and the sale of the downstream."

Asked about the movement of the Abitibi share price as a result of Gordon's buying, Powis said: "It bothered me too. I don't know anything about it. I can't comment on that. I guess all you can say is that the whole thing is vindicated by the fact that they are doing a very large share issue at $26. [In March, 1986, Abitibi issued a prospectus to raise $137.5 million through the issue of common shares and warrants at a price per common share and per half common share warrant of $27.50. Once again, the move was preceded by pronounced upward movement in the share price.]"

Although Powis maintained that the Reichmanns' package was fair from the Gulf shareholders' point of view, which was his main concern, his comments raise broader issues. Looked at another way, Gulf could afford to overpay for Abitibi only because Petrocan was perceived to be coughing up a handsome price for Gulf's downstream, and because the Canadian taxpayer was effectively subsidizing the deal through the Little Egypt Bump.

Paul Reichmann was running away with it, playing all his advantages to the full. On August 2, O&Y signed the new deal with Chevron under which it would pay the American company $2.8 billion for its Gulf Canada shares. Gulf's purchase of 90 percent of Abitibi was also set in motion. On August 31, the Little Egypt Bump partnership between Norcen and Gulf was signed. On September 30, the sale to Petrocan of Gulf's Ontario and Western refining and marketing assets was made official and, effective January 1, 1986, the deal with Ultramar was concluded.

Nevertheless, there was still one piece of outstanding business, and that was the issue of the Gulf minority.

Looking Out for the Minority

One of the main concerns of securities regulators is fairness to shareholders, in particular minority shareholders. In a case like that of Gulf, where the Reichmanns were buying 60 percent of Gulf Canada from its owner Chevron, there are guidelines set out for the bidder's obligation to the minority. When the Reichmanns had made their offer to Chevron in the spring of 1985, they had one to the Ontario Securities Commission in order to gain an exemption from making a follow-up offer to Gulf minority shareholders. Under existing laws, if the price they paid to Chevron worked out at 15 percent more than the price of Gulf shares in the market, then the Reichmanns would automatically have had to offer the same price to the shareholders who held the other 40 percent of Gulf Canada shares. This, needless to say, would have been enormously expensive. The OSC granted the exemption on the grounds that the offer was, at that time, not more than 15 percent above the price of the market.

Following the cratering of the deal in July, the Reichmanns went back to the OSC for another exemption. This time their grounds were somewhat unusual, although at first sight their plan appeared fair to the minority. O&Y told the OSC that it would use its reasonable efforts'' to get Gulf to offer its minority shareholders a cash deal similar to that given to Chevron. This arrangement placed the burden of financing the other half of the Reichmanns' takeover on the takeover target itself. The Reichmanns seemed to be treating Gulf as if it were already part of their private family fiefdom. There were no squawks from investment authorities.

Under a complex plan of arrangement revealed toward the end of 1985, Gulf's minority shareholders could opt to either take a cash and debenture deal, effectively selling out of Gulf, or switch their old Gulf shares for shares in a new Reichmann-controlled Gulf. The circular nature of the deal made it difficult to assess. The more shareholders who opted for new shares, the stronger would Gulf's balance sheet be; the more who opted for the cash option — 10.40 in cash and $10.40 of Gulf debentures — the greater Gulf's debt burden. The Reichmanns were obviously hoping that shareholders would be persuaded to swap their old Gulf shares for shares in the new, reformulated Gulf.

However, just as the plan was being formulated, the Organization of Petroleum Countries, OPEC, once again reared its ugly head. Only this time it was crying for help. Petroleum futures prices began weakening in early December as the cracks in OPEC's façade turned into gaping holes. In the second week of December, OPEC announced that it would accept lower prices in order to maintain its market share. The writing seemed to be on the wall.

As the world oil price, and prospects for world oil prices, weak-

ened, it became apparent that the cash and debenture offer w
the more attractive option. As a result, the Reichmanns in Decen
ber persuaded the Gulf board to sweeten the pot by adding a $
preferred share for those who agreed to take a share in the ne
Gulf for a share in the old Gulf. This, of course, included the 6
percent of Gulf shares owned by O&Y, so the greatest beneficiari
of the preferred shares, which would further weaken Gulf's finan
cial position, were the Reichmanns.

Despite the sweetening of the pot, the disintegration of world c
prices throughout January continued to make the cash offer loc
more and more attractive. In the twenty-five-day period betwee
the issuing of the document outlining the plan of arrangement an
the meeting to vote on it, there was a sharp drop in the world -
and Canadian — price of oil. The projected financial informatio
provided in the plan of arrangement document, which had bee
prepared as of November 7, 1985, assumed a Canadian wellhea
oil price of $33.75 in 1986 and $35.00 in 1987. However, by the tim
of the meeting, Canadian prices had fallen below $30 in respons
to a fall in world prices to below U.S.$20. They would go muc
lower.

The meeting at which the plan of arrangement to swap th
minority shares for new Gulf shares or cash was to be formall
ratified by Gulf shareholders was held on January 31, 1986, in th
concert hall of Toronto's Royal York Hotel. The Reichmanns wer
conspicuously absent. The meeting was an exercise in shareholde
somnolence. Not a single voice was raised to question any aspec
of the deal. But in any case the vote was virtually a formality, sinc
all that was required for the plan to be approved was for th
Reichmanns and 6 percent of the remaining shareholders to vot
for it. Once that arrangement was ratified, shareholders had unt
5 P.M. on Monday, February 3, to opt for the cash/debenture offer

Friendly Persuasion

Gulf Canada's own directors were firmly convinced that the over
whelming majority of shareholders would opt for the cash anc
debentures. They even had a betting pool among themselves tc
guess how many shares would be left outstanding after the share
holders' options had been exercised. Most predicted that 80 per
cent or 90 percent would go for the cash. In any event, only 6

rcent did. Says Powis, "We were amazed at how many people
yed in. Why didn't people tender? I don't know. Inertia? Capi-
gains? There were also a bunch of people out there saying,
ell, we'll stay with the Reichmanns. They know how to make
oney . . .' "

Given the deteriorating oil price background, this amounted to a
mendous act of faith in the Reichmanns. There was no doubt
at their mystique remained. Also, they were still drawing a posi-
ely gushing press, although some of the examples were now
ginning to look a little embarrassing. In July, 1985, the editor of a
ominent Canadian business publication had written of the Gulf
al: "People who can pounce on bargains like this must be real
ers, one-dimensional workaholics with telephones extending
om their ears. Somehow they have to be objectionable, right?
ot so. The Reichmanns are the antithesis of Sammy Glick: quiet,
urtly men who keep their own counsel and whose word is their
nd. In an era when you can't trust your banker, they're the
ception. Budding entrepreneurs should use them as role mod-
s, because sometimes, the biggest are the best."

In the middle of January, even as the price of oil was beginning
fall seriously out of bed, analysts were still doing their own
shing. One was quoted in the *Globe and Mail* as saying: "Invest-
s will be looking at the outlook for Gulf, comparing it with other
vestments and asking themselves, 'Does Gulf have something
e others don't?. . . Gulf's biggest edge is that it is owned by
lympia & York. . . . Hopefully, some of that profit-making abil-
will show up at Gulf.' "

But the Reichmanns were also receiving a more direct helping
nd. An act of faith was being very strongly recommended by
me of the investment dealers. In the weeks before the deal,
uch of the investment community reportedly put in a powerful
fort to persuade shareholders to go for the share swap. One
en observer of the Bay Street scene told the author: "They
id every dealer on the street to do fairness opinions. Burns Fry,
errill Lynch and McLeod Young Weir were paid millions and I
spect that they were all on the phone that last week. The
eichmanns certainly wanted everybody to stay in. That's the way
e street works and really the investors who stayed in should not
mplain of lack of disclosure."

When the smoke cleared, 38 percent of Gulf's minority share-
olders had agreed to go with the Reichmanns and accept com-

mon and preferred shares. Most of those who stayed in we
smaller shareholders who believed their brokers when they sai
"Stay with the Reichmanns. They know how to make money . .

The completion of the deal left the Reichmanns with 80 perce
of the new, more heavily endebted Gulf. In the weeks followi
the plan of arrangement, the world price of oil dived further, h
ting a low of less than U.S.$13 and forcing Gulf, and indeed all
companies, to cut back drastically on planned expenditures.

For the Reichmanns, meanwhile, the financing of their ow
share of the Gulf takeover had not been completed. They ha
planned a $1 billion preference share issue — typically, the bigge
in Canadian history — in order to finance most of the acquisitic
cost not covered by the sale of Abitibi to Gulf. Market conditior
had forced that issue to be shelved.

In cash flow terms, their return from Gulf consisted of commc
and preferred share dividends amounting to little more than $1
million. Compared with the purchase price of $2.8 billion f
Chevron's Gulf shares, that did not look like a particularly han
some return. Moreover, there inevitably had to be some pressu
on Gulf's ability to continue paying its common share dividend
The tax advantages of the Little Egypt Bump improved Gulf
financial position for the immediate future, but that improveme
would be offset by the deterioration in the market. Of course, th
Reichmanns' rationale for diversification into natural resource
had always been that of capital gains rather than income. Th
world price outlook seemed to place those capital gains in sever
doubt.

Shortly after the minority deal had been completed, Alf Powi
who remained on the Gulf Canada board, said: "Sure they've ha
to borrow from the banks for this deal, but I don't think they are i
an uncomfortable position. The banks aren't uncomfortable. .
But it is obviously a cash drain. Even when and if they did th
preferred it would still be a cash drain. Whether debt or preferree
it's still a negative carry. Over time, they are counting that Gu
will be worth a lot more than they paid for it. . . . Gulf will surviv
at $12 oil but they won't be nearly as profitable. But if you hav
faith that owning oil and gas in the ground is a good thing, the
it's a good deal."

Alf Powis didn't sound convinced.

To most people, the Gulf takeover looked like a disaster. "Ca
you imagine what price we'd get for Gulf now?" asked Chevro
Canada's Gerry Henderson.

Still, supposedly knowledgeable analysts refused to believe that the Reichmanns' crystal ball had cracked. ''Just remember the New York deal,'' they said. Some of them even imagined that the Gulf Canada deal was *like* the New York deal, in that the Reichmanns had snapped up oil and gas assets at the bottom of the market. But the fact was that they had missed the bottom by a long way. During the year or so it took to pull the convoluted parts of the takeover together, the world oil price halved. After the deal, it dropped another third.

The reason the Reichmanns *weren't* in more trouble was the structuring of the deal. At one level, the Gulf takeover could be viewed as a strategic masterpiece, pulled off in the most difficult circumstances. But at another, it had been a game of tax smoke and market mirrors, a masterful exercise in the art of corporate arm-twisting, political manipulation, and the exploitation of bad tax policy. The Canadian public paid as much toward the Reichmanns' takeover of Gulf Canada as the Reichmanns.

Their complex manoeuvrings also seemed somehow out of character, or at least out of the character they had so successfully nurtured. But the Gulf deal hadn't been out of character at all. Those who had dealt with the Reichmanns always knew that they were the toughest negotiators around. In Manhattan, the real estate community told a story that, if you were negotiating with the Reichmanns and there were ten points of contention, then the brothers would stand tough on five and give on five. At the end of the day you'd feel pretty happy with your skills. But the next day the Reichmanns would be back to go over the five points that you'd won, and they'd perhaps let you have two and a half, but they'd stand firm on the other two and a half. And you'd begin to wonder. And then the next day, the Reichmanns would be back again. . . .

It was just that they had never done a deal which had — if only partially — been subject to such public scrutiny. They had always squeezed every last drop out of negotiations and played their cards close to their chest, keeping those they dealt with in the dark as much as possible. They showed no particular sensitivity toward shareholders. Fellow shareholders were a relatively new phenomenon for them. Abitibi's minority had been largely dormant since the Reichmanns had acquired control of the company. And the inevitable redundancies in personnel when Gulf Canada's downstream operations were sold — including the closing of the Montreal refinery — appeared to be of little concern to them.

The Reichmanns weren't quite as saintly as they'd been painted in the press. Paul Reichmann now seemed almost obsessed with corporate growth, despite staunch denials that such was any part of his motivation. Also, perhaps he *was* like a great corporate automaton. He was relentless and he was brilliant, but he had blind spots. Soon, those blind spots would become glaringly apparent.

It seemed reasonable that, given what had happened to oil prices, a period of retrenchment might now be appropriate for O&Y. After all, they had executed the biggest takeover in Canadian history in the most complex and trying of circumstances. However, one of the Reichmanns' rationales for the Canadianization of Gulf was that it would enable the company to be acquisitive, and Paul Reichmann wasn't going to let a little thing like the collapse of world oil prices stop him. In fact, he couldn't afford to stop. The momentum had to be kept up.

Otherwise, like the shark, he might sink.

14
HIRAM WALKER: THE REICHMANNS ARE COMING

Cliff Hatch didn't mind having Paul and Albert Reichmann as landlords, but he certainly didn't want them sitting on his board.

Bud Downing, chairman and chief executive of conglomerate Hiram Walker Resources, was on holiday in California the morning of Wednesday, March 19, 1986, when he was awakened just after 5 A.M. by a call from his secretary in Toronto. She told him that Albert Reichmann had just called Downing's office and asked him to return his call immediately. Downing was sleepy and puzzled. A thought crossed his mind. No, it couldn't be. He'd asked Albert Reichmann the question not many months ago, and Albert Reichmann had told him it wasn't so. *That* couldn't be it. He dialled Reichmann's number.

Albert Reichmann revealed that Gulf Canada would, that morning, be making an offer for common and preference shares of Hiram Walker. He indicated that he wished the offer to be friendly, and that he liked the management of Hiram Walker, in particular that of Home Oil. Downing said that he couldn't be sure about his reaction until he saw the details, but he pointed out that no management liked to be taken over. Nevertheless, if there had to be a takeover, he said, he would as soon that it be by Olympia & York as anybody else. Downing recited the corporate catechism for Albert Reichmann. He told him that his responsibility was to maximize the value of any offer to shareholders, and that entrenchment of himself and his management should not be a consideration.

Albert thanked him and hung up.

So it was that after all. Hiram Walker's management had partly expected and partly feared for several years that the Reichmanns would one day come after them. But not now. Or at least Bud Downing hadn't expected it now. The truth was that Bud Downing had been told some weeks earlier that the Reichmanns were coming, and he had simply refused to believe it. Now the pressure was on in the biggest way.

Bud Downing had taken over the reins of liquor, petroleum, and pipeline conglomerate Hiram Walker Resources, HWR, two years previously. A chemical engineer by training, he had spent his whole career with Hiram Walker's liquor business. He was the most solid of solid citizens, a pillar of both the corporate and local community. Born in Mount Elgin, Ontario, he had interrupted his studies at the University of Toronto to serve with the Canadian Navy in World War II. Then he had returned to work his way through the management of HW-GW's worldwide liquor operations. His most exotic assignment had been a two-year stint turning round the company's flagging distilling operation in Argentina, from which he had returned fluent in Spanish.

Downing was well liked, but many thought him of insufficient breadth to be the chief executive of such a divers company. Like Jimmy Lee back at Gulf, Downing was not well versed in the Byzantine intricacies of the stock market, and that — especially when the Reichmanns came to call — was inevitably where any battles would be fought.

But Bud Downing's strength in the coming battle would be the corporate credo he had already chanted for Albert Reichmann: his concern was with getting the best price for his shareholders. It is uncertain if the Reichmanns appreciated either the nature or the depth of that conviction. They would certainly be surprised at the strategy to which the conviction would lead. Downing's statement that entrenching management was no part of his concern may also have been difficult for the Reichmanns to appreciate. Downing's attitude, if genuine, marked a powerful contrast to that of Clifford

Hatch, Sr., from whom Downing had taken over, and whose protégé Downing was. Cliff Hatch saw Hiram Walker as more than just the company he had significantly helped to create, he saw it almost as his possession. In recent years, the whole company had been structured with entrenchment in mind. The irony now was that Downing believed part of that defensive structure was instrumental in the attack. Clifford Hatch, Sr., the man who had masterminded the defences, would not be happy.

A Family Affair

H. Clifford Hatch, Sr., could be forgiven for thinking that Hiram Walker was *his* company. After all, his father, Harry Hatch, had put it together in 1926 by merging Gooderham & Worts Ltd., Canada's oldest distilling firm — which he had bought in 1913 — with Hiram Walker & Sons Ltd. Hiram Walker & Sons had always been a profoundly paternalistic company. It inherited that ethos from its founder.

Hiram Walker was a classic nineteenth-century entrepreneur and philanthropist. Born in Massachusetts, he had headed west and settled in the city of Detroit, which had been founded in 1701 by the Frenchman Cadillac. Starting with a general store, Walker moved into the grain and whisky business and developed a plan to build a combined mill and distillery. In 1856, he bought his first land on the Canadian side of the Detroit River in what would become Walkerville. It was there that he developed "Canadian Club," a brand that became world-famous. Walker was the model employer. He laid out Walkerville's streets, built housing for the workers, and created a waterworks, as well as fire and police departments, to serve his new town. He developed model farms; he laid a railway; he provided three ferries to serve the new industries.

He also built the distillery's magnificent headquarters, modelled after a sixteenth-century Italian Renaissance villa. That magnificent building, which remains the liquor empire's head office, was a constant reminder of the company's historic place within the local community.

Walkerville had been absorbed into the growing town of Windsor, but in many ways it had been a reverse takeover. As the plants of the big auto-makers, GM, Ford, and Chrysler, had spread across from Detroit and become Windsor's biggest employers, Windsor had become a lunch-bucket, blue collar town, but the cream of the factory jobs were at Hiram Walker's riverside plant. There, work was infinitely more pleasant than on the noisy production lines of the auto makers (although the United Auto Workers, the UAW, was the plant's main union). One of the few potential industrial hazards seemed to be the danger of getting tipsy just from breathing in the atmosphere of the bottling line.

The employees felt like a family. There was no great gap between the production line and office workers. And, in more recent years, if you worked at the plant and your son or daughter was at the University of Windsor, then they'd have no trouble getting a summer job at the plant. And everybody got a turkey at Christmas.

Down in Windsor, Cliff Hatch, Sr., had been king. But he felt he had earned his monarchy.

Hatch had entered the business via the leading Canadian wine firm, T.G. Bright & Co. Ltd., when he was seventeen. He joined his father's company the year he came of age, 1937. During the war years, he hunted U-boats in the North Atlantic as commander of the HMCS *Drummondville* and HMCS *Ville de Quebec*. Then he rejoined Walker, rising through the ranks until, in 1964, he was named president. The move was not unexpected. Hatch was already a full-fledged member of the Canadian Establishment. His directorships included the Toronto-Dominion Bank and the Canada Permanent Trust Company. In December, 1978, Hatch added Walker's chairmanship. Although he and his family by that time owned only a very small percentage of the company's shares, the founding role of his father and his own long relationship with the business gave him a perhaps understandably proprietary attitude.

Clifford Hatch, Sr., was a man of moderation. Although he had a good sense of humour, some colleagues poked a little fun at his modest taste. "Cliff's idea of a good time," they'd say, not without affection, "is to take his parish priest across to the Detroit Athletic Club for lunch." And Clifford Hatch didn't like to waste money. He always looked for somebody to share cabs to the airport.

His management style, too, seemed to come from another era. Cliff Hatch didn't hold with the "professional" management notions of having planning committees and acquisition committees and stacks of policy manuals. Often he'd bemoan to colleagues the fact that the business world was sinking beneath mounds of paper. He liked to keep the organization lean and the margins high.

Over the years he had watched and helped his company extend its global interests, purchasing distilleries and businesses in Canada, Scotland, the United States, Argentina, France, and Mexico. It had become one of the largest liquor operations in the world.

Back in 1979, Clifford Hatch began to get an uneasy feeling that somebody out there was casting acquisitive glances at *his* company. It was inevitable that his empire, solidly established on booze and throwing off hefty cash flow, would be attractive to corporate predators. Analysts were saying the stock was undervalued. For any company, that was like having an open cut in shark-infested waters.

Among the predatory fish who had first sensed Walker's vulnerability back in 1979 was, appropriately, "the Piranha," Gordon Securities' Jimmy Connacher. In the fall of 1979, Connacher was doing the rounds of big ticket investors trying to stir up interest in Hiram Walker as an acquisition candidate.

Connacher's pitch was that Walker had undergone a fundamental shift noticed only so far by a few discerning analysts. He told potential investors that Walker had reached a stage of maturity where it was producing more cash than it needed. It was a cash cow, begging to be milked. One of the financiers to whom he brought the story was Bay Street guru Andy Sarlos. Sarlos, who specialized in such situations and who had made a great deal of money from dabbling in Abitibi's troubled waters, brought in a couple of his major clients to help finance the purchase of 1.8 million Hiram Walker shares. When Hatch found out, he became understandably concerned. He became even more concerned when he discovered that a far bigger predator, cash-rich Brascan, newly acquired by the Edper Bronfmans, might be sizing up Walker.

Hatch immediately set about launching a defensive strategy. His first move was to find another company with sympathetic management with whom he could merge and thus become too big to swallow. He found his partner and kindred spirit in Bill Wilder, the recently appointed head of Consumers' Gas.

Consumers' Gas had been established in 1848 to distribute manufactured gas in the City of Toronto. The system had switched to natural gas with the construction of the TransCanada PipeLines from Alberta in the mid-1950s. Consumers' now carried gas to customers throughout central and eastern Ontario, western Quebec, and northern New York State. The area it served embraced a fifth of the population of Canada and it employed 3,000 people. In the early 1970s, it had greatly expanded its corporate empire by gaining control of Home Oil.

Home Oil had its origins in the earliest days of the Alberta oil business just after the turn of the century. The man who brought the company to national prominence, and then near-disaster, after World War II was the flamboyant and legendary Bobby Brown. Brown was a classic risk taker whose vision knew few bounds and who spent the last years of his life fighting the demon of alcoholism. Under his leadership, Home had made some of Canada's most important discoveries, including that of Swan Hills, Alberta.

Brown lived like a king, jetting back and forth in his Grumman Gulfstream II between Calgary and his second home at Toronto's Royal York Hotel. (The sleek jet even had dolphin-shaped gold-plated bathtaps.) But he also frequently had to be physically carried out of Calgary's Petroleum Club, and once nodded off in an alcohol-induced stupor at dinner with the president of Mexico.

Brown's relentless pursuit of bigger and bigger acquisitions, and more and more expensive exploration ventures, almost inevitably led to his undoing. In the late 1950s, he spent more than $30 million in an abortive attempt to gain control of TransCanada PipeLines, an act of corporate hubris that had almost been his downfall. Following the 1968 discovery of Prudhoe Bay, he had effectively "bet the company" on expensive land purchases and in buying shares in Atlantic Richfield, which was involved in the find. But Brown never found his Alaskan bonanza. The Prudhoe bubble had burst and Home's stock plummeted.

He was forced to sell out and only narrowly avoided falling under government control. Canadian economic nationalism was stirring, and the Liberal government of Pierre Trudeau made it clear to Brown that they would not countenance a sale to a foreign company. The Cabinet in fact gave approval to a government purchase, but at last Brown found a Canadian-owned saviour in Consumers' Gas and its then head, the "rock-ribbed Boston Yankee," Oakah Jones. Oakah Jones wasn't exactly a white knight, but Brown considered him a whole lot better than the federal government.

Wilder was offered the Consumers' job when it fell open following a hushed-up scandal in its executive suite — which just happened to be in the Reichmanns' First Canadian Place. In 1978, Ted Creber, the chief executive, was unceremoniously removed when he was discovered to have been receiving hefty fees from a small company that was in turn receiving hefty fees from Consumers'. The job was offered to Wilder and Wilder, who, with only the prospect of managerial civil war if he stayed at Gulf, accepted. Not long after he had taken the reins of control, he had received a visit from Allen Lambert, a Hiram Walker board member who had recently retired as head of the Toronto-Dominion Bank. Lambert wanted to sound Wilder out on his attitude toward a merger with Hiram Walker. Wilder agreed, and Hatch had the amalgamation that he hoped would make his company too big to swallow.

As eager shareholders gathered at Walker's traditional December annual meeting in 1979 to taste the company's products, the finishing touches were being put on the merger that would create a company with the fifth-largest profits of any Canadian corporation.

Apart from making hostile acquisition more difficult, the fit between booze and petroleum was not intuitively obvious. Nevertheless, there was a financial synergism between the cash needs and tax coverage of an oil company and the steady stream of earnings thrown off by a liquor producer. From a business point of view, the marriage was made not in the products but in the profit and loss statements and the balance sheets.

In April, 1980, the Consumers' Gas Company Ltd. and its wholly owned subsidiary, Home Oil Company Limited, officially amalgamated with Hiram Walker/Gooderham & Worts Limited to become Hiram Walker/Consumers Home Ltd. The amalgamation was by a share swap in which each Hiram Walker share was exchanged for 1.375 shares of Consumers'. In June, 1981, following a further internal reorganization, the company became Hiram Walker Resources Ltd.

The merger created a company with worldwide assets of $3.6 billion and revenues of $2.6 billion. It had almost 12,000 employees and earned net income in 1980 of $239.5 million. But there were marital problems, and, as in many marriages, the difficulties arose because one of the partners went on a spending spree that left the joint account with a headache. Home went shopping in the United States and was taken for a ride by a big, beefy oilman named Marvin Davis, whose word turned out to be less than his bond.

Taken Down South

The new Hiram Walker announced within just a few months of the merger that it was planning to invest up to $1 billion in a U.S. acquisition. The announcement of the NEP in October, 1980, added momentum to this move. Early in 1981, the company bought most of Davis Oil Company for a whopping $759 million. The enormously intricate purchase consisted of more than 20,000 oil and gas leases covering 767,000 gross acres of land in Wyoming, Louisiana, Oklahoma, and Texas. It was not a good buy. There was no way in which a thorough evaluation could be made of the properties in the time available. Home Oil executives simply trusted Davis, one of whose declared reasons for selling was that he had incurable cancer. Home thought it was buying proved reserves of 11 million barrels of oil and 173 billion cubic feet of gas. When it eventually had an independent appraisal done, the figures were found to be closer to 8 million barrels of oil and 83 billion cubic feet of gas.

Marvin Davis had cleverly pressured Hiram Walker into a quick decision on the basis that half a dozen other companies were bidding for his properties. Said the chastened Bill Wilder, in a masterpiece of understatement, "Mr. Davis is a pretty good salesman." Wilder also announced that the company was considering legal action for misrepresentation. Davis meanwhile turned around and used most of the proceeds of his killing to purchase Twentieth Century-Fox Film Corp. of Los Angeles. He also staged a remarkable recovery from his terminal condition.

Hiram Walker had borrowed heavily for the purchase and the surge in interest rates in 1981 and 1982, combined with write-offs on the Davis properties, decimated profits. Even before the Davis write-offs, net income plummeted to $99 million in 1982 from $222 million in 1981. The Davis disaster led to a final loss for the year of $78 million. Clifford Hatch was not happy. The merger that was meant to give him stability had led him into a financial morass. Somebody had to pay the price.

There were swift corporate retributions. Al McIntosh, Home Oil's president, had already been fired, but then Bill Wilder found himself stripped of his titles and made deputy chairman to Cliff Hatch, who assumed the role of chief executive and president. True to the restrained rules of executive suite etiquette, McIntosh's firing was to be inferred from the statement in the annual report that "A number of significant steps were initiated during 1982 to improve the performance of the natural resource segment." The chief of these was the appointment as Home's head of Dick Haskayne, a well-regarded oil executive who had been president of Hudson's Bay Oil & Gas and had left after its takeover by Dome Petroleum in 1981. A management committee, consisting of Hatch, Wilder, and the three presidents of the operating subsidiaries — Haskayne, Bud Downing from the distilling side, and Robert Martin from the gas utility business — was also set up "to assist in the monitoring of the three business segments."

The company's 1983 annual meeting was a unique experience for Clifford Hatch. Hiram Walker annual meetings had previously been a quasi-religious celebration of the company's stability and success, a ritual reappointment of auditors, and re-election of directors. But at this meeting the congregation turned fractious. There were a lot of angry questions from shareholders. A flustered and affronted Hatch was deluged with demands for an explanation of the Davis deal. He told shareholders that the Davis purchase had been based on "the best advice money can buy."

Hatch, who was then sixty-six, had hoped to retire before the Davis deal. Now, however, he declared that he planned to stay on as chairman, president, and chief executive until the company's balance sheet had recovered. In any event, he announced toward the end of 1983 that he would be giving up the titles of president and chief executive to his protégé Bud Downing.

That was not, however, the end of the Hatch dynasty, for Downing's previous job as head of the liquor division was taken over by Clifford, Jr., Hatch's son. Cliff, Jr., was to the manor born. He had been educated in Switzerland and at McGill and Harvard, where he got his MBA. He was a member of the Mount Royal and St. Denis clubs in Montreal and of the best yacht clubs in Toronto, Detroit, and Windsor. Cliff, Jr., had worked his way through the company and it was no secret that both he and his father hoped that Hiram Walker management would be kept in the family. However, new threats had in the meantime appeared on the horizon: specifically, a little-known firm of Toronto Jewish real estate developers called the Reichmanns.

Since Hiram Walker's head office was in First Canadian Place, Bill Wilder often ran into the Reichmanns in the building's elevators. In the spring of 1981, he received a call from Paul Reichmann saying that he wanted to come for "a brief chat." Reichmann didn't specify his purpose, but Wilder knew what he wanted to talk about. As Reichmann walked into his office, Wilder thought he would try to put the developer at ease with a touch of humour. "Have you come to collect the rent, Mr. Reichmann?" he asked.

Reichmann didn't laugh. "No," he said, "I checked before I came and it's fully paid." Wilder wasn't sure whether he was joking or not.

Reichmann outlined his intentions of taking a "friendly" minority stake in the company. After he had left, Wilder told Hatch about the conversation, and, once again flippantly, said "You'd better dust off your homburg." Clifford Hatch didn't laugh either, and there was no doubt that he didn't find it a laughing matter. Clifford Hatch didn't want the Reichmanns taking a stake in his company. An analyst would later ask Hatch what he thought of the Reichmanns' move. Hatch just could not bring himself to say what he should have said: that he was delighted to have attracted the confidence of such a worthy investor. He just snapped back, "What would you have me think?"

Paul Reichmann's subsequent quiet request for board representation was turned down firmly by Hatch. Cliff Hatch didn't mind having Paul and Albert Reichmann as landlords, but he certainly didn't want them sitting on his board. The rejection did not please the Reichmanns.

Throughout 1982 and most of 1983, the Reichmanns were preoccupied with financing and refinancing O&Y projects in a high interest rate environment. Diversifications were temporarily put on hold. However, by 1983 this process was complete. Hiram Walker began to feel vulnerable once again. New defensive measures were called for.

One way to strengthen control of a company is to make sure that large blocks of its stock are in friendly hands. The Reichmanns had a large block, and they had indicated that they wanted to be friendly. But the Reichmanns weren't Hatch's idea of friends. He found a company that was much more his idea of a worthy corporate ally, Interprovincial Pipe Line Limited, which, it just so happened, also had its offices in First Canadian Place.

A Chip Off the Old Block

Interprovincial was Canada's largest oil pipeline company, but it was far more than that, it was a chip off the old corporate block of its founder, Imperial Oil, Canada's if not most loved, at least most respected oil company. Interprovincial, created by a special act of Parliament in April, 1949, had grown in step with Alberta's booming production, shipping it to its major markets in Central Canada and the United States.

By 1982, Interprovincial carried 1.2 million of barrels of oil and other liquids through its 2,300-mile system daily. The company was run by engineers who took pride in their level heads and their technical expertise. In 1983, they took particular pride in starting work on a 540-mile line to bring oil from Imperial oilfields at Norman Wells in the Northwest Territories.

Interprovincial was a big, solid company, but, like Hiram Walker, it had reached a level of maturity where it needed to diversify to grow. One major barrier to its diversification was its foreign control, and not merely foreign control, but control by Imperial Oil, which held 33.3 percent of its stock (Gulf Canada and Shell Canada held smaller percentages). For Ottawa's nationalists, and in particular the men who controlled the Foreign Investment Review Agency, Imperial was the greatest symbol of foreign domination of the Canadian economy. The fact that the men who ran Imperial were all Canadians, and were mightily affronted at the suggestion that they would ever act in anything but the country's best interests, only irked the nationalists more. Nevertheless, Hiram Walker's desire to find a friendly shareholder and Interprovincial's desire to become technically "Canadian" dovetailed nicely. Canadianization of Interprovincial meant not only that it would be able to acquire other companies, but also that it would be eligible for higher levels of the NEP's PIP grants. All Hiram Walker and IPL had to do was execute a nice, friendly share swap; not so much "You watch my back and I'll watch yours," as "I'll watch your back while I'm running up this Maple Leaf flag."

Hiram Walker Resources would take 34 percent of Interprovincial's equity; in return, IPL would receive 15.7 percent of HWR. The deal was nominally worth $354 million. As a result, Imperial's stake in Interprovincial was reduced to 22 percent. Nevertheless, Ottawa was concerned that the foreign-controlled giant would still control Interprovincial. The passage of the transaction through FIRA was less than smooth.

Hiram Walker's 1983 annual report detailed the share swap and noted that it had put five directors on Interprovincial's board. A message under the names of Hatch and Wilder declared "we look forward to having appropriate Interprovincial representation on our Board." One might have wondered why Walker had put its representation on Interprovincial's board, but Interprovincial had not gained its representation on Walker's. The answer was that FIRA thought IPL representatives on Walker's board would be, in the words of one of those close to the negotiations, "spies and fifth columnists." Liberal industry minister Ed Lumley thus insisted that all IPL's "independent" directors be sacked. Only one Inter-provincial board member, Doug Gardiner, was allowed onto the Walker board.

But Imperial may well have had a hidden agenda in organizing the share swap. The oil giant was attracted by the assets of Home Oil, and it may well have hoped that over time a way could be found to prise them loose from Walker, or at least run them in conjunction with the liquor-based company. This was perhaps less deviousness than recognition of the perceived attitudes of Hiram Walker management. Imperial and Interprovincial thought that Hatch and the other Walker men from the distilling side had, since the Davis debacle, developed a profound mistrust of the oil business, and might well want to distance themselves from it. Such was not to be the case. The corporate marriage of convenience became bogged down in mutual distrust and a managerial dead-lock. It would end in what Hiram Walker regarded as the worst kind of infidelity, and what IPL thought was the worst kind of managerial incompetence.

When Bud Downing took over as chief executive at Hiram Walker, he carried out a strategic review of the company and decided that Hiram Walker Resources *was* going to live up to its name and be in the oil and gas business. Home was not for sale, or for sharing. Meanwhile, IPL management grew to believe that the presence of Walker management on its board, far from helping it expand and diversify in oil and gas, tended to suppress such moves. Walker management was looking out for choice prospects for its own oil and gas activities. Diversification was also difficult for Interprovincial because of the corporate view of Imperial Oil, largely supported by IPL management, that there were few bar-gains in the oil and gas business any more. IPL would examine potential deals and pursue them for a couple of months, but then the initiative would die either because the deal didn't fit Home's interests or because it didn't suit Imperial's strict investment cri-teria. The company was frustrated because there was no strategy that would fit both investors. The upshot was that two years after the share exchange, IPL's Canadianization had been virtually meaningless, except in terms of the proportion of Hiram Walker's earnings that IPL was able to add to its own. Then, suddenly, even that benefit suddenly appeared endangered.

By the fall of 1985, Interprovincial found itself with bulging cash resources of more than $600 million and still no major diversification. Interprovincial had also became concerned that if it went after a major acquisition, it would have no way of defending its investment in Hiram Walker if anyone took a run at the conglomerate. The most likely candidate to make such a move was still Paul Reichmann. The word was that, despite the complexities of the Gulf Canada deal, Hiram Walker was still on his shopping list.

But there was also another, technical, reason for IPL to increase its Hiram Walker stake. Auditors were becoming a lot tougher in the wake of the banking debacles of the CCB and Northland banks in Alberta, where the supposed guardians of accurate financial reporting had failed to signal the tenuous financial condition of their clients. IPL became concerned that a tightening up of auditing standards would mean that it would no longer be able to "equity account" for its Walker stake.

A company is allowed to equity account — that is, take a percentage of another company's earnings into its own earnings, proportionate to a stake that it holds in that company — provided that it has a minimum equity holding of 20 percent, or, has an "influential position" on the company's board. IPL held 15 percent of HWR's equity, and took 15 percent of Hiram Walker's earnings into its own accounts on the basis of its "influential position," but that basis was highly tenuous. Interprovincial had only one director on the Hiram Walker board and its say in Walker's activities was a moot point. If it could no longer equity account for Walker, then it would only be able to take Walker dividends, that is, the actual cash it received from the company, into its earnings. That would slash its Walker-derived income in half, cut its earnings, and almost inevitably damage its share price.

IPL's position was in danger of being diluted because of the conversion of HWR preferred shares into common stock — which was now an attractive option because of the share price — and also because of a stock dividend program whereby shareholders could take their dividends as additional shares of Hiram Walker instead of cash.

The final rationale for increasing its Hiram Walker stake —

related to its fear of Walker's vulnerability to a takeover — was that Walker was undervalued. According to Interprovincial's evaluation, declining oil prices, insofar as they went hand in hand with lower interest rates, could actually benefit Walker. The impact of lower oil and gas prices on Home was, in IPL's thinking, more than offset by the beneficial impact of lower discount rates on the present values of the company's other earnings. IPL decided therefore, with the approval both of its Walker and its Imperial directors, to increase its Walker stake to 20 percent.

Interprovincial started buying Hiram Walker stock in the fall of 1985 and eventually accumulated another 1.9 million shares, which brought their holding up to 17.7 percent. They were still worried about the Reichmanns. Then, some not unexpected, but nevertheless chilling, news arrived at IPL's First Canadian Place headquarters.

15

THE PIRANHA
COMES TO CALL

*Blaming the Reichmanns' assault on Heule was
a convenient way for Hiram Walker's management
to sidestep the fact that they had been warned
that the Reichmanns were coming, and had done
absolutely nothing about it.*

Early in February, 1986, Jimmy Connacher and Bob Fung of
Gordon Capital Corporation went up to Imperial Oil's head
office on St. Clair Avenue West in Toronto to meet with
senior executives of the giant oil company. Connacher had some
disturbing news to impart that affected Imperial through its 22
percent stake in Interprovincial Pipe Line. Soon after, he delivered
the same news to Interprovincial's chairman, Bob Heule: the
Reichmanns were about to take a run at Hiram Walker Resources.

The source was as surprising as it was credible. The Reichmanns' share dealings had for a number of years accounted for a
good chunk of Gordon's income. Most recently, Gordon had been
involved in the purchase of shares and warrants of Hiram Walker.
Purchasing warrants — that is, the rights to buy the shares of a
company at a fixed price at a later date—is a way of ''creeping up''
on a corporate target, since there are no lists of warrant holders, as
there are of shareholders. Warrants can be accumulated and then
converted rapidly to give a raider a potentially significant stock-
holding. Also, shortly before Christmas, 1985, Connacher had
done a swap deal with the Reichmanns whereby Gordon took 1
million shares of MacMillan Bloedel from the Reichmanns for $26 a

share in return for the promise to deliver 1 million shares of Hiram Walker at the same price.

Just as Connacher had taken a bath on his purchase of 1 million Bow Valley shares from Paul Reichmann at the height of the market back in 1983, he had taken a "kiss" of several million dollars on this deal too. Nevertheless, baths and kisses were part of the territory, and insufficient reason for switching sides in the way in which Connacher appeared to be doing. However, there was more to it than that. The relationship between Connacher and the Reichmanns had cooled considerably in recent months.

The Reichmanns had been extremely angry because, during the Gulf Canada takeover, a story had appeared in the *Toronto Star* which they believed could only have come out of Gordon. They expressed their displeasure both verbally and, even more painfully, with the withdrawal of stock purchases.

Connacher, meanwhile, was equally miffed with the Reichmanns. After working so assiduously for them over the years, he saw them putting business in the way of other investment dealers, in particular Merrill Lynch, which of course just happened to be the Reichmanns' largest real estate tenant down in New York. He felt suddenly shut out.

Imperial Oil and Interprovincial were obviously more than a little interested in what Connacher had to say. Hiram Walker had a shareholder agreement with Imperial Oil dictating a hands-off approach to their stakes in Interprovincial, so the change of ownership was not so threatening on that account. Of more concern was Interprovincial's stake in Walker. Interprovincial didn't want to be left holding a minority of Hiram Walker if the Reichmanns seized control. Jimmy Connacher's bottom line was that Interprovincial should hire him as an investment advisor to think about a strategy. Gordon was duly hired.

Paul Reichmann, if he had known, would presumably have been less than happy.

Imperial would play a neutral role in upcoming events. As the biggest foreign-owned oil company in Canada, its executives were acutely aware that their actions were ever subject to political scrutiny. They reminded Interprovincial, if Interprovincial needed reminding, that their responsibility was to look after the interests of their shareholders. Interprovincial began to plot a strategy to do just that, but they didn't have much time. And they didn't get much co-operation from the company to which Connacher's news should have been of much greater significance, Hiram Walker.

Bob Heule, Interprovincial's affable, slow-talking, engineer chairman, was, like Bud Downing and all the other nuts-and-bolts operating executives of the world, less than sophisticated when it came to dealing with the stock market. But he saw his first course of action as clear. He passed on Connacher's news to Downing. Downing's response astonished Heule. Hiram Walker's chairman told him he just didn't believe it. He had spoken to Albert Reichmann quite recently, and Albert had told him that O&Y had no plans for its Hiram Walker stake at that time. And of course the ink was barely dry on the Gulf Canada acquisition. The Reichmanns were hardly likely to go for another acquisition so quickly. Downing may even have suggested that if Heule had any doubts or suspicions, why didn't he just go and see the Reichmanns?

Heule came away a confused man. Downing, whom he respected, a fellow engineer, the head of one of the largest companies in Canada, had told him that what Connacher said wasn't so. The Reichmanns weren't coming. Back up at Interprovincial, however, Heule's senior executives tended to believe Connacher, and Interprovincial had some pretty smart executives.

Imperial's continuing strong influence over the company had been clearly demonstrated in the summer of 1985, when a successor had been picked for Heule. The man chosen to be Interprovincial's president and heir-apparent, George "Ted" Courtnage, had come straight out of the Imperial/Exxon system. Courtnage had run refineries, he had been in charge of Imperial's heavy oil project at Cold Lake, Alberta, and he had most recently been running the logistics for Imperial's parent, Exxon Corporation, in Europe. Courtnage was hard-working and talented, as was every man on the Imperial/Exxon fast track, and he almost certainly came to Interprovincial with a mandate to get things moving. Another key executive was Doug Martin, a very bright former senior employee of Dome Petroleum, who had been brought in to oversee Interprovincial's frustrated attempts at diversification. Courtnage and Martin told Heule they had to keep pursuing a strategy on the basis that the Reichmanns *were* coming.

Heule decided at least to follow Downing's advice. He went to see Paul Reichmann. Heule tentatively suggested to Reichmann that they might act together in order to preserve the status quo at HWR. Interprovincial, as the largest shareholder in Hiram Walker, would accumulate no further shares as long as O&Y, as the second-largest shareholder, made a similar commitment. Heule wanted a standstill agreement. But Paul Reichmann had no desire to be part of a convoy at which everybody moved at the pace of the slowest thinker. Reichmann told Heule he'd have to think about it; he'd get back to him. Heule left to take one of First Canadian Place's double-banked elevators back up to his office. He was still a confused man.

Later, Hiram Walker management would suggest that Heule's move had been stupid, that by going to see Paul Reichmann, he had virtually *guaranteed* HWR's takeover, because even if Paul Reichmann hadn't been thinking about going for control of Hiram Walker before the visit, he would surely be thinking about it now. But that attitude was an *ex post facto* rationalization. Blaming the Reichmanns' assault on Heule was a convenient way for Hiram Walker's management to sidestep the fact that they had been warned that the Reichmanns were coming, and had done absolutely nothing about it. There was no doubt that Paul Reichmann was firmly set on gaining control of the company that had rebuffed him back in 1981.

Advised by Gordon Capital and its traditional investment house, Wood Gundy, Interprovincial began to cast about frantically for means of defence against a Reichmann attack on HWR. It seemed astonishing that Interprovincial, now that it was proposing to Hiram Walker that it fulfill the defensive role for which it had been brought in, was being rebuffed.

Interprovincial had a lot of cash, but it didn't have enough to attempt a complete takeover of Walker, although that option was examined in some depth. It considered going to 35 percent of Walker, a position that, although still not control, would at least put it in a much stronger position. Interprovincial management went to Walker and suggested an issue of Walker treasury shares, but they were soundly rejected by Walker's executive committee. HWR didn't need a stronger shareholder. There was no danger on the horizon.

Interprovincial's persistence in their fears merely served to annoy Walker's management. The Walker members on Interprovincial's board were also, because of conflict of interest, excluded from deliberations on strategy with regard to Interprovincial's ownership of Walker shares. This inevitably increased tensions between the two companies.

Interprovincial found itself cast in the role of Cassandra, the ancient Greek prophetess doomed to tell the truth but never to be believed. Without Hiram Walker's co-operation, there was very little that the pipeline could do but wait for the other shoe to drop.

Interprovincial would have to decide on strategy after any battle broke out. Although outside observers would be astonished at the course Interprovincial took, it was less surprising once Hiram Walker's bland disregard for Interprovincial's warnings was taken into account.

Dusting Off the Files

O&Y had been looking at Hiram Walker as an acquisition candidate throughout the takeover of Gulf Canada. Late in 1985, while preparing to complete the Gulf Canada acquisition, Paul Reichmann had "dusted off" the Walker files. The Reichmanns had decided to go for Hiram Walker once they had seized control of Gulf Canada, using Gulf as the instrument of acquisition. The principal reason for drawing a bead on Hiram Walker was simple: they already controlled 10 percent of it. Its corporate attractions, however, were a moveable feast. One thing was for sure: Hiram Walker was another very big company. Its value was not far short of that of Gulf Canada. By drawing a bead on it, Paul Reichmann was attempting what no Canadian and few businessmen anywhere had ever attempted before: to seize control of corporate assets worth close to $10 billion in less than a year, thus doubling the size of the Reichmann empire. Gulf Canada ranked tenth by sales in the 1986 *Financial Post 500* listing of the largest Canadian industrial companies. Hiram Walker ranked twenty-third. Combined, they would leap to fifth place, behind only General Motors of Canada, Canadian Pacific, Ford Motor Company of Canada, and Bell Canada Enterprises.

Hiram Walker's original attraction for the Reichmanns lay in its resource assets, that is, Home Oil; but as the price of oil continued to drop in the early months of 1986, Home became a less desirable prize. Emphasis switched to the liquor business. If the Reichmanns knew very little about oil and gas, they knew even less about liquor. Paul Reichmann sounded out a number of other liquor company representatives and executives, including Seagram's Edgar Bronfman, in an attempt to gauge the value of HWR's liquor operations.

Liquor contributed the largest element of Hiram Walker's profits. Of its $665 million operating profit on sales of $3.8 billion in 1985, the liquor business had contributed 42.4 percent, natural resources 25.1 percent, and the utilities 32.4 percent. The liquor subsidiary, Hiram Walker/Gooderham & Worts, still had Canadian Club whisky as its flagship product, but it also produced Ballantine's Scotch, Kahlúa, Tia Maria, Drambuie, and Courvoisier. Meagher's Distillery Limited, which was wholly owned by Walker's 52.7-percent-owned subsidiary Corby Distilleries Ltd., marketed a number of brands including Beefeater gin and Southern Comfort. As well as three major Canadian facilities, the company also had large plants in Loretto, Kentucky; Dumbarton, Scotland; and Buenos Aires, Argentina. The aggregate daily capacity of its distilleries in 1985 was about two hundred eighty thousand U.S. proof gallons. It matured, blended, and bottled cognac in France, it produced premium wines in California, it manufactured Tia Maria in Kingston, Jamaica, and it made Kahlúa in Mexico City. These and other nondistilling operations produced 155,000 cases a day. Hiram Walker, although Clifford Hatch, Sr., would probably have rejected the terminology, produced a sea of booze. But it was high-quality, and more important high-margin, booze.

Liquor was more than just Hiram Walker Resources' biggest money spinner, it was the company's heart, the business around which oil and gas pipelines had been drawn up as a defence, and because of which the ''defensive'' share swap with Interprovincial had been arranged. Ironically, Walker's diversifications had provided many sleepless nights for Clifford Hatch. The link with Consumers-Home had led Walker into the morass of Davis Oil, which, if anything, had weakened the company. Now, the second line of defence was being ignored.

Gulf Discovers It's Getting Married

Before its acquisition by the Reichmanns, there was about as much chance of Gulf Canada going after Hiram Walker as there was of John Stoik, its heavy-set former chief executive, flying around Gulf's downtown Toronto boardroom. It had long been restricted by its foreign ownership, but in addition its management had not been renowned for its qualities of lateral thinking. A Gulf under Reichmann control was a different matter. Gulf's uneasy and somewhat bewildered management, led by Stoik's successor Keith McWalter, suddenly found themselves once more in the limelight. In reality, they felt less like actors than puppets with strange — and unusually active — new hands suddenly working the strings. They were in the schizophrenic position of not knowing what they would do next.

The Reichmanns had always kept information and decisions to the smallest possible group, the main member of which had for a long time been Gil Newman, their roly-poly number-cruncher. However, a new member had been added to the group in October, 1985, when the Reichmanns, acutely aware of the need to build some kind of structure to manage their non real estate holdings, appointed former finance deputy minister Mickey Cohen head of Olympia & York Enterprises, the holding company for the Reichmanns' public interests. Cohen came straight into the decision-making holy of holies, and this inevitably created its own tensions.

Newman now saw his position as number-one non-family henchman threatened. He had been disturbed when David Brown had been brought in from Burns Fry in 1984. But Brown had reportedly grown tired of being kept in the dark and left.

The questions of personal ego, and office politics, seemed to be either beyond the Reichmanns' comprehension or of no concern to them. Newman, almost obsessed with keeping abreast, developed severe worries about his own access to Paul Reichmann. He had given his secretary instructions to inform him about visitors to Paul Reichmann's office, and when Mickey Cohen turned up for one of his first sessions with Paul Reichmann, Newman was hot on his heels. Cohen told him he wasn't expected at the meeting, and the old retainer reportedly left in confusion.

However, without consulting Cohen, Paul Reichmann subsequently appointed Newman to the number two position at O&Y Enterprises but gave no indication of what kind of working relationship Cohen was expected to have with Newman. To Cohen, a man delicately versed in the nuances of power, Paul Reichmann's style and O&Y's organization, or rather lack of it, came as a profound shock. In Ottawa, he could assemble squadrons of Ph.D. economists and lawyers with a phone call. Moreover, financial decisions in Ottawa had been made with the money of far-distant taxpayers, to whom there was an only vague sense of responsibility. On the thirty-second floor of First Canadian Place, where it had taken several months even to be allocated an office, there were no squadrons of high-priced staff. Moreover, those on whose behalf financial decisions were being made were down the hall. And they very much liked the right decisions to be made with their money.

Since Gulf was to bid for Hiram Walker, it seemed only appropriate, in the interests of etiquette as well as obeisance to Gulf's minority shareholders, to let Gulf know what was going on. Gulf's surprised top management were informed of their next move. Moreover, to preserve appearances, when the proposal that Gulf should bid for Hiram Walker was made to the Gulf board on March 17, it was made by Gulf's chief financial officer, Lionel Dodd. Paul and Albert, however, were both on hand to answer questions. Cohen and Newman were, of course, now present as Gulf directors.

There was some concern that Gulf's outside directors might oppose the bid, since it would involve Gulf increasing its already hefty debt burden. Not all the outside board members were there. Perhaps the most prominent, Alf Powis, was on a cruise ship off the coast of Uruguay, where Paul reached him to inform him about the proposed bid. However, neither Powis nor any of the other outside directors raised any serious questions. Paul and Albert were eager to reassure the Gulf board that O&Y's financial strength would be behind the bid. But it was Gulf's financial neck that was on the line. To make the initial planned offer, Gulf would have to borrow $1.2 billion at a time when it was meant to be reducing its debt, and when the company was inevitably weakened by the slump in petroleum prices.

The Reichmanns' rationale turned arguments about the weakness of the oil business on their head. Depressed oil markets meant that Gulf would not be spending so much money on exploration, so it should be directing its cash flow and its borrowing power elsewhere. After Gulf had completed the sales of its Edmonton refinery, its Eastern marketing and refining assets, and Superior Propane, it would still have $400 to $500 million in cash. Gulf was being told that because it was crippled, it had to move faster.

Another reason for going for control now was that the Hiram Walker shares were depressed. Their recent low of $26.50 compared with a twelve-month high of $34.87. One of the reasons for their recent slump, somewhat ironically, was that Interprovincial's open market purchases of Walker shares, which had been part of the plan launched the previous fall to bring its holding in HWR up to the 20 percent level, had now been stopped. Interprovincial's purchases had been holding up the share price.

The Gulf board, whatever their misgivings, gave the go ahead. One critical error on the Reichmanns' part, however, was their underestimation of Walker's opposition to a bid. Paul Reichmann could have been forgiven for his error. Both he and his brother Albert had finally been invited onto the Hiram Walker board a year previously. In fact, they had indicated that they would join at the 1986 annual meeting. However, they had been invited not so much out of friendship as out of a desire on the part of Walker management to have them where they could see them. In the end, the Reichmanns had turned down the board places. The move provided still another indication that Hiram Walker was on the Reichmanns' hit list, an indication that Hiram Walker's board and management again ignored. On March 19, their blindness to the obvious was revealed.

Courtesy Calls

On that Wednesday morning, the Reichmanns put through many calls before the stock markets opened. Paul, after the Gulf affair now much better versed in the intricacies and importance of politics in Canadian business, spoke to a number of federal and provincial politicians, including Ontario premier David Peterson. He also called a number of Hiram Walker directors. He spoke to Allen Lambert, the former TD bank head who was also chairman of financial conglomerate Trilon, which had been created by Brascan's Trevor Eyton and in which the Reichmanns had a major stake. He called Gordon Gray, the chairman of Royal LePage, the giant real estate broker which was also now part of the Trilon empire, and he reached Bill Wilder, Hiram Walker's deputy chairman, just as Wilder was going into a board meeting of the Canada Development Corporation. Albert called Dick Haskayne, the chief executive of Home Oil, whose talents he had praised that morning to Bud Downing.

Paul Reichmann sounded the directors out on what the remaining board members would think of the offer. He was given no indication of powerful resistance, although he was told that the board was bound to seek a higher price. Reichmann also asked the directors what they thought the attitude of Interprovincial and Imperial Oil would be. At least one of the directors told him that he thought they would be pretty upset. The men up at Imperial's headquarters on St. Clair Avenue would inevitably regard Gulf-Reichmann control as a challenge. The director didn't tell him that

Interprovincial and Imperial had now had some time to consider that challenge but had been frustrated by Hiram Walker. That would have been acutely embarrassing.

To get a more direct view of their attitude on that Wednesday morning, Paul Reichmann called Interprovincial's Bob Heule and said he'd like to drop by. Heule wondered if this was the long-awaited response to his suggestion for a standstill agreement. Reichmann took the elevator up the five floors from O&Y's offices to those of Interprovincial and was shown into Heule's office. He sat down and handed Bob Heule O&Y's press release. They were, he explained, going for control of Walker. Bob Heule's worst fear had come to pass. Connacher had been right. Hiram Walker had been dumb.

Heule's 17 percent of Hiram Walker stock was obviously extremely important to Reichmann's bid for control of HWR. Reichmann knew that Interprovincial's main interest in HWR was Home Oil, and obviously realized that the oil and gas subsidiary could be used as a lever to gain Interprovincial's co-operation. He knew that he had another lever, which he had already applied simply by making a bid for less than all Hiram Walker's share. IPL's fear of an impotent minority position in HWR. He told Heule that he would like his support, that he was aware of Interprovincial's interests, and that if Interprovincial gave its support, then he would try and accommodate those interests. Then he left. Although Heule had been warned, he still felt stunned.

The details of the offer were announced to the Montreal and Toronto stock exchanges that morning and trading in Walker shares was temporarily suspended. Gulf's offer was $32 a share for 26 million Hiram Walker common shares and $28.62 for all the first series of the class D convertible preferreds. If fewer than all the outstanding class D preferred shares were tendered, Gulf would buy additional common shares to make up a 38 percent voting interest, so that, when added to O&Y's 10.7 percent of Walker, the combined Gulf-O&Y block would represent 49.7 per cent of the company's equity. The offer, worth $1.2 billion, would be made through the Toronto and Montreal stock exchanges on April 4. It would be limited to Canadian investors, which presented certain problems. A recent U.S. judgement had implied that any information concerning a takeover offer given to the U.S. media could constitute an offer to U.S. shareholders and thus trigger the need for a formal offer in the United States. That would require far more time and also much more disclosure. So Gulf

om the start imposed a news blackout on the takeover south of
ne border, withholding news releases and not returning U.S.
nedia phone calls.

When trading in Hiram Walker shares was resumed around
oon, they jumped $3 to $31, while the class D preferred closed at
28.36, up $2.50. Gulf Canada dropped 25 cents to $16.62.

One newspaper reporter asked Paul Reichmann how he felt
bout working hard and long on such deals. Reichmann re-
ponded simply, "It's fun." But this particular deal would not
rove fun for long.

The Gulf acquisition had been a "friendly" affair. For Gulf Can-
da, no other attitude had been possible. Hiram Walker was differ-
nt. Despite its reprehensible state of unpreparedness, the
ompany had no intention of rolling over and playing dead. The
Valker takeover would turn into a battle. Moreover, by the time
ne Reichmanns' appointees had replaced the old board at Hiram
Valker, the brothers found themselves in the bizarre position of
aking over a company that was now committed to sell the very
ssets for which they were acquiring it.

Their Walker bid unleashed a Pandora's box whose corporate
vhirlwinds were felt around the globe. What started as an issue of
ower in Canada's ruling business élite turned into a worldwide
usiness war with few precedents. In Canada, deep and bitter rifts
vere created between companies that had supposedly been allies.
nternationally, the reverberations were felt in stock markets from
oronto to Melbourne, from New York to London.

At the local Canadian level, the old guard would, in the end, go
own, but they would not go down without a fight. They were
arried off the field clad in the armour of righteousness, because
ney could unequivocally claim that they had done their duty
oward their shareholders. They also left the battlefield with a
arthian shot that threatened to sting the Reichmanns. The shaft
vas provided by their allies from London, who would attempt the
argest ever takeover of a North American business by a British
ompany. The British, some said, were protecting their own
efined rears against unwelcome Australian corporate invaders.
he Aussies, meanwhile, were busy fighting their own civil war
down under."

It turned out to be a corporate soap opera without precedent,
nd if there was one thing Paul Reichmann had never wanted to
e, it was a soap opera star.

16

HIRAM WALKER FINALLY GIRDS ITS LOINS

*Part of the Saturday Night Special's rationale
is its short time-fuse, which, like having a
snub-nosed revolver shoved in one's face, tends
to induce a certain sense of panic.*

As soon as Bud Downing had put down the phone to Albe
Reichmann in the California dawn of March 19, his min
had to switch into a quite unaccustomed mode: comba
Downing was an engineer, not a fighter, and he had been caug
both figuratively and literally with his pants down. Now he had
gird his loins for battle. His good fortune would be that he ha
some whip-smart advisors. He called the Toronto office and to
Archibald McCallum, HWR's chief financial officer, about Albert
call. Then he told him to start marshalling the troops for battle.

Downing also called Hiram Walker's Toronto legal firm, McCa
thy & McCarthy. Peter Beattie, the senior partner on the Hira
Walker account, was also on holiday, in Barbados, and it took hi
a couple of days to get back. But two other high-powered lawye
who worked on Walker, Gary Girvan and Bob Forbes, soon gath
ered up their briefcases and hustled across King Street from the
offices in the Toronto-Dominion Bank Tower to Hiram Walker
sixth-floor boardroom to begin the defensive brainstorming. Th
other key legal counsel called was George "Chip" Reid, an a
lawyer from the Washington, D.C., firm of Covington & Burlin

which had represented Hiram Walker/Gooderham & Worts for thirty years.

Chief financial officer McCallum, as soon as he had spoken to Downing, called Walker's financial advisors at Toronto's Dominion Securities Pitfield (DSP), and New York's Morgan Guaranty Trust Co. Two of the investment firms' leading corporate strategists, Jimmy Pitblado for DSP and Roberto Mendoza for Morgan, took command.

Pitblado had a reputation for being tough and smart. He also had a sense of humour. The previous year he had helped mastermind the sale of more than $100 million of equity in the financially crippled Dome Petroleum. During the negotiations over the issue, Dome's chairman, Howard Macdonald, himself renowned for his wry wit, had spotted a fast food truck that used to park near DSP's Commerce Court West offices. The truck bore the legend "Jimmy's Fine Foods on Wheels." Macdonald ribbed Pitblado about running the business on the side. At the closing of Dome's share issue in May, 1985, Pitblado presented Macdonald with a framed photograph of himself standing with his foot on the fender of the truck. Beneath the picture was a little plaque with the words "It's Jimmy's for a Quick Meal and a Good Deal." Now Pitblado had to come up with not just a good deal for his clients at Hiram Walker Resources, he had to come up with a *better* deal.

Morgan's Mendoza, too, was a lot more than just an *éminence grise*. He liked to get up and take on the opposition *mano a mano*. Later in the battle, he would have an opportunity to do just that. And blood would be left all over the floor.

Later that day, by the time Downing was back from California, the group had its first full meeting. HWR's management wanted to know how much time they had and what their best strategy would be. They asked the lawyers if they had to respond immediately, whether a press release should be issued and if so what it should say, and whether it would be appropriate to speak to the Reichmanns.

The lawyers told them that they didn't have to respond at once, and that until the board had been gathered and the directors had been sounded out, they shouldn't seek out the Reichmanns. However, they told Bud Downing that if Paul Reichmann should attempt to make contact, then he should speak to him. Paul Reichmann made no contact. The U.S. counsel was questioned about the bid not being eligible in the United States. That discus-

sion went around and around the table. Downing, as always, di
more listening than talking. His bottom line remained simple: h
wasn't prepared to fight the bid for the sake of staying in powe
but he was if the price was too low. The group soon came to
consensus on that issue.

U.S. counsel Chip Reid knew all the fancy angles of takeove
defence, which, in the United States was almost an art form. Tha
was where all the elaborate terminology, like "white knights
and "poison pills," had arisen. There was another term ofte
used in takeovers south of the border. It was called the "Saturda
Night Special." Named after a cheap handgun of the kind used i
the hold-up of low rent neighbourhood liquor stores, it referred t
takeover bids that were considered attempted corporate robber
Such bids were usually launched quickly and unexpectedly in th
hope of grabbing control of a company before its management ha
time to organize its defences. The predator hoped to make off wit
the prize while its executives were still staring open-mouthe
down the figurative gun barrel. The group soon decided that th
Reichmanns were trying to pull a Saturday Night Special.

Looking for White Knights

From that Wednesday afternoon onward, the core group: Down
ing, McCallum, and Bill Fatt, Walker's treasurer, for the company
Girvan, Forbes, and soon Beattie, for McCarthy & McCarthy; Rei
from Covington & Burling; Pitblado from Dominion Securitie
Pitfield; and Mendoza for Morgan Guaranty, met once or twice
day.

An immediate priority was to work out what the Reichmanns
bid was really worth, since it was only for 38 percent of the shares
An estimate had to be made of what price the shares of Hiran
Walker would subsequently trade at, and then average that ou
with the bid price. DSP and Morgan believed that HWR share
would fall to $25 if the Reichmanns were successful, so th
Reichmann bid was worth an average to each shareholder o
around $29. That was the figure they had to better. DSP analyst
were sent off to carry out a valuation of Hiram Walker so that th
company had a firm basis on which to reject the Reichmann offer

Most important, Pitblado and Mendoza were sent forth as her
alds to find white knights. DSP was to concentrate its search i
Canada, Morgan was to look elsewhere. A Canadian knight wa

obviously preferable because of potential problems with a foreign bidder. Investment Canada was still seen as the sharp-toothed FIRA watchdog in one of Prime Minister Brian Mulroney's cosy, lambswool sweaters.

There were problems with evaluating Hiram Walker's component parts. The value of Home Oil was as uncertain as the future of OPEC and world oil prices. The second problem was the value of the liquor business, which was on the books at $1.2 billion, but which was felt to be worth more, perhaps considerably more. The value of the holdings in Consumers' Gas and Interprovincial were easy to work out because both shares were traded in the market.

Pitblado began approaching obvious candidates for white knighthood, big Canadian companies like Bell Canada, Canadian Pacific, and Power Corporation. All expressed some interest, particularly Bell, but there was concern about whether they would be able to move quickly enough. Part of the Saturday Night Special's rationale is its short time-fuse, which, like having a snub-nosed revolver shoved in one's face, tends to induce a certain sense of panic.

On Sunday, March 23, Hiram Walker got its board together for the first time since the Reichmanns' bid. The legal and investment advisors brought them up to speed on strategy. Legal roadblocks would be thrown in the Reichmanns' way while the search for a white knight continued. Walker's lawyers would appeal to the Toronto Stock Exchange (TSE) on the basis of technical deficiencies in the Gulf offer. The company would also take action against Gulf in U.S. District Court in Washington for alleged violation of U.S. federal securities laws. HWR had a number of U.S. subsidiaries and about 11 percent of its common shares were owned by U.S. residents. The basis of the suit would be the exclusion of U.S. investors.

On Monday, as an OPEC meeting broke up and oil prices slumped to new lows, a terse press release, dated Sunday, March 23, appeared from Hiram Walker. It declared that the company was "continuing its analysis and evaluation of all of the financial, regulatory and operational implications of the unsolicited Gulf Canada takeover bid for Hiram Walker shares. . . . The Board is expected to make a recommendation on the current offer to the shareholders within a week. At today's meeting, the Board unanimously authorized the management to take financial actions that will strengthen the Company's ability to enhance value for all its shareholders and to commence appropriate legal and regulatory actions to protect the vital best interest of Hiram Walker shareholders.''

One of the "financial actions" was the setting up of a war chest Walker's banks would be asked to arrange a $2.5 billion line of credit, the corporate world's equivalent of a little muscle-flexing before a fight.

There was speculation that O&Y was really after Home Oil, and perhaps Consumers' as well, and that it wanted to sell off the distilling business, but Paul Reichmann told the *Financial Post* Dunnery Best: "A year ago oil would have been the attraction with Hiram Walker. This time the attraction is diversification. When we made our initial evaluation of Gulf, we never looked at this oil price. We considered U.S.$18 (per barrel) as a minimum. Now there is a good possibility that the price will settle below that for a number of years. If the price settles below U.S.$15, or at U.S.$15 the returns will be meagre for a lengthy period. . . Gulf's cash flow will have to be invested to protect the company's reserve base. This is the reason for the bid: to bring other components into Gulf, where hopefully they will enable Gulf to be more patient in its investing.''

The statement that Gulf's cash flow would have to be "invested to protect the company's reserve base," if correctly quoted was financial gobbledygook. Nevertheless, Paul Reichmann had clearly implied that he was after Walker for the liquor.

Meanwhile, HWR's first roadblock was in the process of being knocked over. The TSE refused the company's attempt to halt Gulf's bid. Hiram Walker's lawyers appealed the decision to the Ontario Securities Commission (OSC), claiming that "the unusually complicated and interrelated offers to its large and geographically diverse shareholder body, make it very important the [Gulf] bid should be made through a 21-day circular bid. Alternatively the time of the offer through the exchanges should have been extended so that there is sufficient time for dissemination of information and proper consideration of the offers.''

Put another way: "The Reichmanns are trying to pull a Saturday Night Special and you should be stopping them.''

On that Monday, March 24, Hiram Walker shares, having hit a high for the day of $33.25 on speculation that a higher bid would be forthcoming, closed at their day's low of $32.25. Volume was heavy, with over 1 million shares changing hands. Gulf closed at

$16.75, up 12 cents. On the New York Stock Exchange, Hiram Walker closed at U.S.$23.25, down 25 cents, and Gulf was unchanged at U.S.$11.75.

On Tuesday, March 25, Hiram Walker's board met once again with its legal advisors at Walker's First Canadian Place offices. DSP had produced an evaluation of HWR of more than $40 a share. With this in hand they could now reject Gulf's offer as too low. The following day, Wednesday, March 26, the Hiram Walker board announced that it was unanimously recommending that shareholders reject O&Y's offer, which "significantly understates the value and does not reflect the prospects of Hiram Walker Resources."

"The acceptance of the Gulf Canada offer," it continued, "would transfer control of Hiram Walker to Gulf without enabling all shareholders to realize full value for all their shares. The board considers the bid to be a coercive attempt to pressure shareholders into a hasty decision to sell their Hiram Walker shares."

These were strong words. The Reichmanns had thought that Walker's resistance was little more than formality, but it was becoming clear that it was something more.

Walker shares hit a high of $34.50 on the TSE, with volume of just over 2 million, the issue's largest daily total since listing in 1960. The market was now clearly expecting a bidding war. Trading included blocks of 441,000 at $32.87 and 142,100 at $34.12.

Walker's legal roadblocks, in the meantime, continued to fall. Their U.S. case was dismissed in Washington and, on Thursday, March 27, the OSC threw out their appeal seeking more time to find an alternative to the Reichmann bid. Frenzied trading in Hiram Walker shares continued as volume hit yet another historic high of 2.1 million shares, including a block of 1 million shares at $33.25. It was clear that the arbitrageurs were wading into the action. Ivan Boesky, Wall Street's biggest and sharpest-toothed arbitrageur, who had in the past pulled off as much as $100 million from individual takeover battles, would, over the next few weeks, lead a group of speculators in accumulating more than 7 percent of Walker's equity at a cost of more than $200 million. He would make his usual killing.

After ten days, going into the 1986 Easter weekend, the contest had still only consisted of minor skirmishes. The Reichmanns still didn't believe they were *in* a real battle. However, behind the scenes, both sides were preparing to unleash surprises. The

Reichmanns, for once, would find themselves at least temporaril
upstaged.

Knight Under Siege

A few days after the Reichmanns' bid, Cliff Hatch, Jr., received
call in his Windsor office from Sir Derrick Holden-Brown, the head
of a British company, Allied-Lyons, with which Walker had some
joint liquor interests. Holden-Brown told Hatch that if Hiram
Walker was interested in selling off its liquor operations, he would
be a very willing buyer.

Allied, which had sales of almost $7 billion in 1985, was a world
scale producer and distributor of food products and drinks. The
company had been formed in 1978 from the amalgamation o
Allied Breweries with J. Lyons & Co., the British company famou
for its tea houses. It operated 7,000 British pubs, 950 liquor stores
or "off licences" as they are called in Britain, and 46 hotels. World
wide, the company had 71,000 employees, and its products
included Tetley Tea, Baskin-Robbins Ice Cream, Harvey's Sher
ries, Double Diamond beer, and Lamb's Navy Rum.

Walker and Allied knew each other well at both the corporate
and personal level. Holden-Brown had known Cliff Hatch, Sr., for
forty years. Allied represented many of Hiram Walker's best
known brands in the U.K., such as Courvoisier, Tia Maria, and
Canadian Club. Allied was also a 49 percent partner in the
Toronto-based wines and spirits distributor, the William Mara
Company, the other 51 percent of which was controlled by Corby
Distillers, which was in turn 52 percent owned by Hiram Walker

Allied had other Canadian interests. It had a cereal mix subsid
iary, DCA Canada Inc., with annual sales of $30 million. And i
had 200 Baskin-Robbins ice cream outlets operated by a franchisee
Silcorp Limited. Hiram Walker and Allied also considered them
selves similar kinds of companies: old, established, decent. They
understood each other. Sir Derrick had at one time even been
trainee with Hiram Walker. He, like Cliff Hatch, Sr., was a navy
man, and had served in the Canadian flotilla in the Mediterranean
during the war.

Although Sir Derrick Holden-Brown strongly denied such asser
tions, a takeover of Hiram Walker's liquor operations would also
serve another purpose: it would make his own organization too
big to swallow. For Allied, too, had recently come under the gaze

of acquisitors who were less than welcome; in particular the Australian company, Elders IXL Ltd., a brewing, agricultural, and consumer products conglomerate. Elders, although it was only one-quarter of Allied's size, had made a $3.7 billion offer for control of the British food and booze giant.

At the time of the bid, in the fall of 1985, Britain was in the grip of "merger mania." Around thirty of the companies listed on the *Financial Times* Stock Exchange 100 Index had either officially or unofficially received takeover offers. Allied had no desire to be one of the statistics.

Elders' head and the man who had built the company, John Elliott, was a rough-talking, rugged-featured corporate brawler who was nevertheless well versed in the intricacies of convoluted, smoke-and-mirror financing. Nicknamed "the Thug" in Australian business circles, Elliott was not at all Sir Derrick's cup of Tetley's.

When Sir Derrick had heard of the bid, he had demanded that Elliott present himself at Allied's City of London headquarters to explain his intentions. When Elliott had the temerity to suggest that he might be going for control of Allied, Holden-Brown didn't even show him the door. He had his secretary do it.

But Sir Derrick had some very valid reasons to be concerned about the Elders' bid, quite apart from the distasteful prospect of uncouth antipodeans gaining control of yet another of Britain's leading companies (Elders' best-known international product was Foster's Lager. Foster's ads in Britain and North America all *rejoiced* in how uncouth the Aussies were!). Elders' bid was to be financed with short-term borrowings, so that, if it was successful, Allied feared that large chunks of the company would inevitably have to be sold off to pay down the debt. Hence the bid had been referred by the Office of Fair Trading, at Allied's request, to British takeover watchdog the Monopolies & Mergers Commission, before which its merits were still being decided. At one point Elders had accumulated 6 percent of Allied-Lyons' equity, but around the end of February, 1986, they had sold out at a gross profit of around $60 million. Nevertheless, Elliott claimed that he wanted to make another bid. The fight had turned nasty. Elders had waged what Allied considered a below-the-belt, personal, press campaign against Sir Derrick and his management.

When Holden-Brown called Hatch, Hatch told him to speak to Bud Downing in Toronto. He did so, and Downing thanked him for his interest and in turn put him in touch with Morgan Guaranty's Mendoza. In these situations, all negotiations with suitors take place via the investment advisors. The reasoning is that you never want to have your principals in a room together where they might be forced into making a firm commitment. It is courting at long distance.

Hiram Walker's initial attitude toward Allied was that it was always good to have prospective buyers lined up, but they didn't want to split up the company. A sale of the liquor business was almost inconceivable to both Hatch Jr. and Downing. They wanted to find a buyer, preferably a Canadian one, who would be prepared to bid for everything.

One potential strategy suggested by Walker's U.S. advisors was a "self-tender" or "issuer bid" whereby Hiram Walker would play its own white knight, making an offer for its own shares superior to that of the Reichmanns. But there were potential tax problems. If a company makes a bid for its own shares, any capital gain in the hands of the shareholders is treated as a dividend, with adverse tax consequences. So then the legal wizards toyed with the idea of making the bid through a subsidiary. That, too, ran into problems because a subsidiary is not allowed to hold shares of its parent. So then they came up with the idea of a friendly third party making the bid. In fact, why didn't they *create* a friendly third party, in which HWR could own 48 percent, meaning that it wasn't a legal subsidiary? Hence a company called Fingas was born. The choosing of the name Fingas was perhaps a stroke of black humour. Although it was not the same company, Fingas had been the name of the Consumers' Gas subsidiary through which Ted Creber had executed the dealings that had led to his sudden ejection from the Consumers' chief executive position.

When the Reichmanns and Interprovincial found out about the manoeuvre, they thought there was more than a passing similarity between the transactions of the two Fingases: they were both blatant instruments to further the interests of the management. Hiram Walker didn't see it that way. Fingas was being created simply to make an offer superior to that of the Reichmanns. This would force the Reichmanns either to make a higher bid, or to go away. If they made another offer, this would also allow more time for white knights to get their acts together and make still higher offers. That was in the shareholders' best interests. The question was: where did the money for Fingas to buy Hiram Walker shares come from? The $2.5 billion line of credit was one possibility, but to borrow the money to buy out the shares would simply cripple the company financially. The other alternative was to sell something.

Hiram Walker management had never wanted to sell the company piecemeal, but the white knights were slow to saddle up. Bell Canada had expressed strong interest in acting via TransCanada PipeLines, the giant natural gas pipeline utility that it controlled, but TransCanada was interested primarily in Home Oil. It wasn't interested in the liquor.

Suddenly it all clicked into place: if HWR could sell the liquor business, then the money could be earmarked to fund an alternative offer for Hiram Walker's own shares via Fingas. But also, a sale agreement for the liquor subsidiary would make Hiram Walker *more* attractive to a suitor like TransCanada, since the problem of disposing of the liquor interests would have been solved already. Meanwhile, if sale of the liquor business did not drive the Reichmanns away, the cash from the sale of the liquor would force them to make a higher bid.

Hiram Walker's management and advisors still thought, despite Paul Reichmann's statements, that he was after Home Oil. They believed the Reichmanns' strategy was based on the fact that HWR's liquor assets were undervalued, and that he planned to acquire HWR cheaply, spin off the liquor for a hefty profit, perhaps also sell the stakes in Consumers' and Interprovincial, and wind up with Home Oil for nothing. The liquor sale/Fingas strategy would prevent such a daylight robbery. All they needed now was a *partial* white knight to take the liquor business. Senator Leo Kolber, representing the Seagram Bronfmans, had approached Bud Downing about buying the liquor operations. However, for Downing and the other executives who had come up through that side of the business, nothing would be more distasteful than selling to their arch rivals. Seagram's corporate ethos was quite different from that of Hiram Walker/Gooderham & Worts, and Windsor wanted no part of it. Fortunately, there was another company prepared to pay more than Seagram, and it was run by a real knight to boot: Allied-Lyons.

17
NO MORE
MR. NICE GUY

*It became clear that if it was a choice between
preserving his non-hostile, non-litigious image
and winning, Paul Reichmann would go for the win.*

Peter Rosewell, the jovial finance director of the wines and
spirits division of Allied-Lyons, was in his office in Allied
House in the City of London on Wednesday, March 26,
when he was given a portfolio of material on Hiram Walker's
liquor division and told to come up with a rough valuation by five
o'clock. The material had been sent across the Atlantic by Morgan
Guaranty. Rosewell beavered through the day, worked out a figure, and showed it to Allied's main finance director, John Clemes.
Clemes agreed with it and it was given to Allied's investment
advisors from the old merchant bank of Baring Brothers to check.
Part of the ongoing activities of a large company like Allied is to
keep a check on the values and market valuations of companies in
similar businesses, so Rosewell, Clemes, and the merchant bankers were pretty sure of their estimates.

Morgan's Roberto Mendoza had been instructed to get a formal
offer from Allied. Clemes spoke to Mendoza that night and
affirmed Allied's interest in Hiram Walker's liquor business. He
suggested that they might come over after the Easter weekend.
Mendoza told him that if he was really interested, he'd better get
over right away. The Reichmann fuse was ticking.

Peter Rosewell had to drive 125 miles down to his home just outside the picturesque town of Yeovil, Somerset, to get his passport and a change of clothes and dash back in time to meet Clemes and Michael Jackaman, the wines and spirits division's chairman and chief executive, in time to catch the Thursday morning flight to Toronto. By this time, Allied had lined up its New York investment advisors, Shearson Lehman, as well as its U.S. counsel, the Wall Street firm of Wilkie Farr & Gallagher, to go to work on the case. The Shearson banker most deeply involved, Robert Hill, was another Wall Street whiz. He already knew Mendoza well, which aided the smoothness of the subsequent negotiations. Jack Nussbaum carried the ball for Wilkie Farr. Allied's Toronto lawyers were Fasken & Calvin, with whom they had also had a long-term relationship.

The jet-lagged Brits spent the next few days in a swirl of meetings at the offices of Hiram Walker, Dominion Securities Pitfield, McCarthy & McCarthy, Fasken & Calvin, and Morgan Guaranty. They hammered out a purchase price for the liquor business of $2.6 billion, a figure with which Walker was well pleased. For Allied, the most unusual part of the deal was Fingas, the entity set up to make the offer to Hiram Walker shareholders. The plan was for Fingas to offer $40 a share for half Hiram Walker's shares, which HWR management believed was clearly superior to the Reichmanns' bid.

On Easter Saturday afternoon, March 29, the men from Allied, along with Shearson's Hill and Wilkie Farr's Nussbaum, met with Hiram Walker's representatives from McCarthy & McCarthy to have Fingas explained to them. They were asked to participate in Fingas. They said they'd have to think about it. The McCarthy guys thought they sounded pretty unenthusiastic. Everybody went home. Then at ten o'clock that same night, the Allied negotiators got back in touch with the men from McCarthy & McCarthy and they agreed to meet again at 11 P.M. By 1 A.M., they had hammered out the basis of an agreement. Allied would participate in Fingas to the tune of $200 million, provided that the money could be counted as a down payment on Walker's liquor business. Fingas's voting shares would be held 49 percent by Hiram Walker, 29 percent by Allied-Lyons, and 11 percent by two Hiram Walker associates who had offered their help, former HWR director Noah Torno and market research wizard Martin Goldfarb, who had done a great deal of work for Hiram Walker over the years. They were required to put up $11 each for their interest. (For their participation, and in Goldfarb's case for other services, Torno and Goldfarb received fees of $25,000 and $75,000 respectively. The Reichmann camp would later cite these fees as evidence that the two men were far from independent. Thus, they would claim, Fingas *was* a subsidiary and the proposed transaction illegal.)

Allied's Peter Rosewell gave up the ghost at 3 A.M. to go back to the Four Seasons and collapse, but the lawyers — McCarthy & McCarthy's Peter Beattie, Bob Forbes, and Gary Girvan, and a team from Fasken & Calvin led by J. Michael Robinson — spent all night drafting documents, finishing around 7 A.M. on Easter Sunday morning. Gary Girvan went home to grab three hours' sleep and returned to go over those drafts and then oversee the documentation of the sale of the liquor business to Allied. This began at noon on Sunday. Girvan finished the drafting at 8 A.M. on Easter Monday morning, just in time to turn up in jeans for the 9 A.M. Hiram Walker board meeting sporting a two-day growth of beard.

Sir Derrick Holden-Brown, having jetted over from the U.K. via the Concorde to New York the previous day, attended the directors' meeting to present the case for Allied's acquisition of the liquor business. It was an emotional meeting for many of those present, who realized that the sale of the liquor operation was the sale of Hiram Walker's heart. It was particularly sad for Bud Downing. He believed that he was doing his duty to the shareholders, but Hiram Walker Resources would never be the same. The board duly approved the sale of its heart to Allied-Lyons.

Interprovincial Changes Sides

During the two nights of work over the Easter weekend, much of it in First Canadian Place, somebody joked that he hoped the Reichmanns wouldn't turn the lights out. But the Reichmanns' lawyers had been doing a lot of work themselves, although not, of course, between sundown on Friday and sundown on Saturday, the Jewish Sabbath. But as soon as the Saturday sun went down, they really went to it.

There was a little irony in that the key players in the battle were all occupants of the same building. The thirty-second floor, where the Reichmanns had their tastefully postmodern executive offices, was seeking control of the sixth floor, where the more traditionally sombre wood-panelling of Hiram Walker's head office was located. But going into the Easter weekend, one big question was what the thirty-seventh floor, where Interprovincial had its headquarters, thought. One thing was for sure, the sixth floor wasn't talking to them.

When the Gulf bid was announced, HWR management had immediately cast Interprovincial in the role of bad guys. The Walker men believed Interprovincial had *promoted* the bid by talking to the Reichmanns. They had to take that stance. The only other alternative was that the Reichmanns had, as Bob Heule had warned them, been coming all the time. In that case they looked pretty stupid.

As for the Interprovincial management, they felt with some justification that they didn't owe too much to Hiram Walker. They had offered help and it had been rejected. Now it was every man for himself, and their own shareholders came first. Of course, the irony was that the largest of those was Hiram Walker. So Heule was still a confused man.

Heule did not speak to Bud Downing for several days after the bid, which Hiram Walker took as further evidence that he had gone over to the Reichmann camp. Heule had a reason for not speaking to Downing, but one that would hardly make Walker's chief executive any happier: Interprovincial was considering whether to tender into the bid or sell its shares in the market. If it decided to sell in the market, Heule claimed that he wanted to avoid any conversations with Downing that could brand him as an "insider." Interprovincial's evaluation of Walker was in fact not much more than the market price, so they looked very carefully at selling out. But then Interprovincial decided against that option and Heule eventually spoke to Downing. Once again, he offered his services to Hiram Walker. Once again they were turned down.

Downing was by now convinced that Interprovincial had been the cause of the Reichmann bid. He even suspected that they may have been fifth columnists. He was antagonistic toward Heule. Where had Heule been? Why hadn't he spoken to him before? He told Heule that if he had any proposals he should speak to Walker's investment advisors.

For Heule, the worst position would be as part of neither camp. Time was running out. Heule went back to Downing again and explained that Interprovincial had made no commitments; they were available as allies. But Downing was again cool. Interprovincial was now fixed in Hiram Walker management's mind as one of the enemy. And besides, Hiram Walker didn't need them. They had their own plan, and it would teach Interprovincial a lesson. Heule came away with the idea that HWR had no clear plan of defence. Certainly, Bud Downing's actions to date had given Interprovincial no convincing reason to believe that he would be able to defend Hiram Walker against the Reichmanns' assault, and then Interprovincial would be left twisting in the wind.

A number of third parties, including TransCanada PipeLines, had approached Interprovincial, but Heule had refused to talk to TransCanada's chairman and chief executive Gerry Maier. He correctly inferred that TransCanada would only be calling to solicit Interprovincial's help in an alternative bid for Hiram Walker. In the end, Interprovincial decided that it had only one option. The ultimate irony was to be played out. One of the main bastions of Hiram Walker's defence, because of a disastrous breakdown in communications, felt compelled to turn its guns on the company it was meant to defend. Downing's belief that Interprovincial was in bed with O&Y became a self-fulfilling prophecy: Bob Heule called Paul Reichmann.

Heule went down to Paul Reichmann's office on the thirty-second floor and told him that he was prepared to work with him. Reichmann asked him what he had in mind. Heule said he wanted Home Oil. Reichmann said they should talk, but he and O&Y's legal advisors would point out that it would be very difficult to give Interprovincial special treatment or make a deal on Home Oil. Securities authorities wouldn't like that. But there was another reason why Paul Reichmann knew there was no particular reason to give too much away to Interprovincial: he knew he had them in the bag.

That Easter weekend, the two sides met. There was an informal Interprovincial board meeting on the Saturday, to which the Hiram Walker directors on Interprovincial's board were not invited, and agreement was finally reached on Easter Sunday.

Under the agreement between the Reichmanns and Interprovincial, Interprovincial would not tender its Hiram Walker shares into a new, marginally better, Gulf bid. In return, Gulf would extend its offer and make a follow-up to all the minority shareholders, including Interprovincial, so that all shareholders had the option of getting out for a mixture of cash and "paper," just as in the Gulf Canada plan of arrangement. There would also be an option for Interprovincial to take control of Home Oil.

HWR shareholders would have the option of getting out for cash and cash-equivalent equal to the highest bid price, or taking an interest in the combined Walker-Gulf, or — which was what Interprovincial had always been after — taking equity in Hiram Walker's oil interests, that is, Home Oil. If a higher bid came along from a third party, Interprovincial was free to tender into it.

Many observers subsequently asked why Interprovincial had jumped into bed with the Reichmanns before Hiram Walker's management had had a chance to respond to the Reichmann bid. Many believed that there had to be some other, secret *quid pro quo* that the Reichmanns had offered Interprovincial. But there was no secret *quid pro quo*. Interprovincial simply thought that Hiram Walker's management had rocks in their head. What chance did they have against the Reichmanns, the mythical men with the bottomless pockets? The Reichmanns always got what they wanted, and now they wanted Hiram Walker. Interprovincial had already decided that was a *fait accompli*. There was no way Bud Downing was going to stop them. Interprovincial's agreement with the Reichmanns was made "subject to board approval." The next board meeting was due for Tuesday, April 1. The meeting would turn out to be far from the usual solemn and sometimes somnolent convocation of directors.

During all these meetings and machinations, there was one other key player waiting in the wings. TransCanada PipeLines was Hiram Walker's ideal suitor; big and Canadian. But TransCanada was still deciding whether to strap on its armour and whether it should reach for the white or the black set.

TransCanada: To Bid or Not to Bid

TransCanada was having a board meeting in Calgary on March 19. Toward the end of the meeting, a message was handed to TransCanada's chairman and chief executive, Gerry Maier, informing him of the Reichmanns' bid for Hiram Walker. The news was of more than passing interest to Maier, for he was both acquainted with Paul Reichmann and more than a little interested in Hiram Walker, or at least parts of it.

Utilities — the big companies that deliver basic services or products under government regulation — are often considered somewhat dull. Boardroom developments at Interprovincial in recent months had certainly belied that stereotype. For TransCanada, Interprovincial's natural gas equivalent, which carried Alberta gas to its main Central Canadian and export markets, nothing could have been further from the truth. Its entire history had been a corporate soap opera. The federal Liberals' forcing through Parliament of a bill to provide government financing for part of the line in 1956 caused almost unprecedented political furor. The following year, the Liberals were thrown out of office after twenty-two years in power. According to one survey, almost 40 percent of the voters who abandoned the Liberals claimed they did so because of the government's high-handed performance during the pipeline debate.

Subsequently, TransCanada, or "Traps" as it is known on Canadian stock markets, became much more than a mere pipeline; it became a focus of Western Canadian political resentment, a powerful symbol of Central Canada's alleged rape of the West. It was seen as the means by which Alberta's natural gas heritage was taken at rock-bottom prices to feed the pampered industries of Ontario and Quebec.

This resentment was exacerbated by the fact that the controlling block of TransCanada was for many years held by Canadian Pacific Investments, the investment subsidiary of Canadian Pacific, perhaps the ultimate corporate focus of discontent for Westerners. The classic, but pointed story was of the Prairie farmer standing beneath a crop-destroying thunderstorm, shaking his fist at the sky, and shouting "Goddamn the CPR!"

Corporate drama had rocked TransCanada's executive suite in Toronto's Commerce Court West many times in the preceding decade. The world's largest pipeline company had seen control change twice, had been dragged into a Canada-wide game of political chess over gas pipeline development, had been sucked into the corporate whirlwind — and then corporate disaster — of Dome Petroleum, and had most recently been shaken by controversy over chief executive Radcliffe Latimer, who left the company in 1985 following a flurry of poison pen letters about his high corporate lifestyle.

Maier, the man who took over from Latimer, had seen his own share of corporate drama. A tough, former hockey-playing farmboy from Saskatchewan, Maier had, in 1980, been the first Canadian to be appointed both chairman and chief executive of Hudson's Bay Oil & Gas (HBOG), then a rock-solid company with extensive landholdings and high-quality oil and gas production. Within little more than a year, his corporate world fell apart as HBOG was taken over by Dome Petroleum. The takeover, funded with $4 billion of bank funds, destroyed HBOG and crippled Dome. It also led to the fall of HBOG's U.S. parent, Conoco.

It was while searching for his own white knight to rescue HBOG during Dome's initial assault that Maier had first approached Paul Reichmann. Reichmann had looked seriously at making an alternative bid, but Dome quickly won its Pyrrhic victory. Maier had then moved from HBOG to take over as chief executive at Bow Valley Industries, in which, of course, the Reichmanns held a significant stake. Thenceforth, Reichmann would call Maier from time to time to consult him on oil and gas matters, such as the value of Gulf Canada. Maier, if he was visiting Toronto, would pop into O&Y's offices to chat with Paul. Maier knew the Reichmanns were potential candidates to acquire control of Bow Valley from its founders, the Seaman brothers, but when the Cemp Bronfmans refused to sell their stake to the Reichmanns, O&Y sold out.

In 1985, once Rad Latimer had pulled his "golden parachute" from TransCanada's headquarters, Maier was offered, and accepted, the top job at the pipeline. TransCanada had some financial problems with gas contracts, but it also had enormous financial clout. It had reported a 1985 profit of $278.1 million on revenues of $4.7 billion. It also had the financial strength of its controlling shareholder, Bell Canada Enterprises, the Montreal-based telecommunications giant with more than $13 billion of assets, behind it (Bell Canada's control bid had been masterminded, yet again, by the ubiquitous Gordon Capital). Part of Maier's Bell-blessed mandate when he joined the company was to expand its activities in the oil and gas business, which already accounted for $1.8 billion of its $6.3 billion in assets. Hiram Walker's subsidiary Home Oil was attractive to Maier not merely for its solid assets. Dick Haskayne, the head of Home, had been president to Maier's chairman back at HBOG, and the two men held a great reciprocal respect and admiration. So when Maier was handed that piece of paper on March 19, 1986, telling him of the Reichmanns' bid for Hiram Walker, his mind clicked into overdrive.

Maier made a brief announcement to the TransCanada board and told them he would be getting a task force together as soon as possible to look at TransCanada's options. He called Trans-Canada's investment advisors, Nesbitt Thomson Bongard in Toronto and Salomon Brothers in New York, and told them to get to work. They began to evaluate all of Hiram Walker, but Maier told them their principal target was Home Oil. He considered keeping the stake in Interprovincial, but that was secondary. They began to look at how they might sell off the different pieces of HWR — in particular the liquor business — and at what kinds of corporate structure might have to be created to maximize the value of the acquisition. A key aspect of this process was seeing how they might minimize taxes. Another was an assessment of risks involved in selling off parts of the business. For example, they spoke to representatives of Seagram but realized that there were potential U.S. federal antitrust problems. They were not aware of Allied's interest but realized that a foreign bidder might have trouble with FIRA.

Maier called Bud Downing and went over to Hiram Walker for a meeting during the first week after the bid. He told Downing, McCallum, and other Walker management of the priority of TransCanada's interests: that they had no interest in the liquor or Consumers', and that if the management and directors wanted to think about a leveraged buyout of those assets, then TransCanada would be open to suggestions.

Maier was most concerned to hear if they were amenable to an offer. He said that he did not want to make a hostile bid. The Hiram Walker management sounded friendly. Short-term financing was lined up for TransCanada via the Royal Bank.

By the Easter weekend, TransCanada had a pretty good handle on Hiram Walker's overall value and the parts of the company that it wanted. Home Oil was the main target; Interprovincial was a subsidiary one; Consumers' Gas would be sold off. The main problem was the liquor business, which TransCanada and its advisors had the most trouble evaluating.

Of course, the other obvious person to talk to about acquiring Home was Paul Reichmann. Maier was brought together with O&Y by a remarkable piece of serendipity. He was out jogging the streets of Toronto's plush Rosedale neighbourhood on Easter Sunday when whom should he meet jogging the other way but Mickey Cohen! Cohen said "How about a deal?" Maier said, "Sure," and not long after he got home, Maier received a call from Paul Reichmann inviting him down to First Canadian Place for a discussion.

The two sides talked in general terms about how HWR might be split up, and if so who should make the offer. Maier pointed out that his main interest was Home, and that he was also interested in Interprovincial. Reichmann pointed out that his main interest was the liquor. There seemed to be room for accommodation. But what Maier didn't know was that the Reichmanns were simultaneously — not just in the same building but in the same offices — negotiating with Interprovincial, which wanted Home too. Interprovincial was none too keen to have another pipeline giant as their major shareholder. Maier had phoned Interprovincial's Heule shortly after the bid, but Heule had refused to talk to him. But then of course Heule hadn't been talking to anyone.

Gerry Maier knew that there was no opposition from Imperial Oil to his bidding for Hiram Walker because he had already checked this out with Bob Peterson, Imperial's executive vice-president/chief operating officer, and then Arden Haynes, Imperial's chairman. The oil giant had no problems with TransCanada taking over Walker's stake in Interprovincial. Maier stressed to them that TransCanada could be a good shareholder for Interprovincial and help it achieve some of its oil and gas objectives. He even suggested that TransCanada might be happy to take merely a larger share of Home, along with its management and its technology, and that a minority share might be available for Interprovincial.

Easter Monday Surprises

Paul Reichmann professed not to understand the apparent hostility of Hiram Walker's management. It never occurred to him that it might look as if he was attempting to steal the company from them and their shareholders. His bid wasn't a Saturday Night Special in his mind. He had repeatedly claimed that he would never become involved in a hostile takeover. But it now became clear that there was an unexpected reasoning behind that stance: when Paul Reichmann decided to take you over, there was just no point in hostility. After all, you were bound to lose. Why fight it? Reichmann had clearly convinced Interprovincial Pipe Line of that.

Over the Easter weekend and on Monday, March 31, Paul Reichmann called several Hiram Walker directors, including Allen Lambert and Bill Wilder, to find out why Walker wasn't rolling over and accepting its fate. Reichmann told them he had thought that the whole thing would be more friendly. The message he received once more was that his offer was too low and that the responsibility of the board was to get the best price for shareholders. He told Allen Lambert that there was ''a little change'' possible in the $32 price. Lambert believed, as he later submitted in an affidavit to the Ontario Supreme Court, that ''there was no indication that any material movement in that price was available.'' Anybody who knew Paul Reichmann's track record knew that he gave nothing away in business negotiations, so his stance was not out of character. Bill Wilder told Reichmann that he should sit down and talk with Bud Downing, Walker's chief executive. Astonishingly, this was not an alternative that Reichmann appeared to have considered before. Perhaps he expected that Bud Downing should by this time have approached him in order to negotiate a peaceful transition of control.

Lambert came away from his telephone conversation with Reichmann with the impression that O&Y was not prepared to offer much more for Hiram Walker. Reichmann, however, imagined that Lambert would carry the message of his willingness to negotiate with Hiram Walker management back to the board, and that they would then, as was only reasonable in Paul Reichmann's mind, sit down with him and sort out terms of surrender. It was not so much that wires were badly crossed as that Reichmann perhaps simply continued to misunderstand the motivations and priorities of Hiram Walker's board. The Reichmanns continued to have a big gap in their knowledge about the implications of having public shareholders, which may well have been the result of operating so long as a privately owned company. Public shareholders implied public accountability. But the Reichmanns still seemed to feel that merely having themselves as the majority shareholders in a company should be all the reassurance that minority shareholders needed.

They had always done their deals in private. Public display was painful to them. Business was something done with senior executives behind closed doors. The media was a nuisance, but it had its purpose, and Paul Reichmann had always used it brilliantly to paint a deft picture of his upright stature and his good intentions.

Most often he used it to clarify what he regarded as public misperceptions. Back in 1982, when rumours had swirled about O&Y being in potential financial trouble, the man who had always declared O&Y's finances to be totally off limits, had "allowed" that the business's net worth might be $5 billion. Despite no independent form of corroboration, the press had printed that figure.

Now, Reichmann told the *Financial Post* that it was really the liquor business that he was after in Hiram Walker rather than oil and gas. Astonishingly, he hadn't clarified his intentions to Hiram Walker.

On Easter Monday, the Reichmanns and Hiram Walker had surprises for each other, and for Gerry Maier. Gulf Canada issued a press release with details of an expanded offer. Gulf's new bid was not at a higher price, but it now embraced all the shares. It would extend its $32 offer from 26 million to 40 million shares, and the remaining shares would be offered a plan of arrangement at a later date. Gulf also announced that Interprovincial had joined the Reichmann camp.

That same day, Hiram Walker dropped its bombshell. Having failed to find a white knight, the company would effectively become its own dashing rescuer. It had lined up Allied-Lyons to pay for $2.6 billion worth of armour. The armour would be forged into a corporate form called Fingas, which would buy up around half of Hiram Walker's shares for $40 a share. Of Fingas's total capital of $2.2 billion, Hiram Walker would provide $2 billion and Allied-Lyons $200 million, the latter amount effectively representing a down payment on the $2.6 billion distilling purchase. Hiram Walker's $2 billion would be used to make the bid.

Both announcements were a surprise to Maier. The first, that the Reichmanns had made an agreement with Interprovincial even as they had been talking to him, was not good news, because Interprovincial wanted the same Hiram Walker asset that he did, Home Oil. But the second surprise, the announcement of the Allied-Fingas deal, was much more promising. If Allied was prepared to pay $2.6 billion for the liquor business, then it would be easy to come to an accommodation with them. TransCanada could make a bid for the whole company and then sell the liquor to Allied. Maier wished he had known about Allied. He felt he could have made an even better deal with them, tax-wise, if they had got together before.

Hiram Walker's management, it seemed, was committing the

ultimate act of managerial dedication to shareholders (although they had arranged multi-million-dollar employment contracts, "golden parachutes," for themselves to ease the bump). They had begun the process of corporate self-liquidation; managerial hari-kari.

Hiram Walker's official release declared: "The Board unanimously and strongly recommends that Hiram Walker shareholders reject" Gulf Canada's "partial offer," which "significantly undervalues Hiram Walker and would transfer control of the Company to Gulf Canada without enabling current shareholders to realize the full value for Hiram Walker shares.

"Hiram Walker's Board and management are committed to maximizing the value of Hiram Walker to its current shareholders. The Hiram Walker program is designed to do exactly that and in an orderly fashion."

Faced with the Hiram Walker announcement about the Allied deal, Gulf simply announced that it was postponing its bid, which had been due to close on April 4. Now Interprovincial and O&Y, which, after all, between them still owned 25.7 percent of Hiram Walker, found themselves in the hot seat. And they were mad.

The first real skirmish between the opposing sides took place at Interprovincial's board meeting on April 1, the one that was meant to vote on Interprovincial's plan to join the Reichmanns. All four Hiram Walker directors — Bud Downing, Archie McCallum, Dick Haskayne, and Doug Gardiner — turned up. Heule asked them to leave because they had an obvious conflict of interest. They refused and called Hiram Walker's lawyer Peter Beattie over from McCarthy & McCarthy. Interprovincial meanwhile called up their man Fred Huycke from his office at Osler Hoskin & Harcourt a few floors below at First Canadian Place. The Walker directors were finally persuaded to depart, but they did not go without some hard words being spoken. Meanwhile, Interprovincial's other directors felt that *they* were the ones who should have been annoyed. Hiram Walker's management had been warned about the Reichmanns, and they had done nothing. They had been offered help by Interprovincial, and they had rejected it. There had never been an Interprovincial board meeting like it.

The Reichmanns meanwhile were even madder. They were intensely annoyed at Hiram Walker's unwillingness to meet its fate. The one thing O&Y and its advisors had never considered was that Hiram Walker would sell its liquor operations. They knew only too well that the defence of Walker's Windsor-based corporate heart had been the key element of corporate strategy since 1979. Hiram Walker's management wasn't playing its preassigned role at all. And if Hiram Walker was going to abandon the script, then the Reichmanns were going to have to abandon the role they had so carefully nurtured for themselves, too.

Paul Reichmann had declared that he would never engage in a hostile bid and had then pulled the Saturday Night Special on Hiram Walker. He had also claimed how much he disliked using lawyers. A profile in the *Globe and Mail* in January, 1984, had declared: "He shies away from putting lawyers in charge because the distrusts 'the teaching of the legal profession, where the adversarial role is prevalent, where the assumption is that what the other side wants is probably not right.'"

But that stance was about to change in the biggest way possible. Paul Reichmann had already installed a lawyer, Mickey Cohen, as the head of O&Y's public interests. It became clear that if it was a choice between preserving his non-hostile, non-litigious image and winning, Paul Reichmann would go for the win. If the win had to come through the courts, so be it. If that's the way Hiram Walker wanted it, then the gloves would have to come off.

No more Mr. Nice Guy.

18

DAVID AND GOLIATH

*That must have been the unkindest cut of all:
Paul Reichmann compared with the giant
Philistine of Gath, scourge of the Hebrews.*

The reaction of the Reichmanns to the news of Hiram Walker's double whammy — the sale of the liquor business and the offer of $40 for 50 million Walker shares through Fingas — was swift. On Tuesday, April 1, weighty injunctions started arriving on the desks of Hiram Walker's directors. The Reichmanns, Gulf Canada, and Interprovincial Pipe Line were all involved in the legal attack on Walker. The injunctions sought to prevent both the sale of the liquor business and the creation of Fingas. On Wednesday, April 2, at the Supreme Court of Ontario on Toronto's University Avenue, the battle commenced. Both sides were represented by their traditional law firms, the heaviest corporate counsel that money could buy. The Reichmanns had Davies, Ward & Beck; Hiram Walker retained McCarthy & McCarthy; Interprovincial's case was put by Osler Hoskin & Harcourt.

The lawyers representing the Reichmann camp unleashed a two-pronged assault. On the one hand, they argued that the sale of the liquor assets could not be made without submission to Walker's shareholders; on the other, they claimed that the creation of Fingas was a mere sham whose main intention was to lock up control of the company in the hands of Hiram Walker management. This latter move in particular infuriated the Reichmann camp. If Fingas was successful in its bid for half of Hiram Walker's shares, the company would be invulnerable to hostile takeover.

Walker's lawyers refuted these charges strongly. To the first allegation they responded that shareholder approval was necessary only if "all or substantially all" of a company's assets were put on the block. The liquor assets were less than half of Walker's total. To the second charge, they said that Fingas had been created, not to entrench management control, but to provide a better tax deal for shareholders.

The Reichmann side produced affidavits from Mickey Cohen and its hired guns at Merrill Lynch accusing Hiram Walker management of acting in their own interests rather than those of the shareholders. The Walker side responded indignantly with its own affidavits and testimony that its only consideration had been to acquire the best value for its shareholders.

Some of the tactics used during the legal battle misfired. One that misfired in particular for the Reichmanns was a letter appended to Mickey Cohen's affidavit. The letter was from Seagram's chairman Edgar Bronfman to Bud Downing. In it, Bronfman expressed Seagram's "strong interest" in buying the liquor business from Walker. The letter was intended to establish that Walker management was acting cosily with Allied-Lyons to pursue its own interests, that is, locking up control via Fingas. But far more intriguing than the letter itself was how it had come to be in Mickey Cohen's hands. It could obviously only have come from the Bronfmans. This implied ongoing negotiations with the Seagram empire. For Hiram Walker's liquor division, nothing could have been more unpalatable than falling under the control of their rivals.

Bronfman's letter noted that "Despite our repeated requests to your representatives, you have thus far refused to make any such information available to us." Downing claimed in his own affidavit that he could not give Seagram information since it was a competitor. Moreover, Seagram's highest offer for the liquor business had been $2.1 billion. Although Bronfman had declared that, given appropriate information, he was likely to offer "substantially in excess" of other purchasers, his $2.1 billion figure was still well short of Allied-Lyons' $2.6 billion.

In the end, the Bronfman letter — and its implications of a Reichmann/Bronfman link — would do far more damage to the Reichmanns than it would to Hiram Walker.

Downing's affidavit declared that the Allied-Fingas deal was a good one for the shareholders, and certainly much better than that offered by the Reichmanns. It stressed that Allied's bid was at the high end of the evaluations of the liquor business carried out by Walker's advisors, and that both Dominion Securities Pitfield and Morgan Guaranty had "strongly recommended" that the board accept the offer. As for Fingas, the board had created the vehicle once again at the advice of its investment specialists because a direct bid for its own shares by Walker would have had adverse tax consequences for shareholders.

Downing pointed out that twelve of Walker's eighteen directors were independent, and he strongly refuted assertions by Cohen that they had acted for any other purpose than to maximize the value of their shareholders' investment.

Interprovincial attacked Hiram Walker on a different front. Walker was claiming that it did not have to take the sale of the liquor business to its shareholders because it did not represent the sale of "all or substantially all" of its assets. Interprovincial's president, Ted Courtnage, said that in fact the sale to Allied was part of a planned liquidation of the whole company. As proof, he pointed out that Walker's oil and gas subsidiary, Home Oil, had set up a "data room" in Calgary to provide information to prospective buyers. Those interested enough to front up $20,000 (just to weed out the window-shoppers) could have a look at Home's figures, provided, of course, they were not on the Reichmanns' side.

Hiram Walker refuted this by claiming that if the whole company was on the block, as it now obviously was, then interested buyers should have a chance to look at its assets.

On stock exchanges, meanwhile, frenzied activity in Walker shares continued. By Thursday, April 3, more than 40 million shares had been traded since the bidding war broke out, over 30 million in the week following Easter. All the shares involved in the Walker battle were experiencing hefty trading and price swings, including the 83 percent Hiram-Walker-owned Consumers' Gas. Interprovincial's shares meanwhile had risen $4 since the announcement of the takeover.

As the first week of the court battle came to a close, the Walker management's strategy produced its first desired effect: on Friday,

April 4, the Reichmanns increased their bid to $35 a share for all
Walker shares. The bid would be made jointly by Gulf and O&Y,
with Gulf paying for the first 60 million shares tendered (at a cost
of $2.1 billion), while O&Y would pay for the rest. However, the
amended offer would proceed only if the competing Fingas bid
was blocked by the courts or withdrawn. This upped the stakes
enormously. The Gulf/Reichmann bid was worth around $3 bil-
lion, plus the cost of taking out Interprovincial's stake.

Hiram Walker responded with a statement declaring that the
company "had been informed by means of a press release of an unsolicited conditional proposal, the nature of which is unclear . . ."

Action moved back to the Supreme Court of Ontario on the
Monday, April 7, when it was revealed that O&Y had rejected an
offer from Hiram Walker to wind up Fingas within a year if O&Y
dropped its litigation. The offer was clearly intended to show that
Hiram Walker management had not created Fingas to entrench
itself, as O&Y claimed.

Hiram Walker's shareholders looked on in confusion. The only
bid officially on the table was still Gulf's revised offer for 40 million
Hiram Walker shares at $32. The higher bid from Gulf and O&Y of
$35 for all the shares was subject to the Fingas bid — $40 for half the
shares — being blocked. The Fingas bid was held up in court by
O&Y's injunctions.

Meanwhile, in a filing with the Washington-based stock market
watchdog, the Securities and Exchange Commission (SEC), O&Y
said that, at the request of third parties, preliminary discussions had taken place about the possible sale of some of Hiram
Walker's non-Canadian liquor assets. Again, this revelation, like
the Bronfman letter, would prove extremely troublesome to the
Reichmanns.

The White Knight Appears

On Wednesday, April 9, Mr. Justice Robert Montgomery brought
down his findings. The injunctions sought by O&Y and Interprovincial were thrown out, and Montgomery delivered a devastating
rejection of the claims of the Reichmann camp. He came down
very hard on Cohen's suggestions of impropriety on the part of
Hiram Walker's directors. "The directors of Walker," said the
Judge, "acted throughout . . . entirely for proper purposes and

entirely in the best interests of Walker and for the purpose of maximizing the value to Walker shareholders of their investment. The fact that the directors of Walker have sought to maximize the value of the shareholders' interest by taking decisive action will, I believe, result in a market price for Walker shares, following the Fingas offer, higher than would be the case if the Gulf offer were successful."

But he did not stop with defending the motives of Hiram Walker. He went on to attack those of the acquisitors, the O&Y-Gulf-IPL side. ". . . this is a battle over money. Gulf and IPL want the company and its assets at the cheapest possible price. The [Hiram Walker] board wants the shareholders to get more . . . IPL feels prejudiced because IPL wants the bargain that is in sight and does not want the directors to keep it from IPL and provide it to all shareholders. The same may be said of Olympia & York."

For the Reichmanns, such words must have stung. They had always taken great care to appear scrupulously fair and upright in all their dealings. Now they were being portrayed as corporate purse-snatchers.

Montgomery had yet harder words. Referring to the legality of the creation of Fingas, he said, "When under attack the target does not have to sit idly by without defending itself. An earlier Goliath was dispatched with a sling shot. Fingas is neither a sham nor a puppet as suggested by the applicants."

That must have been the unkindest cut of all: Paul Reichmann compared with the giant Philistine of Gath, scourge of the Hebrews.

Montgomery continued: "Neither Olympia & York nor IPL can represent [Hiram Walker] shareholders. They are antagonistic to and totally opposed to the interests of other shareholders. The applicants cannot identify with the acquisitor [Gulf] and at the same time purport to represent the shareholders it seeks to vanquish." His conclusion was that the sale to Allied and the Fingas deal could go ahead. However, his findings appeared almost immediately academic.

All along it had been suggested that the Fingas part of the Allied-Fingas deal was in fact merely a delaying tactic. Judge Montgomery had cast the Walker board in the role of David vs. the Gulf-Reichmann Goliath, but the historical figure that Walker really wanted now finally appeared: the white knight. Trans-Canada PipeLines, armour glinting in the sun, finally rode up.

On the same day as the Ontario Supreme Court decision, April 9, the natural gas pipeline giant offered to buy all Hiram Walker's common and preferred shares for $36.50 in cash. The bid, at $4.1 billion, was the biggest in Canadian history. Bell Canada Enterprises, TransCanada's major shareholder, flexed its muscles on TransCanada's behalf by announcing that it would raise its stake in the pipeline to 53 percent from 48 percent by buying $200 million worth of TransCanada common shares to help finance the deal. The offer was subject to the condition that 50.1 percent of Walker's fully diluted common shares be tendered.

TransCanada declared that the sale of the distilling interests would go ahead, as planned, to Allied-Lyons. The controlling interest in Consumers' Gas would be sold off, while the 34 percent interest in Interprovincial Pipe Line might be increased. The TransCanada offer was conditional upon the withdrawal of the Fingas offer and also the agreement of Walker's directors.

There was one controversial aspect to Maier's bid that was not revealed at the time. Hiram Walker agreed to pay TransCanada $10 million if its offer was unsuccessful. That hardly fit the chivalrous image, but Maier knew that he was getting into a potentially messy situation, and one that would have considerable costs in terms of legal and investment advice. From Walker's point of view, the $10 million could be considered well spent. Of course it made it clear that, as usual, there was really a mercenary inside the armour. But the Walker board was paying 10 cents a share to hoist the bid price $1.50 above the Reichmanns' most recent, conditional offer. The shareholders could have no complaints about that.

Twisting the Knife

One further corporate event took place on April 9 that was significant in terms of the hostility engendered by the battle. It occurred at Interprovincial's annual meeting. Interprovincial's chairman, Bob Heule, felt a little uncomfortable at the turn of events. He was free to tender to TransCanada under his agreement with the Reichmanns. But he would also have been free to do so if he had never made the agreement. His agreement was still the subject of intense antagonism from Hiram Walker's management and board. Although HWR now had its higher bid, its management seemed determined to twist the knife into Heule. Roberto Mendoza from

Morgan Guaranty was dispatched to the Interprovincial meeting with one mandate: to make a monkey out of Heule.

The meeting followed its usual course of prearranged nominations and elections. Heule told shareholders that Interprovincial would consider both the TransCanada bid and that from Gulf/O&Y. However, he was unequivocal in rejecting Hiram Walker's alternative bid through Fingas. He reiterated that the attraction of the Reichmann bid was that it would give Interprovincial an option to exchange its Walker shares for an equity position in Home Oil. But he made the mistake of suggesting that Interprovincial had done a deal on the basis of an offer from the Reichmanns of $35 a share when the deal was done with the offer at $32. Mendoza rose from the audience and proceeded verbally to tear Heule to pieces.

Heule had no idea who Mendoza was, but the New York banker peppered the slow-talking engineer with questions about his actions. Heule became tongue-tied and had to call up lawyer Fred Huycke for help. The Interprovincial directors present thought it was "dirty pool." But whoever had sent Mendoza obviously thought it was what the IPL chairman deserved.

Heule, however, made one prescient statement. "It isn't over yet," he said. "If there's a higher bid on the table . . . we clearly can take advantage of the higher bid. We have complete flexibility."

TransCanada's bid involved a great deal of paperwork. In fact, the company wouldn't be able to get it out "on the street" until the following Monday. But it seemed now that, failing another higher bid from someone prepared to bid on the same basis as TransCanada — that is, of acquiring HWR with the liquor assets stripped out — the battle was over. Paul Reichmann had said that what he was after was the liquor, and the liquor was now sold. But Paul Reichmann wasn't accustomed to losing.

Business decisions are always about far more than economics and bottom lines. Corporate life is driven far more by ego and personal likes and dislikes than executives will ever admit. There was now more at stake in the Hiram Walker affair than mere money. Paul Reichmann's legal challenge to Walker's surprisingly innovative escape plan had been crushed. He had been cast by the Ontario Supreme Court as a predator, while Hiram Walker's management and board were portrayed as models of responsibility to shareholders. They had even been prepared to commit corporate hari-kari in the name of their shareholders. And now TransCanada PipeLines had finally ridden onto the scene, willing not only to top Gulf's last bid, but also to honour the sale of the liquor business to Allied. To tender O&Y's 11 percent of Walker into TransCanada's $36.50 a share offer would mean a tidy profit. But this was now about more than profit.

Coup de grâce

In Toronto's *Globe and Mail* of Friday, April 11, there appeared an extraordinary interview with Paul Reichmann. In it, Reichmann did what, for senior executives, was almost unheard of: he admitted that he'd made a mistake.

"My brother and I goofed somewhere along the line," he was quoted as saying. "A misunderstanding developed . . . Had we known it would be unfriendly, we would not have gone near it. It's not our style."

Reichmann declared that the problem had arisen because of a misunderstanding about O&Y's intentions for Walker. "They [Walker] thought we were going to dismember the company. Our purpose was the opposite. We wanted to diversify. . . . We goofed because we didn't get the message across clearly enough until they were too deep into another route. . . . It's the first time in 30 years we have gone to court. It's not the kind of thing we do."

Reichmann seemed to be bending over backward to put the Walker directors in a good light: "I personally think that Walker directors thought what they did was in the best interests of their shareholders."

"On March 31 [Easter Monday]," went the story, "O&Y told Walker that it was planning to improve its offer and expected Walker to sit down and negotiate a price. Instead, Walker executives telephoned O&Y to say they had other plans.

" 'They should have listened to us,' Mr. Reichmann said. 'They could have negotiated with us and got the same result as with TransCanada without too much ado.' "

Why didn't Hiram Walker listen to him? It was all in the submissions to the Ontario Supreme Court. It went back to Walker director Allen Lambert's conclusion after speaking to Paul Reichmann on the Easter weekend that Reichmann was prepared to offer little more than his revised partial bid of $32 a share. But some people believed, and Paul Reichmann might well have been one of them, that HWR's resistance came from a long-felt aversion to the Reichmanns seizing control of their company. But of course he could never say that in public. He might not even be able to admit it to himself.

At Walker's board meeting on Thursday, April 10, there was a self-congratulatory air to the proceedings. The formal decision was made to drop the Fingas offer and go with the TransCanada offer, even though it had not yet officially been made.

"Based upon information now available and the advice of its investment bankers," ran a Walker press release, "the directors of Hiram Walker have agreed that they will recommend to shareholders acceptance of the TransCanada offer when it is made."

But the TransCanada offer would never be made.

Paul Reichmann had decided that he would not be denied. His interview in the *Globe and Mail* had not been an attempt at a graceful exit from what had turned into an ugly situation. It had not been a *mea culpa*. It had been part of the groundwork for the final *coup de grâce*. The same day on which the interview appeared, Gulf upped its bid for all Hiram Walker shares to $38 a share.

The market felt that the bidding war was not over. On Friday, April 11, the Walker battle led share prices on the TSE to their third consecutive daily record. Trading in the stock was halted for more than an hour pending the revised Reichmann offer, but once the new offer was out, the shares leaped to $38.62. More than 1 million HWR shares were traded on the TSE, making it, once again, the exchange's most active stock.

On Tuesday, April 15, TransCanada announced that it had pulled its $4.1 billion offer and was reviewing "all available options." Walker meanwhile had revealed in a filing with the Securities Exchange Commission that it had arranged golden parachutes for management in the event of a sale or takeover of the company. Under these contracts, eight of Walker's senior executives were entitled to receive three years' salary and other benefits if they resigned or had their employment terminated within two years after a number of so-called "triggering events." These triggering events were sales of certain assets of the company or a change in the company's control. Alternatively, if a senior officer remained employed for two years following one of the triggering events, he would become entitled to receive a year's salary as bonus. Executives' stock options were also to be accelerated.

Golden parachutes are often criticized. They appear to confirm the notion that management's first concern is themselves. But they do provide security so that management can concentrate on their main objective of providing the best deal for shareholders. Given what was already known or suspected about the Reichmanns' intentions before the battle began, the only question was why management had not strapped on golden parachutes before.

The filing also revealed that Walker's investment advisors would be well taken care of. If the bid price was $38 or higher, Dominion Securities Pitfield and Morgan Guaranty Trust would share equally in a $22.5 million windfall. Their initial fee had been $2.5 million.

On Wednesday, April 16, the TSE 300 Composite Index set yet another new record of 3,118.78. Hiram Walker stayed unchanged at $38.50, but was, once again, the most traded stock on the exchange, with a volume of almost a million shares.

On Thursday morning, April 17, the Hiram Walker board approved the Reichmann bid, "failing a higher bid." They had not approved the TransCanada in such terms. They had not been expecting a higher bid. Moreover, they had approved the Trans-Canada bid before it had officially been made, while ignoring bids from Gulf. Now they looked to TransCanada to come back for a second tilt and rescue them once more. The pipeline's board held a number of meetings on April 16, 17, and 18. After the final meeting on the Friday, TransCanada decided not to up its offer for Walker. Gerry Maier would not get involved in a battle of business egos.

Once again, Walker shares were the the most active on the TSE, but now they were on the way down. The stock dropped $1.25 to $37.12. The market knew the battle was over.

Acquiring Problems

Paul Reichmann had made the high bid and won. But had he won the war? Hiram Walker's distilling interests, the very asset the Reichmanns claimed they most desired, had been sold, and the Ontario Supreme Court's Mr. Justice Robert Montgomery had dismissed the injunctions of both the Reichmanns and Interprovincial Pipe Line to halt the sale. Paul Reichmann appeared to have made a quite uncharacteristic move. Had his actions been inspired by emotion rather than economics? If the sale to Allied went through — as it now appeared that it would — then instead of diversifying, all the Reichmanns' acquisition of Hiram Walker would have achieved was the acquisition of more oil and gas assets and a gas distribution system. In fact, it looked as if they wouldn't even end up with the oil and gas assets. Interprovincial's Heule had climbed into bed with the Reichmanns in the hope of emerging with Home Oil. This liaison had been complicated by suggestions that Home had also been offered to TransCanada. But whatever the conclusion to these Byzantine manoeuvrings, it seemed that Home was sure to wind up in other hands. That would leave the Reichmanns with Consumers' Gas. It might be the largest local gas distribution utility in the country, but it would appear a small prize for such a complex and acrimonious battle.

There were good, though unannounced, financial reasons for the Reichmanns to fight the sale to Allied. The best was that, if the sale went through, they would be lumbered with an estimated $300 million tax bill. But there was more to be saved than cash. There was also face. Olympia & York Enterprises went back to court to challenge Judge Montgomery's decision.

Another unusual interview with Paul Reichmann appeared in the *Globe*. He appeared to admit that he had made another gaffe: "Had we been advised that the spirits business was irretrievably sold, we still would have made an offer, but we would have pursued it less aggressively." Then he admitted that if the distillery was sold, "the purpose of our offer will be defeated."

Was it really possible that Reichmann had made his $3.3 billion bid without checking whether the distillery was "irretrievably sold"? Did he think that the Allied sale was a mere delaying tactic? If so, he was terribly wrong. Allied-Lyons wanted Hiram Walker/Gooderham & Worts. In fact, now the British company wanted it more than ever. Hiram Walker/Gooderham & Worts, meanwhile, more than ever wanted to avoid the clutches of the Reichmanns.

And there was another problem; financing the deal. Contrary to popular belief, the Reichmanns' pockets were not bottomless, and Hiram Walker could turn out to be a very expensive acquisition.

19

THE EPISTLE ACCORDING TO PAUL

The right hand's cards were being played so close to the chest that not even the left hand knew the state of play. But then that had always been the Reichmann way.

On the morning of Sunday, April 20, Bill Shields, the business editor of the *Windsor Star*, received one of those phone calls of which newsmen dream. The caller announced that Paul Reichmann wished to give an exclusive interview to the *Star*. He wanted specifically to give it to Brian Bannon, the young business reporter who had been covering the Hiram Walker story. When did Mr. Reichmann have in mind? asked Shields. Today, Sunday, came the reply. Well, hold on now, said Shields, it wasn't that easy to get to Toronto on a Sunday. No matter, said the O&Y representative. Paul Reichmann would send down the company jet.

For some hours, Shields couldn't contact Bannon, who was with his wife visiting Midland, Michigan, but he finally reached him that night. Bannon's adrenalin started pumping. He called the Reichmann people and told them he could come down the next morning. At first, Paul Reichmann said that would not be possible because the Abitibi-Price annual meeting was to take place that day. However, he then decided that it was so important that his side of the story be told that he reshuffled his schedule.

Reichmann was mightily upset because of a letter that had been brought to his attention the previous Friday. Under the name of Hiram Walker liquor executive Dennis Stoakes, it had been sent to one of the distillery's customers. It asked for the customer's support in gaining approval for the sale to Allied-Lyons and in rebuffing the legal roadblocks of the Reichmanns. Not only did it point to the enormous layoffs at Gulf Canada in the wake of its acquisition by O&Y and the sale of the downstream to Petro-Canada, but it also suggested that the Reichmanns were in league with the Seagram Bronfmans and planned to split up the Hiram Walker liquor business. These allegations, in Reichmann's mind, were all "lies, falsehoods or misconceptions." It wasn't so much the details that offended him as the implication that he had been less than honourable and forthright in his dealings.

The Stoakes letter was in fact part of a larger campaign. As soon as Allied-Lyons had made their bid for the liquor business, with the full support of Hiram Walker management, the Windsor headquarters organized a campaign of letters to local businesses and organizations, from the Chamber of Commerce to the art gallery, asking them to write to Investment Canada in support of Allied's bid. The local community had responded quickly and positively. Cliff Hatch, Jr., the head of the liquor arm, had himself written to Investment Canada asking them to allow the Allied takeover.

There was widespread fear in Windsor that Reichmann control would mean the splitting up and selling off of the liquor division. Local unions were afraid the Reichmanns would sell to Seagram, with the prospect of rationalization and job losses.

Once again, the Reichmanns' natural secretiveness was causing problems. This time, however, part of the problem was that the Reichmanns themselves didn't appear to have their strategy clearly laid out. Paul Reichmann had had little experience of public relations. His efforts only served to muddy the waters. The right hand's cards were being played so close to the chest that not even the left hand knew the state of play. But then that had always been the Reichmann way.

Paul Reichmann was now claiming through his press conduits that he had never intended to split up Walker and that he had always wanted the liquor business. Why were people not believing him? Why were they doubting his word? The simple answer was that Gulf had admitted talking to third parties about sales of parts of the liquor business, while Reichmann himself had admitted talking to Edgar Bronfman and half a dozen other prospective purchasers of the liquor assets. Everybody, he said, should now just forget those details. In the rarified atmosphere of Paul Reichmann's business world, his word was simply to be believed. That people were refusing to do so, although he appeared to be speaking in riddles, was intensely annoying.

The contentious sale of the liquor business to Allied was now a matter of government approval and legality, but Reichmann — while his staff lobbied away in Ottawa and his phalanxes of lawyers dreamed up obstructions to the sale — appeared to want something else: he wanted Windsor to want him.

Paul Gives a Lecture

On Monday morning, April 21, Bannon turned up at the thirty-second-floor reception area of O&Y in First Canadian Place. He had butterflies. It wasn't every day that you got to interview Paul Reichmann. Come to think of it, nobody *ever* got to interview him unless he had a message to give or a misapprehension to correct. He didn't give interviews simply for the purpose of general enlightenment. Still, Bannon didn't have Paul Reichmann's skilful manipulation of the press uppermost in his mind when he was ushered into the O&Y executive vice-president's plush office. This was a scoop, and Bannon wasn't about to pass it up.

Reichmann kept him for an hour, during which, in Bannon's own words, he "spoke like a school teacher." The reporter noted that he could "narrow his deep-set, sad eyes when something annoyed him and then, a minute later, chuckle over the foibles of big business."

Paul Reichmann's eyes were particularly sad over "misunderstandings" about his intentions. He noted that he had called Ontario Premier David Peterson to inform him of the offer for Hiram Walker Resources and to assure him that there would be no negative impact from the takeover, but then he admitted that he should have followed this up "with calls to Windsor and so on, but, in time, circumstances came about — what is referred to as the takeover battle — which then made us attach our focus to other aspects and we were remiss in not communicating this properly."

But, as with his earlier attempts to set the record straight over Hiram Walker, these *mea culpas* were a prelude to something else. That something else was the "lies, falsehoods and misconceptions" of the Stoakes letter. Reichmann admitted that he had spoken to Edgar Bronfman, but claimed that he had called him in Europe before the opening bid for Walker in order "to tell him that the bid is for the purpose of diversification and it's not to buy Home Oil to make Gulf stronger in oil and gas, just so there is no misunderstanding. Unfortunately, we were not aware some people were going by that rumor and we failed to communicate."

How people were expected to know about Reichmann's secret conversation and his apparent change of intentions was not laid out.

Bannon brought up the issue of how Edgar Bronfman's letter to Bud Downing had found its way into the hands of the Reichmanns. Reichmann did not explain. Then Bannon asked the $5 billion question: "So the idea of selling the spirits business in whole or selling off a number of brands was never a part of the plan?"

Reichmann said no.

Earlier in the interview Paul Reichmann had said, "[Gulf] does not intend to dispose of the parts of the *Canadian* business of Hiram Walker Resources, with the exception of Home Oil." (Author's italics.)

If Reichmann had never considered selling off foreign parts of the business, why had he specifically said "Canadian?" He went on to say, "Gulf and myself as the controlling shareholder of Gulf, are making statements that the operations of Hiram Walker will not be affected *in the Windsor area, nor will they be in British Columbia.*" (Author's italics.)

Reichmann's statements also indicated ignorance about Hiram Walker's structure. He didn't appear to realize that a healthy part of the Windsor head office's employment related to the legal, financial, and management functions of the international organization. If overseas assets were sold off, how could their Windsor head office functions be maintained?

Reichmann went on to indicate that there could be adverse implications if Elders' attack on Allied-Lyons was successful: ". . . it may look like the British company will take Hiram Walker and everything will be fine from here on after. But the facts are that Allied-Lyons and Hiram Walker will be too large and if the Australians are successful, the first thing they will do is dump Hiram Walker and who will get it is anyone's guess. You could say if they dump it to another foreign company, it means Investment Canada

THE EPISTLE ACCORDING TO PAUL 215

can take a second look at it, but what if they dump it to a Canadian company like Seagrams or anybody else.''

For a man who had always taken the high road, these statements seemed very close to scare tactics.

Pitching the Paper

There was another issue that Paul Reichmann was very keen to address in the press: that of the proposed plan of arrangement by which Hiram Walker shareholders could take ''paper,'' or some mixture of cash and paper, at a later date instead of tendering for $38 in cash immediately. Reichmann wanted to sell the plan because if everybody tendered for cash, the total cost to Gulf and O&Y would be $3.3 billion. Neither Gulf nor O&Y wanted that. O&Y still planned to lend Gulf any cash above $2.1 billion it needed to buy Walker shares, with repayment through the issue by Gulf to O&Y of Walker shares. O&Y's potential cash liability was thus $1.2 billion. But the more paper that shareholders could be persuaded to take, the less O&Y would have to fork out. If just over one-third could be persuaded to take paper, then Gulf would still have to find $2.1 billion, but the Reichmanns would have to put up nothing. In the heat of the battle, there had been insufficient time to address the issue.

Following O&Y's agreement with Interprovincial Pipe Line, Gulf Canada had outlined a plan of arrangement for shareholders not tendering to the cash offer. This was similar to that used by Gulf — once it was under Reichmann control — to buy out its own minority. Even Gulf's own board had been astonished at how successful the move had been the first time. Gulf now announced that such a plan would be available to all Hiram Walker sharehold- ers. Gulf and Hiram Walker would be merged and the merged entity would offer shareholders who did not tender their shares various cash alternatives. They would be allowed a tax-free share exchange into shares of either a combined Gulf/Hiram Walker or Home Oil, or a package of cash and debentures.

Reichmann had already done some selling of this still vague plan through the press. He had told the *Financial Post*: ''We are giving an all-cash offer. But we are also saying, 'Have a look at the plan of arrangement.' In our view, the great majority of shareholders would prefer to stay with the company, and therefore become shareholders in a larger and stronger company . . . That is part of our strategy; to widen the shareholder base of Gulf. O&Y could end up with 50% to 60% of Gulf."

That was hardly the primary rationale for the plan from the Reichmanns' point of view, however. They realized that if enough shareholders could be persuaded to take paper, then O&Y could avoid the hefty debt attached to a cash purchase. The Reichmanns' stake in Gulf would be reduced, but the family would retain control. However, Reichmann's view of what the "majority of shareholders would prefer" turned out to be almost embarrassingly transparent wishful thinking.

The proposed plan of arrangement was extremely fuzzy, but $38 in hard cash was very clear. The New York "arbs" were rumoured to have now accumulated up to 30 percent of Hiram Walker's shares. They certainly weren't interested in any plan of arrangement. The bid was still to be made only on Canadian stock exchanges, but the arbs could get over that simply by selling in Canada.

Now, while Paul Reichmann was giving his "exclusive" to the *Windsor Star*, time was running out. The *Star* was perhaps not the best medium to address Bay Street. Nevertheless, there were likely to be large numbers of shareholders in the city, to whom Reichmann, through Bannon, now attempted to pitch the plan: "As I said, we hope many of the shareholders will, instead of taking cash, take shares in the new company. This message has not gotten across well enough because our minds and the minds of our advisors were occupied with the takeover disagreements or battles. But we will find a way to rectify that in the future."

With regard to Gulf Canada's mounting debt, and mounting debt prospects, Reichmann continued: "As shareholders in Gulf, we will be pushing the company and directing it to finance this so that its final debt to total capitalization ratio should be 35 to 40 percent which is adequate for a strong, healthy company."

Reichmann seemed to be speaking like King Canute. Debt ratios, like the tide, could not be turned by "pushing and directing." If shareholders opted for the cash, then the debt of both Gulf and O&Y would be significantly increased. Insofar as Gulf's debt was greater, it was, from Hiram Walker's point of view, a less desirable owner. Fears that it would try to use HW-GW's finances to prop up its own would inevitably increase.

Paul Reichmann went on to respond to some questions about

corporate concentration, and then the interview was over.

Paul Reichmann may have satisfied himself that he had set the record straight, but his answers were less than satisfactory from the Windsor distillery's point of view. He had spoken of "lies and misconceptions" about a possible sale to Seagram, and yet he had admitted speaking to Edgar Bronfman. Moreover, he had given no adequate explanation of how Bronfman's letter to Downing had found its way into the hands of O&Y's lawyers. He had denied that selling off either all of Hiram Walker or any of its brands was ever part of his plans, and yet he had emphasized the safety of the Canadian part of the business rather than the business as a whole.

McWalter's Alligators

Tuesday, April 22, the day the Reichmann interview appeared in the *Windsor Star*, was also the day of Gulf Canada's annual meeting. This would be Keith McWalter's chance to muddy the waters. At the meeting Paul, Albert, and Ralph voted themselves onto the board, where they joined their executives Gil Newman and Mickey Cohen, and then, typically, they disappeared. McWalter gave the appearance of a man up to his hip-wallet in alligators. He had to put a brave corporate face on a series of events outside Gulf's control. The company's first-quarter earnings had in fact increased by 66 percent to $166 million, but this was more than totally accounted for by asset sales related to the previous year's Reichmann takeover of Gulf Canada. By far the largest element, $118 million, came from the sale of Gulf's Edmonton refinery to Petro-Canada. Another $13 million came from the sale of Gulf's remaining downstream assets of Ultramar, and a final $74 million from the transfer of Gulf properties to Norcen Energy Resources. These gains were partially offset by a $72 million loss on the redemption of some U.S. debentures.

Once these elements were stripped out, Gulf's results were a disaster. After excluding earnings from discontinued operations, earnings for the first quarter of 1986 were a slim $9 million, down from $52 million the previous year. Oil and gas earnings had been hit by lower prices, but the main reason for the precipitous dip was the increase in Gulf's debt and related interest expenses.

Gulf's long-term debt had climbed from $1.3 billion to $2.8 billion since the end of 1985. Moreover, if Hiram Walker shareholders accepted Gulf's cash offer, it was going to climb further. McWalter, not surprisingly, made an enthusiastic pitch to Hiram Walker shareholders to hang on and wait for the paper.

He pointed out that the board had maintained its 13-cent-a-share dividend, and, that once the dividend on the preferred share (offered as the "sweetener" back in January to get Gulf shareholders to take new Gulf paper) had been taken into account, "the combined yield to our shareholders has increased over the yield a year ago." McWalter did not elaborate on how dividends on the common shares would be maintained in the face of such depressed financial results. He went on to point out that the majority of Gulf Canada's individual shareholders had held their shares at the time of the earlier Reichmann-masterminded plan of arrangement. But that statement was at once both misleading and telling. It was misleading because in fact holders of 56 million of the 90 million minority shares, that is, 62 percent, had opted to cash in. If in fact the smaller number of shares that had opted to stay in had been owned by a larger number of shareholders, then that meant that it was the smaller — and less sophisticated — investors who, either through inertia or investment dealer persuasion, had stuck with the Reichmanns. Said McWalter, "The performance of our stock since then certainly indicates a wise decision on their part." The day he made his statement to the meeting, Gulf common shares were trading at $16 and the Gulf preferred "sweetener" was trading at $4.60 for a total of $20.60 vs. the cash and debenture exit price, for those who had opted out of Gulf, of $20.80. In other words, those who had stayed in were just about holding their own. It was difficult to see how an assessment that they had made "a wise decision" could be justified.

McWalter went on to say that "a similar situation is developing with Hiram Walker. . . . There has been a great deal of trading in recent weeks, but apparently many of the non-institutional shareholders have retained their stock. . . I think this is a prudent decision." McWalter was again effectively pitching the small, unsophisticated, non-institutional shareholders to hang on to their paper so that Gulf's balance sheet would not suffer. But he was whistling in the dark.

Although the claim that Gulf shareholders had done well to hang on to Gulf shares looked arguable, McWalter might well have claimed that the Gulf ordinary share price had held up remarkably well in relative terms. In fact, what was truly remarkable was that the Gulf plan of arrangement had been hatched when the oil price was more than U.S.$30 a barrel, but had been put into effect as OPEC's collapse was sending it tumbling below U.S.$18. Looked at in those terms, it was amazing that anybody had been persuaded to switch into the equity of the "new" Gulf at all. Just as awe-inspiring was that although the oil price had subsequently slumped below U.S.$10·and, as McWàlter spoke, was trading below U.S.$15, the share price was still holding up.

It looked like more than a remarkable act of faith in the Reichmanns' ability to wave their magic wand over a slumping oil business and somehow make it attractive. It looked like somebody, or perhaps several entities, were engaged in that old practice of "stabilizing the market," which, when it was done by any lesser entity than a major investment house, is known as stock manipulation.

Meanwhile, as if it were not enough to be attempting to fulfil the unaccustomed role of sweet-talking deal-salesman while facing an abysmal business outlook, McWalter also had to address the concerns that the Reichmann puppet Gulf would start splitting up and selling off Hiram Walker's liquor business. The day of the annual meeting, a letter under McWalter's name was sent to lawyers representing the United Auto Workers Local 2027, whose 500 workers were employed at Walker's Windsor, Ontario, distillery.

McWalter pointed out that the sale of the liquor business to Allied was not a foregone conclusion. His letter claimed: "It is unfortunate there have been recent rumors misrepresenting our intentions and creating undue concern among Hiram Walker's employees. Let me assure you and your client that if we are the eventual owner of Hiram Walker's distilled spirits business it would be our intention to retain the operations affecting your client." The Gulf-O&Y camp had done it again. By qualifying the word "operations" with the phrase "affecting your client," McWalter had once more raised the spectre of a sale of foreign assets. Again, what he, like Reichmann, apparently failed to appreciate was that the sale of *any* of the liquor assets affected the employment prospects in Windsor.

At the meeting, McWalter increased the confusion by telling the audience: "If, ultimately, Gulf is the owner of the Hiram Walker distilled spirits business, it would be our intention to retain the *Canadian* operations." (Author's italics.) If Gulf-O&Y had no intention of selling off any foreign liquor operations, why did

McWalter emphasize the retention of Canadian assets? After the meeting, he flatly contradicted Reichmann's *Star* interview. When asked directly about Gulf-O&Y's intentions for the foreign liquor operations, he said that the options were "open."

Gulf and O&Y were able to get some parts of their strategy co-ordinated. Like Reichmann, McWalter raised the bugbear that Allied was under attack from Elders. What might Elders do to Hiram Walker if it succeeded in its bid for the British-based company? "Elders has not made its intentions public but, if the Hiram Walker distillery assets were to be sold to them, this could indeed produce the situation about which the employees are concerned."

"Our aim at Gulf Canada," he concluded, "is to build a strong, diversified, Canadian-owned company with a stable earnings base to make solid and lasting contributions to the Canadian economy. . . Such a Canadian company, we are confident, will have an extremely broad Canadian ownership, including, we hope, many present Hiram Walker shareholders. Our offer for Hiram Walker is in support of that strategy and if we become the owner of its distillery business, assumes the continuation of the Windsor operations."

On stock exchanges, ahead of the closing of the offer the next day, Wednesday, April 23, Hiram Walker trading increased to unprecedented volumes. But now it was not frantic trading; it was the trading of the arbitrageurs' massive blocks, selling into the cash offer. On the Monday, Dominion Securities Pitfield "crossed" — that is, acted for both the buyer and the seller of — a single block of 3 million shares.

O&Y's advisors, Merrill Lynch and McLeod Young Weir, meanwhile were eagerly trying to forestall investors from tendering into the cash offer. They were receiving no help from Hiram Walker's board and management. The previous week, on April 17, Hiram Walker had mailed a letter to shareholders recommending acceptance of Gulf's cash offer. The letter had also, pointedly, made reference to the proposed Gulf/Hiram Walker plan of arrangement. An original draft of the letter had recommended outright rejection of the fuzzy alternatives. But the final version was damning enough. "In view of the limited disclosure and uncertainties regarding the options that would be available to continuing shareholders under any such plan of arrangement, the Board is unable to express an opinion as to any such options." On Monday, April 21, Walker had the letter printed in a number of newspapers.

On April 22, in an attempt to sway shareholders the other way, a notice under the name of Merrill Lynch and McLeod Young Weir was placed in various Canadian newspapers.

"In connection with your decision whether to tender your Hiram Walker shares into Gulf's Offers, consider that, following the Offers, Gulf intends to formulate a plan of arrangement to combine Gulf and Hiram Walker in which you will have the following options:

1. A ROLLOVER FREE OF CANADIAN CAPITAL GAINS TAXES into equity securities of the combined company (which may include or exclude Hiram Walker's oil and gas assets)
OR
2. A CASH-AND-DEBENTURE PACKAGE totalling $38.00 ($19.00 cash/$19.00 debenture) for each Common Share and $34 ($17.00 cash/$17.00 debenture) for each Class D Preference Share, First Series. . ."

The day before the offer, trading in Hiram Walker stock reached an all-time record. On the TSE alone, 5.8 million shares were traded, including the largest-ever block trade, when McLeod Young Weir crossed 5.2 million shares at $37.75. That day, the TSE fell 32.7 points to 3,098.1, largely as a result of share price declines by the major refining companies, Imperial, Shell, and Texaco, in the wake of dismal news about downstream profits. At one time, the news would have driven down Gulf too, but the Reichmanns had sold off Gulf's downstream activities, so the move, on this day at least, seemed particularly shrewd. Petro-Canada, of course, appeared correspondingly less shrewd.

On Wednesday, April 23, at 8:30 A.M., on the floors of the Toronto and Montreal stock exchanges, Hiram Walker shareholders gave their response to Reichmann's and McWalter's appeal that they hang in. The industry's traders went to the men from Merrill Lynch and McLeod Young Weir who were responsible for taking in Hiram Walker shares and quietly placed their sell orders. When it was all over, the answer was unequivocal: just over 90 percent of the minority shares were tendered for cash. The Walker shareholders were voting with their feet. In droves.

Gulf-O&Y was now another $3 billion in the hole.

20

BLUE BLOOD MEETS BLUE COLLAR

*McWalter was now dancing to the Reichmanns'
tune. The difficulty was in getting Paul
Reichmann to play for him. The unions, meanwhile,
found Sir Derrick's tune much more beguiling.*

On July 12, 1812, Brigadier-General William Hull, Commander of the North Western Army of the United States, crossed the Detroit River and landed with 2,000 men on the site of what is today the Hiram Walker distillery in Windsor. Like Paul Reichmann, General Hull considered himself a man of good intention, convinced that he had come to "liberate Canada from oppression." But British-controlled Canada, rather like Hiram Walker/Gooderham & Worts, didn't want liberating. In less than three weeks, after British General Isaac Brock had appeared with reinforcements, Hull and his men were forced to take to their boats and retreat across the river.

When Sir Derrick Holden-Brown arrived in Windsor on the afternoon of Wednesday, April 30, 1986, he received a welcome similar to that of his military fellow countryman 174 years before. He was seen as a saviour.

Some thought that Windsor might be able to save Sir Derrick, too. They believed that events in the international arena had made Allied's enthusiasm for the Hiram Walker acquisition even greater. Even though Elders' first bid was still stalled in front of the British Monopolies & Mergers Commission, and the Australian company had disposed of its initial Allied holding in the market at a profit, Elders' John Elliott had not given up. In late February, he had set up a battle headquarters in London. Early in April, there was a flurry of activity "down under" that had stock markets buzzing. Allied was a keen observer.

Australia was in the throes of its own corporate civil war. One of the country's richest and most intriguing businessman, Robert Holmes a Court, whom even Edward de Bono, the man who invented the term, described as a "lateral thinker," had several times bid for control of the Australian resource giant The Broken Hill Proprietary Co. Ltd. (BHP), known as "The Big Australian." However, the Melbourne-based BHP had consistently rebuffed him. On April 7, Holmes a Court made another assault, bidding around $2 billion to gain control of the company by doubling his BHP stake to 40 percent. Three days later, Elder's Elliott stunned the business community by picking up almost 19 percent of BHP's stock—at a cost of $1.8 billion—on the Melbourne stock exchange. His move sent trading through the roof.

On April 14, the other shoe dropped. Broken Hill bought rights to 20 percent of Elders' stock and injected $1 billion of new capital into the company. Elders and Broken Hill were acting as back-to-back white knights, each protecting the other's corporate posterior.

Elliott claimed that the BHP deal strengthened his company. He clearly regarded it as part of his strategy to go back to London and take another run at Allied. As for Allied's purchase of Walker, Elliott, obviously hoping that the Reichmanns' court challenge would be successful, was quoted in the *Financial Post* as saying that the Allied-Walker deal "has been put together in altogether indecent haste, and contributes nothing to either company."

Sir Derrick Holden-Brown begged to differ.

Sir Derrick's Royal Tour

On Wednesday, April 30, before heading for Windsor, Sir Derrick brought his case to Toronto. At 11 A.M. he appeared at a press conference at the Westin Hotel as part of a strategy to acquaint Canadians with his company. Full-page Allied-Lyons ads had appeared in the media that morning, emphasizing the wide range of the company's products.

Sir Derrick, who had flown into New York via the Concorde the previous evening, sported a Canadian Maple Leaf tie given him by the man who had been his commanding officer during the war, Tommy Ladner, a well-known Vancouver lawyer.

He told those assembled, in his well-modulated tones, that Hiram Walker would form a major part of a new, larger Allied-Lyons. He promised that with Hiram Walker's liquor side under Allied control, the company could look forward to increased exports, stable employment, and an opportunity for new products and markets.

Sir Derrick pointed out that any notion that the wedding with Walker was part of an Allied defensive strategy against the unwelcome advances of the Elders IXL group was quite erroneous. "I can state," he said, "that our company is under no serious threat of a takeover by either Elders IXL of Australia, or anyone else." He admitted that there was a "short-lived attempt," but that the bid had lapsed, and that Elders had disposed of its stake. Allied was also exploring arrangements to gain a listing for Allied shares on Canadian stock exchanges with a view to a Canadian share-offering as part of the financing package for Hiram Walker.

He ended with a subtle dig at the O&Y group, obviously intended to stir fears that the Reichmanns might be corporate vampires, interested only in sucking off the financial lifeblood of the liquor business. "There will be no draining off of the cashflow or net earnings of Hiram Walker to finance adventures in other industries, be it aerospace, energy, or anything else."

Aerospace was just thrown in. Holden-Brown meant energy.

Sir Derrick's resolve, in his deferentially British way, seemed total, "Gulf . . . has indicated that they are not interested in the whole of Hiram Walker," he said. "I have indicated that I'm not interested in part of it."

That afternoon he flew to Windsor to receive his saviour's welcome.

At a press conference at Windsor's riverfront Hilton Hotel, he delivered a message similar to the one he had given that morning in Toronto: Hiram Walker/Gooderham & Worts under Allied-Lyons control would remain a "Canadian-directed" business under its current management. Although Holden-Brown acknowledged that the local executives were in a "very difficult and delicate position," they made no effort to restrain their enthusiasm for him. When he went to the distillery to speak to them the next day, his brief presentation to management was greeted with a standing ovation.

Holden-Brown seemed almost embarrassed by the level of local support. Even the Windsor City Council had sent a letter on Allied's behalf to Investment Canada. When Windsor Mayor David Burr offered a second letter, the British knight said that such overt lobbying was perhaps not necessary so long as strong local support was visible. Local politicians of all stripes showered good wishes upon the gratified British executive.

Pressed once again by the local media on the sensitive issue of the Walker takeover being a defensive move for Allied-Lyons against Elders, Sir Derrick called Elders a "very brash, cheeky Australian company . . . a small fish trying to swallow a whale."

Sir Derrick skilfully played his long-term connections with Walker, not just in corporate terms, but in personal ones. He noted that when he had been a management trainee with Walker back in 1951, he had contracted tuberculosis. The company had paid him for seven months, a paternalism that was then unusual.

Holden-Brown's blue blood might have seemed a little out of place in Windsor, where blue was the colour of collars rather than corpuscles, but the Hiram Walker workers could identify with his example of corporate paternalism. And his emphasis on tradition was not out of place in Hiram Walker's headquarters. When Sir Derrick stepped into those headquarters on May 1, he felt very much at home. With their wood trimmings and their glass office partitions, they looked very much like a British merchant bank. Indeed, at one time the ground floor had been taken up by a bank.

Holden-Brown departed Walkerville in no doubt that the community was 100 percent behind his bid. From Windsor airport, he headed with his entourage for Ottawa to meet with industry minister Sinclair Stevens and officials from Investment Canada. Investment Canada knew about Sir Derrick. They also knew how enthusiastic Windsor was to have him as the owner of its oldest and most beloved local business. The government agency had been inundated with letters supporting the Allied bid.

That weekend, Sir Derrick flew home. He hoped to spend the following Monday, a British bank holiday, on his ten-ton sloop moored at Lymington, Hampshire. He needed a brief period of relaxation, for he was facing a hectic three-week period leading up to the extraordinary shareholders' meeting in London on May 27 at which his bid for Hiram Walker/Gooderham & Worts was to be put to shareholders.

Sir Derrick's reception in Canada could not have been warmer. There was less sweetness and light in the Reichmann camp.

Cleaning Out the Boardroom

While Sir Derrick was making what was almost a royal tour, back in Toronto, the Reichmanns were moving in on Hiram Walker. Mickey Cohen called Bud Downing and told him that he wanted all capital expenditures halted; he also wanted the resignations of all board members except for Downing and the heads of the three operating subsidiaries.

On Friday, May 2, there was a brief meeting of the board at Hiram Walker's First Canadian Place head office. The outside directors handed in their resignations and were replaced by the Reichmanns' nominees, most of whom were Gulf directors. They were: John Allan, the head of Hamilton-based steel giant Stelco; Howard Blauvelt, the consultant and former head of oil giant Conoco; Bob Butler, the chairman of Toronto's Urban Transportation Development Corporation Ltd.; Ed Crawford, the head of Canada Life Assurance; Gar Emerson, the lawyer from Davies, Ward & Beck; Mickey Cohen; Keith McWalter; Gil Newman; Alf Powis, and Bob Heule.

Those of the new directors present filed in and went round the table shaking hands with the departing members of the board, as if they had just played a good game of tennis or round of golf. On the surface it was all very gentlemanly, although Cliff Hatch, Jr., looked visibly upset. But this wasn't a friendly end to a diverting game. For the outgoing Walker board it was the end of a battle, but Hiram Walker still had a battle on its hands.

The new directors, since they were there to serve the interests of the shareholders, had little real part to play. Paul Reichmann controlled the majority of Walker shares, and he had never felt that his interests needed looking after by a board of directors. Nevertheless, one new board subcommittee was set up to look at potential loopholes in the contract under which the liquor business was to be sold to Allied-Lyons. It consisted of Cohen, Newman, McWalter, and Powis.

Paul Reichmann had claimed that he had never wanted a battle.
Now he had a corporate civil war on his hands. He found it all very
hard to understand.

The question now was whether he would meet his Waterloo in
Windsor.

Unhappy Union

On the day after the Gulf annual meeting, Wednesday, April 23,
Paul and Albert met for eighty minutes with Howard McCurdy,
the New Democrat MP for Windsor-Walkerville. Said McCurdy
after his audience, ''They certainly did seem anxious to reassure
the people of Windsor that their acquisition does not spell out a
threat to employment levels.''

Nevertheless, McCurdy would later refute a story in the *Windsor
Star*, which he claimed suggested that he might support the Gulf
bid. After all, McCurdy was the NDP member, and had to keep an
eye on union opinion. Union opinion was firmly behind Allied-
Lyons. Once again, that support had increased because the union
couldn't get a straight answer out of Gulf-O&Y.

Hiram Walker/Gooderham & Worts got on well with its union.
The company had been plagued by strikes in the early 1970s, but
the last two wage agreements had been signed almost a year ahead
of schedule. Local 2027 of the UAW was headed by Scottish-born
Ron Dickson, a feisty but highly articulate representative. When
the bidding war had broken out, Cliff Hatch, Jr., had called
Dickson in to brief him on the state of affairs, and had laid out
clearly why management supported the Allied alternative.

At first, Dickson was inclined to follow the lead of management,
but then decided it would be prudent to gain outside help. The
union retained the prestigious local law firm of Paroian Courey
Cohen & Houston (Dickson joked that if a law firm could be
described as ''prestigious,'' it could double its fees). Leon Paroian
told Dickson that he should take independent action to gauge the
quality of the alternatives. Dickson was supporting Allied, but
what did he know about Allied? Dickson determined to approach
the rival bidders. Allied proved a model of amenability. The
Reichmanns did not.

Paul Reichmann had said in his *Windsor Star* interview ''. . . . we
did communicate to a number of people but not well enough for

the people directly affected to be informed." Dickson represented
the people "directly affected." Thus he felt it not unreasonable
that if Paul Reichmann could give exclusive interviews to the *Windsor Star*, then somebody senior from Gulf-O&Y should speak to
him, too. Since it was Gulf who was making the bid, and since
Keith McWalter, the president, chairman, and chief executive of
Gulf, had written to him on the day of Gulf's annual meeting
seeking to reassure Walker's labour force, Dickson and Paroian
thought it appropriate that McWalter might make himself available. Between April 22 and May 4, Paroian had three conversations with McWalter. In the last, McWalter had said that he wanted
to meet with union representatives, and would be calling back
within a day or so to confirm the time and place.

Ten days later, they had heard nothing. But they were all,
including McWalter, being somewhat naive about the realities of
power within the Reichmann corporate empire. How could Keith
McWalter take the initiative in speaking for Gulf? The Reichmanns' acquisition had effectively emasculated management.
McWalter was now dancing to the Reichmanns' tune. The difficulty was in getting Paul Reichmann to play for him. The unions,
meanwhile, found Sir Derrick's tune much more beguiling.

The week of Reichmann's *Windsor Star* interview and the Gulf
annual meeting, Dickson and two colleagues had crossed the
Atlantic to meet with Allied's unions and management and visit
the company's facilities in London, Bristol, and Shepton Mallet.
The representatives of the British Transport & General Workers
Union, the TGWU, spoke in glowing terms about Allied and were
enthusiastic for a link with Walker, which they thought would
increase the markets for British products. Dickson met briefly with
Sir Derrick Holden-Brown and Allied's board. He subsequently
joked that when he had been growing up in Scotland, anybody
with a double-barrelled name was either the landlord or the local
Tory candidate, which gave him a natural adverse bias. But he was
impressed by Holden-Brown's sincerity, and he came away from
Britain even more enthusiastic for the Allied alternative.

As a result of Paroian's lack of success in tying down McWalter,
the union decided to draw some attention to itself. It chose to do
so, as Dickson put it, "on the home ground of the adversary." On
May 14, Dickson held a press conference at Toronto's Sheraton
Centre at which he delivered an impassioned attack on the
Reichmann bid. The union leader pointed out that he had sought
and was in the process of obtaining, written undertakings from

Allied-Lyons about the future of all of HW-GW's Canadian operations and its workers, not just the members of the UAW. Allied was being co-operative; Gulf and the Reichmanns were not.

Dickson outlined his union's problems in obtaining a response from the Reichmanns and made a devastating attack on their way of doing business. He said the union had looked "with great concern, to the manner in which employees of Gulf Canada were treated when the Reichmann group acquired Gulf and then immediately sold off a substantial part to Petro-Canada. The new owners of Gulf arbitrarily discarded the policy of the former management regarding terminations and ordered that the surplus employees (3,000 of them) could either resign without further compensation or be transferred to Petro-Canada and be subject to any of its policies for those transferred employees."

Then he turned on the Reichmanns' apparent ignorance about the structure of Windsor employment, bringing up McWalter's statement that the options were still open on the non-Canadian assets. Dickson pointed out that 90 percent of operating income from the distilled spirits division of HW-GW came from international activities. "The sale of all or any part of brands such as Ballantine's, Kahlúa, Courvoisier . . . would result in orphaning the Canadian distilled products to such an extent as to make them unattractive from a wholesale and distributing marketing perspective on a worldwide basis. In addition, Canadian distillery operations would sustain significant losses in production as a result of the loss of sale of distilled alcohol supplied to the non-Canadian operations."

Dickson also stressed that the legal, financial, and management functions for all the non-Canadian brands were located at Walkerville.

"Without giving assurances that the non-Canadian assets will not be sold off," said Dickson, "we ask Mr. Paul Reichmann how he could give assurances to Premier Peterson '. . . that there would be absolutely no negative impact and that business will continue'?"

Hidden Agenda

Dickson's bottom line was that the union believed that the Reichmann group had "a hidden agenda which is not in the best interests of the employees, or the community." As evidence, he pointed yet again to the Reichmanns' possession of the Bronfman letter and to Gulf's admission of third party talks about the disposal of Hiram Walker assets. "Both of these, of course, immediately raised suspicions and concerns that, if the Reichmanns got control of Hiram Walker, they intended to sell all or part of the Hiram Walker distillery operations to Seagram's or some other distillery." The inference not only seemed reasonable, it seemed unavoidable.

Dickson made a number of other stinging accusations at the press conference. Pointing back to the Little Egypt Bump, Dickson said: "In restructuring Gulf, the Reichmanns avoided $500,000,000 in taxes. What will be the tax cost of the Hiram Walker restructuring? Will that 'savings' be used to the benefit of Canada by creating new industry (and therefore jobs) or will it be used to provide the financing of more takeovers to the benefit of the ever expanding Reichmann empire?"

The time had obviously come to correct Dickson's "misconceptions" too. Cliff Hatch, Jr., relayed a message to the union leader that he should call Mickey Cohen at O&Y, which Dickson did the day of the press conference. Cohen assured him that Gulf was going to issue a press release the following week, on May 20, that would allay all the union's fears. Dickson waited.

On Tuesday, May 20, the press release came, but it did anything but allay the union's fears. In fact, it exacerbated them. The release referred to two developments, one legal and one concerning a planned reorganization of Gulf. On the legal side, the Reichmanns were taking their fight beyond a mere appeal of the Supreme Court of Ontario's judgement against them. Gulf and Hiram Walker Resources were "to commence legal proceedings seeking a declaration from the Supreme Court of Ontario that the purported purchase agreement with Allied-Lyons for the distilled spirits business is unenforceable, not binding, and of no force and effect."

That Gulf should be upping the legal stakes was perhaps not surprising, but to drag in Hiram Walker's surviving managerial board members — Downing, Hatch, Jr., Haskayne, and Martin — placed them in the most difficult of positions. They were the very people who had approved the sale in the first place. The rightness of their actions had been supported in the strongest terms in Justice Montgomery's Ontario Supreme Court judgement. Now they were apparently being forced to reverse themselves. In fact, hey had had nothing to do with the decision to take the court ffensive. That had come out of the subcommittee consisting of Newman, Cohen, McWalter, and Powis. But the management's osition appeared more than difficult.

Corporate etiquette prevented the surviving Walker board members from making any public statement, but Cliff Hatch, Jr., two days after the Reichmann interview had appeared in the *Windsor tar* and the day after Gulf had become Hiram Walker's official ew owner, had issued a message to employees declaring that the Reichmanns' statements about employment were "encouraging s far as they go. Unfortunately," it continued, "their intentions oncerning the remainder of our operations remain unclear. At his juncture, the proposed sale of Hiram Walker/Gooderham & Worts to Allied-Lyons is proceeding on schedule."

The statement, although guarded in its wording, was a bold act f defiance. Within his now strangely appropriate ivy-clad Renaisance palace Windsor headquarters, Hatch, Jr., was like some nedieval prince determined to fight a distant and despised monrch. He was supported by both his local subjects and his father, who had once been king. His opposition was made all the more ointed because he had hoped one day to be king himself.

Bud Downing, meanwhile, who had equally strong support mong the workers and management down at Walkerville, had to ake a more diplomatic line. He was much closer to the Reichnanns. In fact, he was sitting in a prize piece of their real estate. When Paul Reichmann had called him after seeing the Stoakes etter, Downing had apparently expressed "shock," and told Reichmann that it had not been authorized. But although the letter nay not have been authorized by him, it could hardly have come s a surprise.

The other part of Gulf's May 20 press release was not likely to omfort either Dickson or any of the distillery's management. Gulf Canada was proposing a reorganization under which the Hiram Walker spirits business would become one of three "legs" of the Gulf organization, alongside forest products and oil and gas. The elease declared that the restructuring plan would "establish within Gulf Canada Corporation a diversified business and earnngs base, which will strengthen the basic businesses and enable hem to expand and compete more effectively in Canadian and nternational business markets."

It said that Gulf intended to "make the spirits business similar to

Abitibi-Price, with its own elected Board of Directors and able to raise its own equity and debt capital for modernization and expansion objectives.

"The Board considered various alternatives for the reorganization of Gulf Canada Corporation all of which would achieve an important improvement in the already financially strong company. The emerging Gulf Canada Corporation will be able to stimulate growth and investment within all its three businesses while at the same time further reduce the ratio of debt to capital."

The release left many questions unanswered. In places it made little sense. How was tying Hiram Walker's spirits division to a deeply indebted Gulf Canada going to help it? Indeed, how could Gulf Canada be "strengthened" unless it was drawing financial support from Hiram Walker and Abitibi? As for "further" reducing the ratio of debt to capital, that ratio — the indication of how saddled a company is with debt and thus how prone to rises in interest rates — had gone up significantly at Gulf since the Reichmanns had gained control.

Hiram Walker's management had good grounds for wariness about being linked with oil companies. There had been much concern back in 1979 when the company had amalgamated with Consumers'-Home. The concern had been justified. They had all lived through the Davis Oil debacle.

When Ron Dickson saw the release, he immediately contacted Cohen and pointed out that it did nothing for his concerns — in fact, just the opposite. Was there perhaps, Dickson asked with pointed sarcasm, another release that he had missed? He said that a meeting was necessary. Keith McWalter had actually planned to go to Windsor on Monday, May 26, but now Paul Reichmann decided that the "lies and misconceptions" had gone far enough. It was time for him to take his message to a wider audience. It was time to meet the people of Windsor.

21

PUBLIC EXPOSURE

*Sir Derrick came back across the Atlantic
like Maggie Thatcher steaming down to the
Falklands. He felt that he had not merely
the locals but the force of justice on his side.*

Tuesday, May 27, dawned damp and grey in Windsor. From his suite in the Windsor Hilton, Paul Reichmann could look across at the black towers of Detroit's giant Renaissance Center, which rose almost menacingly above the mists of the Detroit River. Today would be an unusual day in his life. The man who claimed never to have courted publicity was calling his first press conference. He was also scheduled to meet with both the management and the unions at Hiram Walker/Gooderham & Worts' head office. Reichmann did not relish the task ahead, but he felt that misconceptions continued to abound. He had come to have another attempt at putting them straight.

He had not been pleased with his exclusive *Windsor Star* interview, even though it had printed almost verbatim what he had said. Perhaps it was because the story had also quoted union leader Ron Dickson's skepticism about Reichmann's intentions and his honesty. Reichmann had agreed to give another exclusive interview to Brian Bannon, but this time he insisted that a third party be present with a tape recorder. But if Reichmann thought that the presence of a tape recorder was going to get him the media coverage he desired, he was wide of the mark. What he really objected to in the press was that they failed to catch the purity of his *intentions*. They kept quoting what he said and then picking holes in it.

As Paul Reichmann prepared himself for the greatest bout of public exposure in his life, 6,000 kilometres away, at noon London time, Sir Derrick Holden-Brown, the chairman of Allied-Lyons, was submitting his proposed acquisition of Hiram Walker's spirits business to his shareholders. The meeting was being held at the ancient Plaisterers Hall in the heart of the City.

The week before, John Elliott's "cheeky" Elders IXL had launched another attack on Allied's planned purchase of Hiram Walker's spirits business, calling it "a defensive move at considerable expense to its shareholders." Holden-Brown had brushed off the attack. At the shareholders' meeting there were some questions about the price that Allied was paying relative to Hiram Walker's book value, but Sir Derrick noted that Walker's conservative accounting considerably undervalued the company. Since Walker's flat earnings performance in recent years had also come under attack, he was forced to point out some shortcomings in Hiram Walker's liquor management that he said would be corrected under Allied control. "It is not a good thing to be critical of your newly found partner. We regard Hiram Walker as a well-run company, but perhaps concentrating too much in recent years on its five key brands and not enough on taking advantage within its major marketplace — which is the United States and Canada — of opportunities to launch new products.

"We think that they have missed a few tricks."

When the vote was taken, support for the Walker deal was overwhelming.

Yet again, the solidity of Holden-Brown's support contrasted sharply with the situation in the Reichmann camp. Reichmann's new legal attack on the Allied deal had infuriated Walker's old management. The previous week, Bud Downing had stepped down from his position as president of Hiram Walker Resources and been replaced by Mickey Cohen. Bill Fatt, Walker's vice-president and treasurer, had resigned. Meanwhile, Reichmann's persistent denials of a sale of all or part of Hiram Walker's liquor business to Seagram received another blow the week before, when, at the Seagram annual meeting in Montreal, Edgar Bronfman had declared that he was still interested in Hiram Walker. If Paul Reichmann had unequivocally told Bronfman that he was not going to sell any of the liquor business, then how could Bronfman still claim to be interested? Unless, that is, he was hoping that Elders' bid would be successful and that he could then buy Hiram Walker's liquor business from the Australians.

Union Dues

At 9.30 A.M. Mickey Cohen stood chatting in the driveway of the Windsor Hilton with the chauffeur of Paul Reichmann's limousine. A couple of minutes later, the tall, looming figure of Paul Reichmann appeared from the elevator and walked his slow, deliberate walk out to the car. The limo pulled off up Riverside Drive for the short trip to the Hiram Walker plant.

At 10 A.M. Reichmann met with Ron Dickson and union representatives, and read them a prepared statement. "I am very pleased," he said in his soft European-accented voice, "to have this opportunity to talk to you about our plans and expectations for Hiram Walker/Gooderham & Worts. This meeting is overdue. But because I wanted to be certain that I could make clear commitments when I spoke to you, and could tell you with conviction about our plans for your company, I could not make this presentation until several important issues had been resolved and clarified. Specifically, we had to complete the purchase before we could gather enough facts to understand the Hiram Walker/Gooderham & Worts business thoroughly and develop firm plans.

"It is perhaps inevitable that in the arrangement and decisions involved in the purchase of a company as large and complex as Hiram Walker Resources, there are uncertainties, even misunderstandings. I am here today to do away with those uncertainties and to make clear to you the exciting future we see for the Hiram Walker spirits business as an individual company within a Canadian-owned Gulf Canada Corporation.

"As employees you have more at stake than anyone else in the future of this company, and I can assure you that we are committed to a course that will see the spirits business grow and will be able to provide stable levels of employment in Windsor, in other parts of Canada and in the overseas operations."

Then Reichmann came to the heart of all the contention, the sale to Allied-Lyons. "I would like to make clear the position regarding ownership of Hiram Walker/Gooderham & Worts. With the purchase of 69 percent of the shares of its parent company, Hiram Walker Resources, Gulf Canada is now the owner of this important distilling business.

"The purported agreement to sell the distilling business to Allied-Lyons PLC was prompted by the mistaken belief that if Gulf Canada acquired control, it would sell the distilled spirits and wines business to The Seagram Company. The notion that we intend to sell the liquor business to Seagram's has plagued this entire matter and is patently untrue."

When Bud Downing read that remark later, his immediate reaction was that it was at best a one-sided interpretation of events. It was uncertain whether Reichmann truly believed what he said, or was peddling the Seagram straw man to provide an excuse for HWR management to bow out gracefully of their sale commitment, but the fact was that they had no desire to bow out of the agreement. They still believed a sale to Allied would be best for the liquor business. Moreover, their agreement to sell to Allied had nothing whatsoever to do with fears about Seagram; it had been a response to the Reichmanns' perceived attempt to pull a Saturday Night Special.

Reichmann went on to tell the workers that "The purported sale agreement with Allied-Lyons is in our view unenforceable and, as the lawyers put it, of no force and effect and Gulf Canada and Hiram Walker Resources have launched legal action to establish this. These legal proceedings may well be protracted and, indeed, could take several years to conclude."

Here was a very clear threat to Allied-Lyons: they might be bogged down for years in the courts. And of course the Reichmanns were obviously putting every obstruction in the way of the "purported" purchase of Hiram Walker's liquor business. That very morning, Allied's finance director John Clemes had admitted at the extraordinary general meeting in London that Allied was being hampered because the new owners were refusing access to information about Hiram Walker. As soon as their acquisition was official, the Reichmanns had "pulled down the shutters."

Nevertheless, Reichmann went on to give what looked like a very solid reassurance to the workers about the future of the company. "As owner, Gulf Canada will work with your management and with you to ensure that all operations continue as before, under the same terms and conditions regarding employment, with the same employees and management, and that manage-

nent's plans for the profitability and growth of the business will
be supported and implemented. It is key to this plan that this
business be developed and expanded both inside and outside
Canada."

He next turned to the corporate restructuring indicated in Gulf
Canada's press release the previous week, under which Hiram
Walker would become one of three separate Gulf divisions with its
own board of directors "and access to the public financial markets
to finance its modernization and expansion objectives. This is an
important point," said Reichmann, "because your management
has told me that as a wholly owned subsidiary of Hiram Walker
Resources, Hiram Walker/Gooderham & Worts had to compete for
capital with the other businesses in the company. As a result it was
not possible to undertake all the projects which management
thought would be good for the business."

Again, Paul Reichmann was getting into a touchy financial area.
Hiram Walker executives were incredulous when they heard these
remarks later in the day. It seemed very hard to believe that they
had been held back by lack of cash. Indeed, one of the reasons for
Hiram Walker/Gooderham & Worts' attractiveness as a takeover
candidate as far back as 1979 was that it was generating more
money than it could utilize.

Paul Reichmann then, at last, clarified the point about the sale of
the non-Canadian parts of the business. "I also would like to
emphasize that we have absolutely no intention of selling any
segment of the spirits business to others. The international spirits
operations will not be sold because, as you know yourselves, its
operations and its revenues are essential to Canadian activities."

His audience certainly knew that. Unionist Ron Dickson's concern had been that, as recently as a few weeks before, neither the
Reichmanns nor Gulf's Keith McWalter appeared to know it.

Reichmann continued: "The importance of the international
operations to the financial health of Hiram Walker/Gooderham &
Worts is brought out by the fact in 1975, the operating profits of the
Canadian portions of Hiram Walker/Gooderham & Worts were
only 35 percent of the total, dropped further to 10 percent in 1985
and are currently forecast to decline further year by year. Urgent
action is required to reverse this trend and it is needed before it is
too late.

"As Canadians running a Canadian-controlled business, we recognize the urgent need for such a reversal and we will encourage

the development of new Canadian-distilled products that will find acceptance at home and abroad and return Canadian operations to their prominence of past years."

Later that day, when the liquor management heard those statements, they almost burst out laughing. Their business was 130 years old. Most of them had worked in it all their lives, and now a family of Toronto real estate developers with a career bureaucrat as their main hired help was going to tell them what new products they should be producing. That didn't sound very convincing.

As part of his pitch for the organization's support, Reichmann pointed to what had happened to Abitibi-Price under his family's control. "As owners," he said, "we committed ourselves to making Abitibi-Price one of the best, perhaps even the best, forest products companies in the world. Over five years, more than $1 billion has been spent in replacing or rebuilding plant and equipment, training employees to achieve higher skill levels, modernizing manufacturing, distribution and administrative activities, and expanding and upgrading its products to fetch higher prices in the marketplace. At the end of 1984 it employed 14,800 people. At the end of 1985 it employed 15,500 men and women . . . Abitibi Price provides a clear example of what we want to happen with Hiram Walker/Gooderham & Worts."

But although Paul Reichmann might point to the success of Abitibi-Price under Reichmann ownership, that success had nothing to do with the Reichmanns' knowledge of lumber or newsprint. It had everything to do with the quality of Abitibi management and with their willingness to operate under Reichmann control. The situation at the rebellious liquor operations of Hiram Walker was quite different.

He also pointed to the family's excellent record in developing Canadian jobs as a result of its international activities, in particular construction in the United States. He finished by saying, "This is a fine company that has raised the Canadian profile around the world. It has become a truly great Canadian multinational built and managed right here in Windsor. When Cliff Hatch, Sr., joined this company . . . the gross assets were about $63 million and annual sales were about $64 million. Currently both assets and sales have increased about 24 times from those 1937 levels. With the help of Cliff Hatch, Jr., and your exceptionally well-qualified management team, and with the vital help of all of you, I have no doubt that this pattern of growth can continue."

In return for his statement, Ron Dickson presented Paul Reichmann with a list of demands regarding employment and the future of the business. Then it was time to meet the press.

Meeting the Press

Shortly after 11 A.M. Reichmann entered Hiram Walker's "Canadian Club" room, resplendent with 1960s art that, twenty years later, is all too clearly not timeless. Reichmann was accompanied to the front of the room by Paul Pearson, a public relations and advertising specialist hired by Olympia & York a couple of weeks earlier. After a brief introduction by Al Milne, Hiram Walker/Gooderham & Worts' PR chief, who joked that he'd never in all his years been so successful at drawing the press to a conference, Paul Reichmann took the podium in front of a very "sixties" ten-foot by twenty-foot tapestry that portrayed the different stages of distilling. As the shutters clicked and the television cameras rolled, he read his prepared statement again.

Reichmann's references to the Hatches indicated that he was doing his best to mollify the family that had most vigorously opposed Reichmann control. But when he came to "the help" of Cliff, Jr., well, where exactly *was* Cliff, Jr.? If he'd really wanted to help Paul Reichmann, he would have been up there on the podium with him. His absence spoke volumes.

There followed a brief question-and-answer period. Reichmann was asked about recent trips by Mickey Cohen to the U.K. Were the Reichmanns trying to make a deal with Allied? Said Reichmann, "We have agreed to listen to suggestions they might have, and they have agreed to listen to suggestions that we may have."

He was also asked about the difficult position of the Hiram Walker management. He said that Bud Downing had decided to hand over the presidency to Mickey Cohen because he wanted a new senior officer to deal with matters "too difficult for anyone directly involved" with the original sale to Allied.

Soon Mickey Cohen, who was sitting at the back of the room, began to make signals to PR man Al Milne to draw the conference to a close. Reichmann was still answering questions, but Cohen knew he wanted to get out of there. He motioned again: close it down. Milne got up, then Paul Pearson got up, and then the conference was over.

Photographers continued to thrust cameras into Reichmann's face as he walked out the side door of the building into the beautifully laid out Hiram Walker garden, whose honey locusts, hawthorns, junipers, and yews stood drinking up the rain. Reichmann and Mickey Cohen and Paul Pearson walked across to the main building and disappeared up its steps to have lunch with Cliff Hatch, Jr., and his executives. From the Hiram Walker point of view, the lunch, which had to be closely supervised by Reichmann's kosher chef, was perhaps the day's most demanding task. The atmosphere at the lunch was, not surprisingly, cool.

After lunch, Reichmann returned to the "Canadian Club" room to give his same speech to Walker's management. He was politely received but did not get the standing ovation that Sir Derrick Holden-Brown had received three weeks earlier. Later in the afternoon, he met with Windsor's mayor, David Burr, who tried to sell Reichmann on supporting his plans for a local aqua-park and wave pool. Reichmann escaped as soon as possible. He also gave another exclusive interview to the *Windsor Star*'s Brian Bannon, this time with his own tape recorder present. And then, gratefully, he drove to the airport.

It had been the most exposed day of Paul Reichmann's life.

Sir Derrick Steams Back

Despite Reichmann's attempt to allay the fears of Windsor, some of his remarks caused concern. One in particular was the prospect of the ownership issue being tied up in the courts for "years." Yet again, he seemed to be unaware that such uncertainty would inevitably damage both the morale and the business outlook of the liquor operation. By threatening Allied-Lyons, he was threatening the whole liquor business. He would realize his mistake, and once again, either because of bad judgement or bad advice, he would have to appear to reverse himself.

In the meantime, however, the legal hold-up of Allied was being escalated by all means possible. The latest move was the unannounced withdrawal by Hiram Walker of a submission to the U.S. Federal Trade Commission and the U.S. Justice Department, under the anti-trust provisions of the Hart-Scott-Rodino act, seeking approval of the Allied takeover. Approval under the act was a necessary precondition of the sale.

When Allied found out about the manoeuvre, its executives were incensed. The week after Reichmann's Windsor press conference, Sir Derrick came back across the Atlantic like Maggie

Thatcher steaming down to the Falklands. He felt that he had not merely the locals but the force of justice on his side. The Reichmanns had to be taught a lesson.

On Monday, June 2, he appeared at a press conference in Toronto to announced that Allied-Lyons was taking a little legal action of its own. It was suing the Reichmanns for $9 billion. Since the award in the United States of more than U.S.$12 billion to Pennzoil in a similar suit against Texaco the preceding year, the action was not to be taken lightly.

Damages of $4 billion were being sought against Gulf Canada Corporation, Olympia & York Enterprises Limited, and the four members of Hiram Walker Resources board's special committee: Cohen, Newman, Powis, and McWalter. Paul and Albert Reichmann were also named. A further $1 billion was sought from all the defendants as punitive damages. In the event that the court did not order fulfillment of the terms of the agreement with Hiram Walker, an additional $4 billion of damages was sought.

In addition to the damages, Allied was seeking an injunction to restrain all defendants from "interfering" with the shares or assets of the liquor business.

Sir Derrick told the news conference that "while it is not in keeping with Allied's philosophy to conduct its business by litigation, it is wholly unreasonable to expect us to stand idly by while hostile attempts are made to frustrate our binding agreement to acquire the spirits and wine division of Hiram Walker."

He pointed out that the agreement between Allied and Hiram Walker Resources clearly stated that both sides should use their "best efforts" to satisfy the pre-completion conditions, but that the Reichmanns were "totally ignoring both the spirit and the wording of the agreement in a blatant attempt to prevent completion." Sir Derrick cited Hiram Walker Resources' withdrawal of the Hart-Scott-Rodino antitrust filing as a "glaring example" of the breach.

Two days later, Sir Derrick addressed the Toronto Society of Financial Analysts. The very model of British probity, he pointed to Allied-Lyons interests in Canada and how well they fitted with those of Hiram Walker. "Our two companies," he said, "also display significant differences which, as in all marriages, will make for a perfect union. Our product lines are complementary, but the traditional marketing spheres of the two companies are dissimilar. "Hiram Walker obtains 73 percent of its business from North America . . . 17 percent in Canada and 56 percent in the United

States, and only 3 percent from the United Kingdom. Allied-Lyons, on the other hand, derives 75 percent of its wines and spirits volume from the United Kingdom, and only 4 percent from North America.''

He pointed out that Allied's products could greatly benefit from Walker's strong distribution networks in North America. Also, Allied had no wines and spirits manufacturing facilities in Canada, and so would need Hiram Walker's facilities.

Sir Derrick then let Michael Jackaman, the managing director of Allied's wines and spirits division, address the group. Jackaman pointed out that in the spirits business, as with so many others, international manufacturing and marketing capability had assumed an overriding importance. "Our business plan for Hiram Walker,'' he said, "calls for both the sharing of management expertise, and the transfer to Canada of our technology, in the form of new wine, spirits and other products not now made in this country.'' Jackaman's polished presentation highlighted new business that the Allied link would bring to Hiram Walker's operations in Canada and the United States. He concluded: "Our plans are quite specific and well advanced. We look forward with confidence to the success of our new Hiram Walker division.''

Sir Derrick returned to the podium to address legal details once more. He noted that the opposition had taken further action in the Supreme Court of Ontario in an attempt to exercise what they claimed to be a right to withdraw from the agreement. "Well, I can assure you,'' said Sir Derrick, "no such right of withdrawal exists.''

With regards Investment Canada approval, Sir Derrick said, "One reason we are entirely confident of gaining approval is the excellent business plan we have developed for Hiram Walker,'' which he then went on to detail.

Sir Derrick asked for questions. The inevitable question about the Elders bid was posed. Sir Derrick outlined the background to the bid, describing the Australian company as one with more "ambition than assets.'' He noted that Elders' proposed bid was not merely highly leveraged, it was "totally leveraged.'' In the event of an Elders' takeover, Allied's assets would have had to be sold off to pay the debt.

"We had to watch the aspect,'' said Sir Derrick with suitable indignation, "of parts of Allied-Lyons being carpet-bagged around the world by an Australian company that at the time had none of our shares. We expressed our displeasure in this matter.''

The audience laughed at Sir Derrick's understatement. They laughed again when he noted that Elders' attempt to sue the Monopolies Commission had been "rather like kicking the referee in the shins."

He concluded by saying that there was "about a 0.1 percent chance of the bid being allowed to proceed."

The audience loved it.

Regarding financing, Sir Derrick said that shareholder approval had been given both for the acquisition and for the issue of 700 million pounds worth of new equity. To find the 1.2 billion sterling necessary for the Hiram Walker liquor takeover, Sir Derrick said Allied was contemplating raising 400 million of equity and 800 million of borrowing. He repeated his earlier statement that he wanted to sell Allied's shares in Canada as part of the equity funding.

Sir Derrick was a big hit with the crowd. His performance was in sharp contrast to the much less polished presentation of Paul Reichmann in Windsor the week before. But at the end of the day the Allied-Reichmann battle was not a beauty contest; it was a legal battle. Both sides were aware that becoming bogged down in an acrimonious dispute in the courts was to nobody's benefit.

Two weeks later, on June 17, Paul Reichmann issued a press release declaring that "The interests of employees and management . . . as well as the health of the business itself, will be served best by ending the uncertainties regarding ownership as quickly as possible."

Hiram Walker/Gooderham & Worts knew that. Allied knew that. Once again, the only person ignorant of the fact a month before, when he had been telling the workers and management in Windsor that the Allied case might take "years," had been Paul Reichmann. Unfortunately for Paul Reichmann, he was doing a lot of his learning in public.

Allied-Lyons, seeking to thwart the Reichmanns' attempts at delay, had, the day before, launched a motion for immediate judgement, but the Reichmann side now stated that it, too, wanted to accelerate the legal process. The Reichmann camp also committed not to "interfere" with the Hiram Walker liquor division's shares or assets, as Allied had requested. The motion for immediate judgement was delayed until July 2, which was also the day on which Investment Canada was to bring down its ruling.

O&Y worked hard to have the Allied bid rejected. Mickey Cohen was spending a great deal of time working his old bureaucratic and political "network" in Ottawa. Although Cohen, because of his close connections with the Trudeau Liberals, was *persona non grata* with most of the Tory government, many of the public servants who had worked for him were still in power. Paul Reichmann was also making the rounds of ministers to put the O&Y case. Again, however, there was a feeling that the Reichmanns had used up all their "credits," and more, in the Gulf Canada acquisition.

In an attempt to turn the political situation to its advantage, the O&Y side came up with the idea of selling 25 percent of the liquor business to the Canadian public if it was retained. O&Y began working behind closed doors with its brokers. It made this suggestion to Investment Canada and Investment Canada in turn tried to spring a Canadian public sale of 25 percent of the liquor business as a condition of allowing the purchase to Allied to go through. Allied's representatives were flabbergasted; they saw the condition as nothing less than attempted sabotage. They pointed out that Allied had already committed to sell its own shares in Canada. They also noted how politically damaging it would be for Investment Canada, and the Tories, if it appeared that a government that was "open for business" was seen to be putting roadblocks in the way of foreign investment. Investment Canada backed down.

Meanwhile, Olympia & York continued to attempt to win over the distillery's workers. Cohen got wind of a meeting, scheduled for June 19, between the UAW's Ron Dickson and representatives of Investment Canada. He called Dickson and asked him to meet with Paul Reichmann that day in Ottawa's Four Seasons hotel. Dickson turned up with Leon Paroian, his counsel, at Reichmann's fifteenth-floor room, and was surprised to find Reichmann alone.

Dickson didn't want to start the meeting on the wrong foot, but he also wanted to make clear to Reichmann where he stood, so he pulled out a copy of a letter he had recently written to the *Windsor Star*. The letter was not designed to please Reichmann. Although it described him as a "man of immense, understated charm which he uses to his great advantage," it went on to declare ". . . one is almost tempted to say the emperor has no clothes when one considers how inept Mr. Reichmann and his colleagues have been throughout the Walker deal. Moreover, it continued, "despite Mr. Reichmann's many attributes as a successful businessman and decent human being, and his devotion to duty, family and religion, he still has something to learn even from a Scottish working man of the old school. That is, to be a part of humankind, one must be a participant in the affairs of humankind and not an aloof observer. Additionally, in the real world of less celebrated men, that part of the planet where most of us dwell, a man's word is not enough unfortunately. That is why, being the unredemptive realists that we are, we at local 2027 prefer Allied-Lyons as our new employer. Anything they say they sign. We invite Mr. Reichmann to do the same . . .''

Reichmann admitted that O&Y had made many gaffes during the affair, but did not seem to regard these as personal errors. Nevertheless, he was able to deal with one of Dickson's problems immediately. He presented him with a letter containing the commitments he had made in Windsor.

Dickson asked Reichmann why he wanted a government-regulated consumer product. Reichmann pointed to the condition of Gulf Canada and the oil industry. Dickson said that sounded as if they just wanted Hiram Walker to tide them over a bad patch, and that they might then sell it off. Reichmann denied that that was his strategy.

Throughout the remainder of the two-hour meeting Reichmann expressed increasing frustration at Dickson's unwillingness to withdraw his support for Allied, ridiculing some of his assertions. The Scottish union man pointed out that the Reichmanns' reputation was that a deal was a deal; why then were they challenging the sale to Allied-Lyons? Reichmann responded that that should be no concern of Dickson, whose sole responsibility was to his union members. He accused Dickson of becoming emotionally involved with the Allied side. Dickson said the workers thought that Allied offered the best prospects for employees. Reichmann then launched into a lengthy diatribe against Hiram Walker's management over the Fingas arrangement, which had obviously made him very mad.

Dickson stuck to his guns. After two hours, Reichmann announced that he had to go off to a meeting with energy minister Pat Carney. He said as the union man and the lawyer left: ''Ron. No matter who wins, I hope that you and I can still be friends.'' The suggestion seemed strangely incongruous.

Dickson came away from the meeting convinced that Paul Reichmann's charm only extended to one's agreeing with him. He found that there was an almost frightening single-mindedness to the O&Y executive.

Decisions Decisions

Investment Canada and its political masters had no desire to be involved in more controversy than was absolutely necessary. They were well aware that if the courts came down against the validity of the Hiram Walker liquor business sale to Allied, then they would not have to make a decision. The Reichmanns' appeal of Mr. Justice Montgomery's Ontario Supreme Court ruling was due to start on June 23. Investment Canada wanted to delay its decision until after that date. On July 9, the Ontario Supreme Court brought down its decision: the Reichmanns' appeal was rejected and the validity of the sale to Allied was upheld.

The following day, Paul Reichmann gave an interview to the *Toronto Star*'s Diane Francis. Again he brought up the Seagram straw man. Pointing to the brothers' successful relationship with Abitibi-Price, he observed: "We were sure that would have happened with Hiram Walker, and it would have, without that silly rumour from Seagram. That's what poisoned the whole thing."

Reichmann said that Dickson's UAW workers were "naive," and claimed that the union only represented 460 workers out of a work force of 1,680. "Dickson and his workers are at no risk, whoever ends up owning it. But the other huge number of head office employees will stand a great risk if Allied-Lyons takes over."

But the fact was that Allied had given written job guarantees to Investment Canada. Moreover, it was uncertain where Reichmann thought he was going to win friends by such statements. He was insulting the union and hardly likely to put himself on a better footing with non-unionized employees because of that.

Speaking of Allied's purchase, he said: "That is not to say Allied did anything wrong. In sum total, it did what a good businessman does: trouble brewing creates an opportunity and a bargain." The statement rather raised questions about the Reichmanns' motivations and methods.

With an eye to the Investment Canada decision, Reichmann commented: "It's quite, quite clear the sale would be a big net detriment. . . . there are statements by Allied it will introduce in Canada pear juice, cider or whatever. But that's an irrelevant kind of matter . . ."

Francis's probing interview continued with a question about Allied's pledges being in writing. She was obviously unaware that Reichmann had given written pledges to the UAW's Dickson.

Nevertheless, Reichmann then made the astonishing statement: "It means nothing to put it in writing. The government knows that whatever they want from us they can have."

This was not the interview of a man who was in charge of events.

On July 11, the day Reichmann's "rare and candid" interview appeared in the *Star*, Investment Canada brought down its decision: the sale to Allied was declared to be of net benefit to Canada and could go ahead.

The same day, the influential CBC radio program *As It Happens* contacted O&Y to see if it could get some comment on the decision. They were hoping that they might get Mickey Cohen, but then, to their surprise and delight, Paul Reichmann's secretary called back and said that Reichmann himself would comment. She gave a number in New York at which he could be reached.

When one of the program's producers, Harry Schachter, called the number, Paul Reichmann answered. Reichmann said he was prepared to speak but he was in a hotel room with some other people. They would be leaving soon and he would call back in half an hour. Schachter typed out a line of questions for the program's host, Dennis Trudeau, and waited. Reichmann called back just as the item was due to be aired. He got to listen to his introduction live: "The wealthy Reichmann family of Toronto has enjoyed spectacular business success for years. Today, they suffered a rare setback. Investment Canada has given the go-ahead to a British company, Allied-Lyons, to take over the Hiram Walker distillery. The Reichmanns, through Gulf Canada Corporation, recently bought Hiram Walker Resources and they badly wanted the Windsor-based liquor business as part of the package. Paul Reichmann is vice-chairman of Olympia & York Enterprises."

Trudeau opened by asking: "Mr. Reichmann. You've been fighting very hard to keep the distiller part of Hiram Walker in your company Hiram Walker Resources. How big a blow to your plans is this Investment Canada decision?"

Paul Reichmann began a convoluted rebuttal. "O.K.," he said, "first I want to react to the introductory comments about the setback. First of all the basic issues are legal. Investment Canada was just one of the conditions that would be required if there were a legally binding agreement. Fundamental issues have to do with the questions: is there a legally binding agreement? If there is one, is there a provision in the agreement whereby by some payment the agreement can be cancelled. Furthermore, is there a requirement on a group that was not party to the agreement to facilitate actions which are conditions that have to be fulfilled. . ."

Trudeau interrupted: "You're talking there to me about the contract that Hiram Walker Resources made to sell the distiller to Allied-Lyons before you took over Hiram Walker. You're contesting that in court . . . You've lost at Investment Canada. You've lost another decision about whether they had to consult the shareholders to sell the distiller. Why are you fighting so hard over this? Why do you want the distiller so badly?"

"First of all," Reichmann responded, "it's very important for Gulf Canada in its present circumstances of the world prices of oil to have a diversification in a stable product and assure its ability in the future to continue its exploration and development of oil reserves. But that is not the principal question at this point in time. Sometimes one might look at this as if it were a soccer game, let's say, where scoring is what counts. That is not the situation. There are five important legal issues before the court. In the first one the court of appeal this week when they dismissed our appeal stated that part of the agreement had a contravention to the Canada Corporation Act and that the er . . . I do not have the document in front of me. . ."

Paul Reichmann had got lost in his own legal web.

Trudeau moved in to help him out. "I understand," he said, "there are very fine legal points being debated here but it remains Mr. Reichmann that you have taken a high profile and you've taken quite many steps to hold onto the distillers. Why is that income so important to you? Why do you think it is even important to Canada? Why do you oppose the Investment Canada decision?"

The response was once again tangential. ". . . As a matter of principle. As an individual. As a Canadian citizen I believe that Canada should have an open door policy and all kinds of investment should be welcome whether it's of benefit or not, because I think that for a nation, the importance of benefit is to the economy as a whole in the long run not every single action as such. . ."

Trudeau interrupted: "Surely though you would have liked to have another decision from Investment Canada?"

Reichmann continued: "All that we have been saying is that as long as there is a statute in our books that says that investment criteria is net benefit to Canada, we are convinced that if Allied-Lyons were successful, this would be of substantial detriment to Canada."

When Trudeau asked him why, his answer was so complicated that the host had to cut him off.

It had been a less than sparkling performance by Paul Reichmann. Nevertheless, this was not an issue that would be decided as a debating contest. It was a legal battle that was soon due to go to the courts. The trial had originally been due to start on July 16, but the lawyers, because of the sheer volume of paper and a number of other contested issues, asked for a delay of the proceedings until July 18. On that day, the start of the case was put back until July 29.

Both sides had declared that they wanted a summary judgement so that Hiram Walker's liquor business could continue without the shadow of contested ownership. Allied wanted a decision enforcing its contract. The Reichmanns wanted the contract thrown out. The July 9 appeal court decision appeared to support Allied's case, but in fact it caused some confusion. The justices had declared that the legality of the Fingas deal had been irrelevant to the sale of the liquor business to Allied. But they had also said that the issue of Fingas's legality could not be decided without a full trial. The Reichmann camp claimed that the legality of Fingas was thus still an issue; the Allied lawyers declared that it had been judged irrelevant and thus could not be adjudicated again. The three appeal court judges were asked to clarify their decision. They declined to do so. Two days later, the Reichmanns sought permission to appeal the rejection of their appeal.

On July 29, the two sides met again in the Ontario Supreme Court. Their declared intentions to boil down the issues and thus expedite judgement had now obviously fallen apart. It was agreed to have a full-scale trial to decide the enforceability of the sale of Hiram Walker's liquor assets, starting on September 29. If the Reichmanns' appeal against the rejection of their earlier appeal was permitted, and then upheld, the issue of the legality of Fingas would form a key part of their case. If not, then they would have to argue against the sale contract's enforceability on other grounds. Allied's $9 billion law suit, meanwhile, unless there was an out-of-court settlement, would be the subject of yet another trial. To accommodate possibly lengthy proceedings, it was agreed to extend the closing date of Allied's proposed purchase of Hiram Walker's liquor business to October 31.

The day the September 29 trial date was set, it was announced that Interprovincial had agreed, in a typically convoluted deal, to pay $1.1 billion for Home Oil. Some $517 million of the purchase price would be accounted for by the redemption by the Reichmanns of most of Interprovincial's stake in Hiram Walker. Another $200 million would take the form of the issue to Hiram Walker of an Interprovincial debenture, whose interest rate would vary with the price of oil. The remainder of the price would be in cash. As for the Hiram Walker shareholders who had not tendered to the Gulf offer, they would receive $38 in cash.

Both TransCanada PipeLines and Texaco Canada had been in the running for Home, but neither had been willing to pay as high a price as IPL in the severely depressed petroleum market. The Reichmanns, through Hiram Walker and Gulf, still held 40 percent of Interprovincial, so Home remained significantly under their control anyway. Nevertheless, there remained uncertainty over the Reichmanns' intentions for their IPL stake. There was uncertainty over almost every aspect of the Hiram Walker deal.

The possibility remained that accommodation might be reached before the September 29 trial, but that seemed increasingly unlikely. Mickey Cohen reportedly had offered Allied a deal whereby the two sides would split Hiram Walker's liquor business 40-40 with the remaining 20 percent sold to the public, but Allied had firmly rejected the suggestion. They wanted the fulfillment of their contract and no part in a move designed to save O&Y's face. A ding-dong battle was brewing in which both Paul and Albert would likely be called to testify, as would Hiram Walker management. O&Y obviously did not want injurious testimony from anybody in Hiram Walker's executive suite, so both Bud Downing and senior financial man Archie McCallum were asked for their resignations. Thus they would be giving testimony as supposedly "disgruntled" former employees. The Reichmanns certainly seemed to be going out of their way to make them disgruntled. O&Y representatives had attempted to freeze the trust account set up by Hiram Walker management to guard the funds for their golden parachutes. Walker's Treasurer, Bill Fatt, had resigned but managed to gain his settlement before the Reichmanns could stop payment. However, this attempt to lock up the parachutes understandably greatly annoyed the remaining proposed recipients.

A more contentious and messy corporate situation could hardly be imagined. Public exposure had not been kind to Paul Reichmann. A public trial was hardly likely to be any kinder. The only winners from the coming battle were likely to be the lawyers.

22

THE PAUL PRINCIPLE

*The Reichmanns have become victims of their
own success in a peculiarly Canadian way;
they had been encouraged by a financial and
political system that loves size . . .*

The conclusion of the Hiram Walker affair would mark the
end of a remarkable period for the Reichmanns. They had
been responsible not merely for the largest and second-
largest takeovers of the year, but for the two largest acquisitions in
Canadian history. One of their peripheral deals, the sale to
Petrocan of Gulf's downstream assets, had been the year's fourth-
largest Canadian corporate purchase.

Within a decade, Paul Reichmann had increased by twentyfold
the assets under the family's control and built an empire that
matched in size those of Canada's largest publicly owned companies, Bell Canada and Canadian Pacific. Half the growth had come
in the past year. Those few people who have been close to
Reichmann have always said that he wanted to create another CP,
and he has done it. But it is a troubled empire.

It has been exposed to the glare of political controversy and it is
deeply in debt. The Reichmanns have, in the course of their two
gigantic public acquisitions, both shattered the myth of their crystal ball and forced a rewriting of the corporate hagiographies.

The Gulf Canada acquisition was not merely disastrously timed
but stirred controversy about the use of taxpayers' funds to facili-

tate the growth of private empires. In Hiram Walker, they proved themselves not only less than omniscient but also indecisive. They underestimated the resolve of Hiram Walker's management and carried through with a hostile takeover, which they had claimed they would never do. They called forth legions of lawyers to assert their right to Hiram Walker's liquor assets, again something they had previously claimed was not their "style." The acquisitions had also weakened their financial position, perhaps severely.

Mountain of Debt

Real estate companies tend to be highly levered. If you are the biggest, it stands to reason, therefore, that your debt load in absolute terms is likely to be the biggest also. Paul Reichmann admitted in 1982 that O&Y's private real estate operations had debt of perhaps $6 billion or $7 billion. Whatever the changes in that figure in the intervening years, there is no denying that the Gulf and Hiram Walker ventures have added around $2.5 billion to their corporate load. The Reichmanns are one of the world's largest corporate borrowers without taking their publicly quoted interests into account.

Gulf borrowed heavily for the Hiram Walker takeover. Even when it had handed over Hiram Walker shares to the Reichmanns to repay the $900 million it had borrowed from O&Y, its debt still totalled $3.3 billion. When combined with Abitibi-Price's $400 million and Hiram Walker's $1.4 billion, the whole Reichmann publicly traded empire held debt of $5.1 billion. The Reichmann creation is thus more outstanding for its debt than its assets. It owes more than the external debt of all but a handful of the most impecunious countries.

The now even more fascinated press wrote stories in the summer of 1986 suggesting that a change had come over the Reichmanns; they were somehow acting — in particular in the Hiram Walker/Allied battle — "out of character." But the Reichmanns had not acted out of character, it was just that few people understood their character, or their limitations. Expectations of the Reichmanns' talents had surpassed anything the brothers could possibly produce.

At the simplest level, the Reichmanns' business acumen has been portrayed in such semi-mystical, almost omniscient, terms that they had almost inevitably at some time to stumble. As they moved from the discreet, private world of their real estate operations to the world of publicly traded companies, that stumble would become more public.

The Reichmanns had built an enviable reputation as honourable men. But you didn't get to be the world's biggest real estate developer by being a boy scout. They have always been very, very tough when it comes to negotiating.

Their reputation has also been blown up because of their personal privacy. In fact, it wasn't so much their personal privacy — there are very few business executives who are desperately keen to have their home lives pried into — as their *separateness* from the business and social establishment that made them so fascinating — the fact that they didn't belong to clubs, or go to cocktail parties or dinners, or play sports.

The less they appeared to want to belong, the more the establishment pursued them. In the end though, it was their odour of success that brought the big money begging. In banking relationships, secrecy tends to be directly proportional to the amount of money involved, although one executive of Citibank Canada, on whose board Paul Reichmann briefly sat, ventured that: "Paul is a real gentleman. If he gave me his word, I'd back it with $100 million of Citibank's money." But by 1986, $100 million had become almost petty cash in the Reichmann scheme of things.

Within the Canadian banking establishment, their oldest and strongest ties have always been with the Canadian Imperial Bank of Commerce. Early in 1986, Paul Reichmann achieved the Canadian corporate equivalent of a knighthood, being invited onto the CIBC's board. On most company boards, the theory is that the directors are there to oversee the performance of the management. On bank boards, directors are there to provide business. When Paul Reichmann moved onto the board of the Commerce, it wasn't clear who was receiving the greater honour.

The greater the Reichmanns' financial clout, the greater their ability to secure secrecy in their financial affairs. They were able to take the unprecedented step of raising money on the Eurodollar market in mid-1985 while revealing virtually no corporate details. They pulled off this feat by having a subsidiary of insurance company Aetna Life guarantee the loan.

The offering circular for that U.S.$125 million financing contained the almost astonishing statement: "Neither the delivery of this Offering Circular nor any sale made hereunder shall, under any circumstances, create any implication that there has been no material change in the affairs'' of O&Y or Aetna ''since the date hereof or that information herein is correct as of any time subsequent to the date hereof.''

In other words: ''Just give us the money.''

And the investors did.

The habits of secrecy die hard. Its pleasures are not easily given up. But secrecy has its downside, too.

Doomed to Diversify

The Reichmanns are hard-working, relentless, and clever. But the events of 1986 are much easier to understand once one realizes not only that they are not supermen, but also that their skill lies overwhelmingly in real estate and real estate finance. That very success has provided the funds whereby they almost *had* to diversify, but it has provided no guarantee that the diversifications would be successful. Most of them weren't. Some, like Brinco, turned out to be utter disasters.

Looked at another way, the Reichmanns are almost inevitably the victims of their own success. The success comes from real estate; the problems have arisen in attempting to utilize the fruits of that success. That basic dichotomy can be seen throughout their operation. Real estate is well organized with strong management; the investment/diversification side has virtually no organization. One is based on being as good as one's word and, although driving hard bargains, delivering a relatively simple package of goods; the other is involved with complex financing, tax-driven acquisitions, and politics. Those who deal with the Reichmanns on real estate almost always come away with heightened respect for their standards and their methods; those who deal with them on their diversifications have often found themselves kept in the dark and filled with trepidation.

Moreover, problems have inevitably arisen in diversification because of an extension of the Reichmanns' attitude that their business is ''nobody's business but their own.'' Their actions have caused what Paul Reichmann euphemistically calls ''misunderstandings'' because ultimately they do not *want* others to understand what they are doing. The communications breakdown in the case of Hiram Walker is far from unique.

When they moved on English Property in 1978, they drove the Edper Bronfmans into a state of near-panic by their failure to communicate. Again, in 1984, when the other branch of the Bronfmans, the Cemps, was in the process of cementing control of Cadillac Fairview, North America's largest publicly traded real estate developer, the Reichmanns stepped in and snapped up big blocks of stock from right under their noses. The Cemp Bronfmans were fit to be tied. After what seemed like another inordinate delay, the Reichmanns assured them that it was just an investment, that they did not want board seats, and what was all the fuss about anyway?

In fact, the early, somewhat tempestuous relationship with the Edper Bronfmans has built into bigger things — not so much through the Reichmanns' relationships with Edward and Peter as through Paul and Albert's mutual admiration society with the Edper's front-line corporate generals, Trevor Eyton and Jack Cockwell. But that relationship, through the shared interests in Trizec and Trilon, is once again an élite affair out of the public eye.

Paul Reichmann claims to understand people, but he understands best certain types of people engaged in certain types of activity. What he really understands is the art of deal-making. The Reichmanns are far more like bankers than operating men; their skill is in making money with money. Paul Reichmann in particular has had little knowledge of dealing directly with workforces, particularly unionized workforces. At the real estate end of the business, that had for decades been the job of subordinates. The Reichmanns also seem to have failed to grasp the notion of public responsibility to public shareholders, not simply doing the right thing, but being *seen* to do the right thing. That was one of the big problems at Hiram Walker.

There is also a peculiarly Canadian element to the Reichmann story. The Reichmanns have become victims of their own success in a uniquely Canadian way; they have been encouraged by a financial and political system that loves size and indulges those with talent and *chutzpah* to the point of folly. It is the Canadian corporate equivalent of the Peter Principle. It might even be called the "Paul Principle." As corporate executives tend to be promoted to the level of their incompetence, so Canadian companies in a prevailing climate of mega-loans and economic nationalism tend to expand to the point of self-destruction.

Dome Petroleum, the company that gave Canada a world-scale basket case, is the classic example of the phenomenon. The

Reichmanns are very different from Jack Gallagher and Bill Richards, but they, too, have been perceived as having "the golden touch." Like Dome, the Reichmanns have been encouraged by the government to expand with the help of public money, and, like Dome in its halcyon days, they have found banks and financial institutions only too glad to open their vaults. It remains to be seen if they proceed, like Dome, to the point of a financial trauma so great that it threatens to bring down the banking system. With perhaps twice Dome's overall debt load, they certainly have the potential.

Once one understands this peculiarly Canadian context, and the nature and limitations of the Reichmanns' business outlook, then the story told in this book becomes not one of brothers acting out of character, but of an almost inevitable move toward, if not disaster, then to corporate problems whose size had to correspond with the brothers' ambitions.

The Not-So-Invisible Hand

The public costs of the Gulf Canada deal are easy to catalogue: nearly $600 million of taxes foregone under the Little Egypt Bump; another $100 million of PIP grants spent on dubiously economic frontier activity, and the expenditure of more than $1 billion by Petrocan to make itself the largest downstream oil company in Canada. The irony of the whole transaction of course is that it left the Reichmanns deeply in debt and in control of an asset of dubious value.

As for Gulf Canada, yet another large Canadian company whose only crime was to be foreign-controlled, it was split up. Of course, Chevron's takeover of its parent was the key to Gulf's sale, but it was the Reichmanns who, with government help, split it up, sold it off, and left the rump burdened with debt. Another corporate culture has been destroyed, albeit a not terribly admired one. Another $2.8 billion has left the country, with adverse implications for the value of the dollar. And all for what?

Said the forthright Alf Powis (before being slapped with part of a $9 billion lawsuit made him less forthright): "Canadianizing Gulf, as far as I'm concerned, does very little for the country. But as a Gulf director, Gulf was suffering because of its ownership."

So, Gulf *had* to be Canadianized because of the NEP. One bad policy decision led to another.

There are critically important lessons to be learned from the Gulf affair. Businessmen are proponents not of free enterprise but of making money. That is a more than subtle distinction. Adam Smith's "invisible hand" of free enterprise guided an individual who sought only selfish profit to promote a collective good "that was no part of his intention." Now, the invisible hand is increasingly replaced by a clumsy government paw that thrusts itself into the marketplace time and again proclaiming to act in the public good. Adam Smith's selfish butchers and bakers have been replaced by the *dirigiste* wisdom of the Scientific Research Tax Credit, which saw the "quick flip" artists laughing all the way to the bank with hundreds of millions of dollars of government money.

Honest businessmen, meanwhile, have to spend an increasing amount of their time either avoiding the paw or deciding whether to try to take advantage of it. But to seek government favour is to embark on a slippery slide. This has particularly been so in the field of energy. The paw doled out money to explore in the frontiers, and billions of dollars were wasted. The paw told Canadian companies to buy out foreigners and encouraged banks to finance the purchases. Thus both the Canadian oil companies and the banks found themselves in severe trouble. In the Gulf case, the government's "assistance" to the Reichmanns' private enterprise meant a heavy public cost. The irony was that in the end the Reichmanns didn't do very well for themselves either.

The bottom line is simple, although not simplistic: bad business environments breed bad business. The Tories were faced with the most glaring object lesson of this in the NEP. The Liberals promoted Canadianization and created a wasteland. The Tories, for some bizarre reason, sought to outdo the Liberals. Unfortunately for Canada, they almost succeeded.

Concentrating Hard

Then there is the question of corporate concentration, the implications of having so much corporate power in so few hands. Most recently, emphasis has been placed in Canada on the adverse implications of conglomerates that control both financial and nonfinancial institutions, and on the resultant potential for self-dealing. Although the Reichmanns have a sizable stake in the financial conglomerate Trilon, criticism there has been concentrated on their senior partner in the company, the Edper controlled Brascan. Brascan was, in the summer of 1986, coming under heavy criticism for some of its dealings.

However, the ultimate argument against corporate concentration and conglomeration is not potential corruption but incompetence: whether collections of companies all lumped together for dubious reasons of "financial strength" or "balancing each others' business cycles" can be run efficiently. To do so requires highly sophisticated management systems and talented management. The Reichmanns' feat of accumulating perhaps the largest family-controlled empire in the world with virtually no management becomes at once both astonishing and worrying.

Paul Reichmann may admire Trevor Eyton and Jack Cockwell and the job they have done in building the Edper interests (an empire, as indicated, not without its own problems) and suggest that he has the same kind of managerial role in mind for Mickey Cohen and Gil Newman. Such a development is extremely unlikely. There were suggestions as the Hiram Walker affair moved toward its messy conclusion that Mickey Cohen had been given his head in handling the deal. If that was so, then his head would surely be on the block and the Reichmanns would be unlikely ever to loosen the reins of power again. But Paul Reichmann has never let anyone else make his mistakes. Mickey Cohen is not Trevor Eyton, but the question is largely academic anyway.

The Reichmann empire is a family company writ gargantuan. If you're not family, then you're not going to run it. Delegation, and the building of a powerful management team, is essential merely to keep the divers empire alive, let alone moving forward, but delegation outside real estate is something the brothers have not yet learned.

Alf Powis, refuting charges about the supposed dangers of corporate concentration, says, "I remember when I was young everybody was worried about the Argus Corporation. Where is it now?"

So, too, one might wonder where the Reichmann empire will be in ten or twenty years' time? In the summer of 1986, not even Paul Reichmann seemed to be sure where it was going.

CHRONOLOGY: STEPS TO EMPIRE

1955–60	The Reichmann family arrives in stages in Toronto from Tangier. They start a tile importing business. This leads to commercial property development.
1965	The family buys Flemingdon Park, some 500 acres of mixed-use land in the northeast corner of Toronto, for around $25 million, and moves into high-rise development.
1965–74	Olympia & York Developments, the family holding company, builds a significant real estate portfolio, as well as building and managing for others. The buildings it owns include: Place Bell Canada, Ottawa (1.5 million square feet) Toronto Star Building, Toronto (900,000 square feet) York Centre, Toronto (900,000 square feet) Bell Canada Data Centre, Toronto (400,000 square feet) Global House, Toronto (380,000 square feet) Texaco Canada Limited Head Office, Toronto (240,000 square feet) Mony Life Insurance Company of Canada Building, Toronto (220,000 square feet) Shell Canada Limited, Data Centre, Toronto (165,000 square feet) Province of Ontario, Ministry of Consumer and Commercial Relations, Toronto (120,000 square feet)
1974	O&Y starts building First Canadian Place. At 72 stories, its main tower is the largest building in the Commonwealth and the tallest bank building in the world.
1977	They buy the "Uris Package," eight Manhattan skyscrapers, for U.S.$320 million. The transaction is subsequently dubbed "the deal of the century."
1978	They purchase 80 percent of Block Brothers, a Vancouver-based company specializing in residential real estate development and real estate brokerage. (They subsequently buy out the minority.)
1979	March. They take control of English Property, one of Britain's largest publicly owned real estate companies for $157.3 million. This gives them a majority interest (although not control) in Trizec, a Canadian real estate company with assets of $1 billion. Trizec is controlled by Edward and Peter Bronfman. They buy, for an unspecified price, just under 10 percent of Canada Northwest Land Ltd., a Calgary-based oil company.
1980	September. They buy 50.1 percent of petroleum and mining company Brinco for $95 million.

The same month, they buy, for around $33 million, 9 percent of Royal Trustco, the parent holding company of Canada's largest trust company, with more than $26 billion under its administration, and the country's largest brokers of residential real estate. They subsequently take their stake up to 23.9 percent.

They win the contract to develop the 8-million-square-foot Battery Park City in Lower Manhattan, the largest private commercial real estate development in the world.

1981   March. Following a bidding war, they acquire 16.8 million shares of Abitibi-Price, the world's largest newsprint manufacturer, at a cost of $537 million. (They subsequently increase their holdings giving a final cost — for 94 percent of Abitibi's stock — of $560 million.)

April. They buy 20 percent of MacMillan Bloedel for $214 million, and then tender it into Noranda's partial offer for MacMillan Bloedel. They are left with just under 10 percent of MacMillan Bloedel and a stake in Noranda.

They accumulate an initial stake in Bow Valley Industries of 5.3 percent for approximately $31 million. (They will later take this stake to 10 percent.)

They buy 5.9 percent of Hiram Walker Resources for around $130 million (again they will later increase this stake to 10 percent).

1983   They swap their 23.9 percent stake in Royal Trust for cash and shares in Brascan-controlled financial conglomerate Trilon. They receive approximately $40 million in cash, an immediate 12.5 percent share in Trilon's common stock, and warrants and convertible shares that can ultimately bring O&Y's voting interest in Trilon to more than 20 percent.

1984   June. They buy 16.2 million shares of Cadillac Fairview (22 percent) for $232 million.

1985   They buy 60.2 percent of Gulf Canada, Canada's second-largest integrated oil company, from Chevron for $2.8 billion.

As part of the deal, they sell 90 percent of Abitibi-Price to Gulf Canada for $1.2 billion, leaving the newsprint producer still effectively under their control.

1986   April. Gulf Canada, now under Reichmann control, pays $3 billion for 69 percent of liquor, petroleum, and gas distribution conglomerate Hiram Walker Resources.

July. Interprovincial PipeLine swaps its Hiram Walker stake plus a package of cash and debentures reportedly worth $1.1 billion for Home Oil. There is also a legal battle over the sale, for $2.6 billion, of Hiram Walker's liquor subsidiary to Allied-Lyons PLC of England for $2.6 billion.

INDEX

ACKNOWLEDGEMENTS

This book grew out of a long article on the Reichmanns' acquisition of Gulf Canada that I began writing in 1985 for *Saturday Night* magazine. Intrigued by the family, I began to delve deeper into their past and their business dealings. The day after they made a $1.2 billion bid for control of Hiram Walker Resources, March 19, 1986, I approached Anna Porter and suggested that I write a book. She was enthusiastic. Over the next four months of frenetic research and writing, I watched first hand as the Hiram Walker story turned out to be stranger than fiction.

I could not have written this book without the invaluable experience and information gleaned from writing my three previous books: *The Blue-Eyed Sheiks, The Sorcerer's Apprentices,* and *Other People's Money.* Through these, I have become well acquainted with the oil business, the financial community and Ottawa/business relations. These three interrelated areas provided critical reference points for telling the Reichmann story. Also, the contacts that I developed in the course of writing these books have been extremely valuable. The Canadian business community is remarkably small and the same characters crop up time and time again. So, astonishingly, do the same mistakes.

The cooperation I received from the Reichmanns' business organization, Olympia & York, was, like the curate's egg, good in parts. Nevertheless, a number of senior employees from O&Y's real estate operations were extremely helpful to me. I name these below but wish to stress that none of the conclusions I have drawn in this book are in any way attributable to them.

There is a very deliberate dearth of public financial information on the Reichmanns, so personal interviews were of critical importance in piecing together the brothers' story. There are at least two dozen people from Toronto, Calgary, Ottawa, and New York who spoke to me on the condition that I not divulge their names. I take this opportunity to thank them. I should also like to thank the following for providing me with valuable assistance: Carol Alkerton, Brian Bannon, Dunnery Best, Gail-Ann Bost, Theresa Butcher, Pat Brasch, Harry Carlyle, William Clark, Howard Cohen, Estelle Nopolsky-Davis, Jamie Deacie, Ron Dickson, Jim Doak, Kathy Duffield, Trevor Eyton, Bob Fenner, Dan Frank, Norm Fraser, Doug Gibson, Ira Gluskin, Jim Hamilton, Dick Haskayne, Gerry Henderson, Bob Heule, Sir Derrick Holden-Brown, Bill Hopper, Peter Hunter, William Kilbourne, Bernd Koken, Gerry Maier, Sheilagh McEvenue, Paul McGoldrick, Bob McGrath, Stephen McLaughlin, Bill Menzell, Dan Mernit, Al Milne, Ed Minskoff, Bill Nankivell, John Norris, Bob Patterson, David Philpotts, Alf Powis, Sheryll Reid, Bill Richards, Keith Roberts, Robert Robinson, Peter Rosewell, Gary Ross, Andy Sarlos, Thorn Savage, Harry Schachter, Tim Sheeres, Bill Shields, Jim Soden, Ron Soskolne, Frank Ternan, Bob Vallance, and Joe Wright.

Again, I must stress that the conclusions I have drawn are entirely my own.

Last but not least, I wish very sincerely to thank Key Porter and Betty Corson for their support and encouragement throughout this high-pressure venture